CONCRETE DREAMLAND

Coming of Age in Underground New York

PATRICK DOUGHER

LB
Little, Brown and Company
New York Boston London

Copyright © 2025 by Patrick Dougher

Hachette Book Group supports the right to free expression and the value of copyright. The purpose of copyright is to encourage writers and artists to produce the creative works that enrich our culture.

The scanning, uploading, and distribution of this book without permission is a theft of the author's intellectual property. If you would like permission to use material from the book (other than for review purposes), please contact permissions@hbgusa.com. Thank you for your support of the author's rights.

Little, Brown and Company
Hachette Book Group
1290 Avenue of the Americas, New York, NY 10104
littlebrown.com

First Edition: April 2025

Little, Brown and Company is a division of Hachette Book Group, Inc. The Little, Brown name and logo are trademarks of Hachette Book Group, Inc.

The publisher is not responsible for websites (or their content) that are not owned by the publisher.

The Hachette Speakers Bureau provides a wide range of authors for speaking events. To find out more, go to hachettespeakersbureau.com or email HachetteSpeakers@hbgusa.com.

Little, Brown and Company books may be purchased in bulk for business, educational, or promotional use. For information, please contact your local bookseller or the Hachette Book Group Special Markets Department at special.markets@hbgusa.com.

Book interior design by Marie Mundaca

ISBN 9780316571029
LCCN 2024949560

Printing 1, 2025

LSC-C

Printed in the United States of America

To my perfectly imperfect family, my progeny and beloveds, and all who have blessed my life. To the Godbodys, the street corner sages and outcast scholars, the exquisite misfits and righteous rebels, the sinner saints and all the angels with dirty faces who have been my teachers and guides. To all who live with trauma and addiction. One day at a time we do together what I could never do alone.

The sins of the father are to be laid upon the children.
—William Shakespeare

Contents

1. Sins of the Father — 3
2. The Wrong N***** — 14
3. Dreamland — 20
4. First Communion — 22
5. Give Thanks — 26
6. Fresh Air — 29
7. Sunday Split — 32
8. Pet Peeve — 36
9. Tar Baby — 49
10. The Cemetery — 53
11. Enter the Dragon — 60
12. Front Line — 75
13. Fallen Boy — 84
14. Godbody I — 90

CONTENTS

15. The Basement	94
16. Broken	99
17. Rose-Colored Glasses	102
18. Gizmo and Gadget	108
19. Ray Ray's Reparations	115
20. Gangsters I	124
21. A Monkey Can't Sell Bananas	128
22. Godbody II	135
23. Native Gun	139
24. Turn Styles	148
25. Speck & Scrapps	154
26. Christmas Miracle I (The Resurrection)	167
27. White Devil	172
28. For the Love of Him	180
29. Psychedelic Shaman	191
30. Express	198
31. Christmas Miracle II (The Nativity Scene)	202
32. The Strand	207
33. Homeless Stew	213
34. Hand of Death	219

CONTENTS

35. Smooth Operator	223
36. Gangsters II	228
37. Over the Hump	232
38. Whitey and Speedy	237
39. Hard Break	243
40. The Messiah	249
41. Yesterday I Died	254
42. Second Chance	264
43. Sober Feet	274
44. From Haiti with Love	281
45. Christmas Miracle III (The Dove)	285
46. Stardust and Rainbows	291
47. Godbody III	302
48. Christmas Miracle IV (The Something)	310
49. Gentrification	315
50. Crawling Back	327
51. Godbody IV	333
Acknowledgments	*339*

CONCRETE DREAMLAND

Sins of the Father

MY DAD WOULD get lonely. He'd sit up late listening to music, drinking his gin and beer, and smoking his unfiltered cigarettes. After a while, he got to the sentimental stage in his drunk and wanted someone to share with. That person was usually me. He'd wake me up and sneak me downstairs, then play music and tell stories about his life. Some funny, some sad, and mostly all inappropriate for my ten-year-old ears.

I cherished these times with him. It was our special secret. He gave me his full attention and talked to me like I was a peer and a friend. I was too young and excited to recognize how sad he was and how much pain he was in. He would often say "I'm feeling no pain" when he reached a certain point in his high, as if that was the goal of his drinking, yet it seemed no amount of gin and beer could truly wash away his pain.

One night, he woke me up to hang out, and even in my youthful, naive excitement, I could feel my father's sadness. Most times when he snuck me downstairs, he had some treat waiting for me. Some candy, a bag of chips. Sometimes it was just a little sip of beer, but on this night, he offered nothing. He was listening to mournful jazz. Slow and heavy. The music matched his mood.

Dad had told me a lot about his life by this time. About the Catholic school he went to as a kid where the cruel nuns beat him daily because he wrote with his left hand. They called it "the devil's hand." He told me about the gang he was in as a teen and the fights he had. He told me about people he'd seen being killed. He told me in great detail about the time he lost his virginity. He even told me about the neighborhood pervert who molested him in a park bathroom when he was just a boy. He told me all kinds of stories from his life, but he rarely, if ever, mentioned his family, and he never mentioned his father.

After the album ended, we sat quietly for some time. He leaned back in his favorite chair next to a table on which sat a pint of Gordon's gin, a shot glass, and a can of Rheingold beer. I sat at his feet, fanning the smoke from his newly lit cigarette away from my face. He started our "rap session," as he called it, with the question "Have I ever told you how your grandfather died?"

For the next hour or so, I learned that Ambrose Francis was a tough yet good-hearted Irishman who worked as a mechanic. He was a father who doted on his son, but his world revolved around my grandmother, whom he loved and cherished above all. I learned that when she died giving birth to my aunt Chris, my grandfather sank into an abyss of grief he was never able to climb out of. Looking at the floor, Dad described how the drink took his father and made him a dark, mean, abusive drunk.

My dad was nine years old when his father became a monster.

Dad paused for a long time, seemingly deep in thought. I felt uncomfortable with his sudden silence because he seemed to completely drift away. Then he did something he'd never done before and never did again. He poured me a shot of gin.

Then he poured himself a shot and told me how my grandfather died.

My dad was twenty years old, and he and my grandfather hadn't been getting along for years. My grandfather would often go on weeklong drunken binges and disappear, leaving my dad to fend for himself and take care of his little sister. When my grandfather returned from these drunken binges, he'd be sullen and violent until the next one. After one of his disappearances, he showed up and demanded my dad pay him rent for the month. They argued and came close to blows.

They were living in Bedford-Stuyvesant at the time. The neighborhood was a mix of poor and working-class Blacks, Whites, and Hispanics. It was a tough neighborhood rife with gangs, and my dad was a member of one of the most notorious gangs, the Bishops. Their turf not only covered all of Bed-Stuy but extended all the way to Downtown Brooklyn. They were known to be more organized and ruthless than their rivals and boasted the largest number of members, all of which accounted for their "success." My father was their only White member. Part of what got him membership in the gang was his ability to make zip guns, homemade single-shot guns constructed from a piece of wood about eight inches long, a thick rubber band, a metal tube, and a nail. It took skill to make them, and when done properly they were quite deadly. Dad was a whiz at making them. He practiced and honed this craft in the woodshop at Boys High School when the teachers weren't looking. He said it was one of the few things he excelled at in school. He had just finished a new zip gun when my grandfather showed up drunk and demanding money.

Again, my dad stopped the story. He seemed on the verge of tears, his face contorted. He bowed his head and struggled to get the rest of his words out. Then he took a big breath and continued. "He was drunk. Yelling, cursing, and throwing things. He wanted the money for booze, so I went into my room and counted out twenty dollars in single bills. When I came back, he was sitting on the couch holding a zip gun I'd been working on and had left on the living room table. I threw the singles at him and said, 'Here! Take your fucking blood money!'"

Those were his last words to his father.

"I went back to my room and slammed the door. A moment later, I heard a sound I thought was a metal folding chair falling. When I came back out, your grandfather was still sitting upright on the couch. A small trickle of blood was dripping from his left eye. He'd shot himself with the zip gun. He was dead."

My father said he left him there and went around the corner to the bar where the Bishops hung out. He got drunk.

That drunk lasted twenty years.

And he hit bottom. By then, he and Mom were sleeping in separate bedrooms. Dad had lost his job at the Saxon paper company. Over the years, he'd worked his way up to the level of shop steward, but he'd simply become too unreliable, too often showing up late and hungover. Coming back drunk after his lunch break. Unemployment left him free to drink around the clock, and he became dark, mean, and abusive. Sullen and violent. He became a wretch. Eyes sunken in, pale, unkempt, and greasy. He reeked of a sour, sweet stink. Old sweat, tobacco, and wine.

Then, seemingly out of nowhere, he had a moment of grace. He said he "got sick and tired of being sick and tired," and he checked himself into a detox. He was away for a month, and when he came out, he started going to AA meetings. He got sober.

He changed.

It was miraculous. It was something I could barely believe I was seeing. I'd spent the first fifteen years of my life in a house dominated by the abuse and neglect of an active alcoholic, but now our home was one of quiet peace and harmony. My father had turned himself into this loving, gentle, wise man.

Back when he was still drinking, I remember him saying if he ever stopped, he'd end up boring and humorless. He got that wrong. After he gave up alcohol, he was funnier than ever. He was beautiful.

For the first year of his sobriety, he was out of work, and I remember him sitting at the kitchen table, reading, doing crossword puzzles, drinking coffee, searching the want ads, and smoking cigarette after cigarette. That's where he was when I walked into the kitchen one day and he asked me to sit with him. He said he noticed I was sad. He said I looked heavy. He was right. I'd just found out my best friend, Chris, was sleeping with my girlfriend, Linda. She was the girl I'd loved with my whole heart. In one moment, I lost my friend and my girl. I was broken. My dad listened to me. I could feel his compassion. I don't remember all of what he said, but I remember the love in his eyes and his soft, reassuring voice.

About a week later, Dad got a job as a foreman in a paper factory. He'd always worked in paper factories, and now after a year of being out of work, he was back doing what he knew best. He was proud, but he was really out of shape. A year of sitting around, smoking cigarettes, and drinking coffee had left him weak.

On the evening of the second day at his new job, Dad came home exhausted. He moved slow and heavy, as if he were still carrying boxes of paper on his shoulders. He made us a quick dinner of his signature dish, which he'd named Slungollian because basically he slung any leftover in the fridge into a pot, added tomato sauce, and served it over rice. Usually, he made a big performance as he cooked this. In his bad fake British accent, he might say, "Here we have last week's beautifully burnt pork chops no one wanted. We'll add those with just the faintest dash of these two-week-old lovely lima beans and allow them to marinate as we mix in a smidgen of whatever this gorgeously green moldy stuff is." It was a whole hilarious cooking show, and the results were always surprisingly delicious.

On this night, though, he was too tired to perform. He cooked and then went to lie down. At about 9 p.m., he called me up to my parents' bedroom. By then, he was back in Mom's good graces and had moved back into the master bedroom. He was under the covers, reading and smoking. He said, "Pat, I'm really tired. Would you please wash the dishes and clean up tonight?"

To my selfish sixteen-year-old mind, this was a great imposition. How dare he ask *me* to clean the kitchen? I shouted at him, "All right! I'll wash the damn dishes then!" I slammed the door.

Those were my last words to my father.

The next day was the last day of school before winter break, and after school I went to hang out with my friend John and his twin sister, Nancy, out in the Rockaways. They ran the little luncheonette by the school where the cool kids hung out. They were about ten years older than me. John and Nancy considered themselves misfits, and in me, I think they recognized a kindred spirit. Like me, they were into new wave and punk rock. We became friends. They took me under their wing and would sometimes sneak me into shows. On this day, we were at their place after hours, smoking joints, sipping wine, and listening to the Ramones and Devo, when my mom called and told me to come home right away.

I was still quite tipsy when she sat me down in the kitchen and held my hand. I couldn't imagine what was happening. I thought I might be in trouble for hanging out. She held my hand and said, "Baby, Daddy's gone."

He wanted to make a good impression at his new job, so he'd been working really hard moving heavy boxes all day. She said, "You know your father was a hard worker. You know how hard he would push himself."

He suffered a massive heart attack and died right there on the floor of the paper factory. He had just turned forty years old.

I went numb. The first thing I said—to my mother, the woman who had just lost her husband—was "Well, he lived a good, long life." I thought I was consoling her.

I was in some kind of denial fog. I didn't really believe my father was dead. I thought all of this might be some sick joke my parents were playing on me, maybe to teach me a lesson for being a selfish little shit who couldn't be bothered to wash dishes without bitching. But no, it was no joke. Dad didn't zip through a doorway and yell "Surprise!" He was gone, and I was never going to see him alive again. I'd never be able to tell my father I was sorry.

I was still numb when my friend Keith showed up. My mom had called him. His father had died suddenly from a heart attack only a year earlier, and she probably thought he would understand what I was feeling.

Keith said, "Let's take a walk." We went outside and wandered quietly until out of his pocket he pulled the biggest spliff I'd ever seen. We lit it up, then walked to one of the schoolyards a few blocks away and sat on a bench. We'd smoked half of the spliff when it really hit me: My father is dead. My father is no longer living. He's not breathing anymore. He's not thinking, being funny, helping support the family, or making me feel okay that my buddy stole my girlfriend. He's gone. Forever.

But they were all just thoughts. I was too high to feel anything.

The day of the funeral, I was in the basement getting dressed. The family was upstairs getting last-minute things together, and I was in my underwear, ironing my pants, when there was a light knock on the back door that led to the basement. The door was always open, and whoever was out there must have known that, because they let themselves in before I could answer. I looked up from the ironing and saw Linda standing before me, dressed for the funeral. Her hair was up in a bun and she wore a dark-colored dress. She looked grown and beautiful. I hadn't seen or spoken to her since the day three weeks before when I found out she was sleeping with my best friend. Seeing her now, dressed that way, left me speechless.

I stood staring at her. It all seemed surreal. My brain couldn't process her being there. I was still in my underwear, unable to move or speak. She said, "I've come for the funeral." Then she did something both erotic and traumatic. She walked over to me, got on her knees, and put me in her mouth.

We had sex. Standing at first, but then we moved to the couch. With my family waiting for me a few short steps above us, we fucked and we exploded together. It was the most powerful and emotionally charged sexual encounter I'd ever had. It left me dizzy, spent, and confused.

Linda got up and adjusted her dress. Then she kissed me on the cheek and left. I never saw her again. I found out weeks later she'd transferred schools.

The funeral parlor was only five blocks away. I called up to my mom and said I'd meet them there, that I needed to walk alone. I took the long way. I needed time to try to process my feelings. The problem was I couldn't identify or feel my feelings. I was empty and lost.

As I approached the funeral home, I heard a horn beep. I looked over to see Bill Gross, my dad's closest drinking buddy, sitting in his beat-up old Volkswagen. He was this big, chubby, lovable Irish guy, and he and my dad were really tight. They'd drink together and talk for hours, but when my dad got sober, they lost contact. I hadn't seen Bill in over a year. He'd always been super kind to me. When he and dad hung out, he always brought me a gift, a comic book or some candy, but what I really loved about him was he'd take time to talk with me, and he would actually seem interested in what I had to say. It made me feel seen. He never spoke to me like I was a dumb kid. He was funny and genuine. I trusted him.

He motioned me over, swung open the car door, and told me to get inside, then he pulled off without a word and started driving. He lit a skinny joint and passed it to me. Didn't even ask me if I smoked. I took a hit. Then another. After a minute, he said, "I'm not going in. I can't stand to see your father like that. I'm here because I need to tell you something that I feel you have a right to know. After I tell you this, you'll never see me again."

I couldn't figure out what was happening. His attitude was almost playful. He was saying these heavy words but he had a tight grin on his face, and he never even bothered to turn down the rock and roll on the radio.

"You know me and your dad were like brothers. We told each other our darkest secrets." He pulled the car over and looked at me directly. "Your father killed your grandfather. They argued about money, and your dad shot him in the face. He got away with it because he covered it up to make it look like your grandfather committed suicide, and the cops were careless."

I couldn't believe what I was hearing. The words seemed to come from far away.

Bill continued, "It tortured your father his whole life. That's why he drank the way he did, and that's why he married your mother. He married a *nigger* to punish himself."

I went numb.

Bill Gross eased the car back in front of the funeral home, let me out, and drove off. True to his word, I never saw him again.

I remember looking at my dad lying in his coffin. I felt nothing.

I remember people hugging me. I felt nothing.

I remember people saying, "It's okay to cry. Let it out!" I felt nothing.

No tears came. I felt nothing.

When it came time for the ride to the cemetery, I opted out. I told my mom I needed to be alone.

I walked back home to an empty house. Relatives had brought over food and bottles of liquor.

I poured myself a drink.

Then another.

Then another.

I got drunk.

That drunk lasted twenty years.

The Wrong N*****

WHEN ANNE LEE Gerald, my African American mother, and Ambrose Francis Dougher, my Irish-German American father, met on a blind date, she was a nineteen-year-old mother of two boys, and he was a twenty-two-year-old virgin.

My grandmother Floree Gerald moved to New York City from South Carolina with my mom and her three younger brothers, Charles, William, and Daniel, in the early '50s as part of the Great Migration north to escape the poverty and oppression of the South. My mom was twelve years old when they arrived. At that tender age, she already carried the baggage of being a rape and abuse survivor, and she was charged with taking care of herself and her brothers while my grandmother worked around the clock as a nanny and domestic servant. Mom grew up fast. By the time she was seventeen, she found herself pregnant with her first son, Darik—the result of being wooed and manipulated by an older neighborhood Casanova who promptly disappeared upon receiving the news of his impending fatherhood. Only a year and a half later, she was pregnant again. This time after being drugged and raped by a slick and ruthless young man who went on to become one of Brooklyn's most celebrated councilmen. Her second son, Michael, was raised by my great-aunt Agnes, and up until we were teens, we thought we were cousins. Despite the trauma, abuse, and hardships of her young life, Mom excelled in school and managed her many responsibilities with positivity, resourcefulness, and strength.

The blind date happened in Bedford-Stuyvesant, Brooklyn, in the early '60s, a time when interracial marriage was still illegal in many states and Black Americans were still segregated under Jim Crow and denied the right to vote in the South. At the time, Bed-Stuy was a multiracial, working-class neighborhood, and it's where my parents fell in love, married, and had me. When I was five years old, they moved us all to Bushwick, where they'd found a three-bedroom railroad apartment for cheap. The building had a Jewish-owned doll factory in the basement. I remember the first-floor hallway being littered with the body parts of discarded dolls. It looked like the aftermath of a bomb blast.

Most of the city's Puerto Rican population lived in Bushwick, so they were the majority on my block. There were still Jewish, German, Italian, and Irish families in the neighborhood, but they were aging out, and their kids were long gone. Most of the families were poor, and when I was a little kid I thought those Spanish-speaking kids must have come from a place called "Tarica" and that's why they were called "poor Taricans."

The hierarchy went like this: The lightest-skinned, straightest-haired Puerto Ricans were at the top of the pyramid, followed by the browner and curlier-haired Puerto Ricans, who were far more common. Then came light-skinned Black kids with the "good hair," going all the way down to the bottom of the pecking order, which was the dark-skinned, nappy-headed kids. No one ever declared the hierarchy out loud, but everybody knew it and acted accordingly.

Because I had curly hair and was considered light-skinned, I would've been near the top of the ghetto privilege pyramid, except my dad was a White man, which immediately made me a White boy. Even my older brother, whose father was Black, called me "White boy." I was perceived as weak and soft because White boys, as everyone knew, were soft and weak. I was a target for teasing and bullying. I had to constantly prove myself.

By the time I was seven, I was fighting pretty much every time I went out to play. It was usually the dark-skinned boys who had it in for me. They'd say, "Look at me again, White boy, and I'll smack them curls out your head!" That only made me look at them harder. Defiant. My dad teased that, true to my blood, I had "the stubborn, hard head of an Irishman and the tough, hard skin of a Black man." After many scraps, I was mostly accepted, and nobody messed with me.

Five days a week, I was bused to attend school in the White neighborhood across the border in Ridgewood, Queens. From first grade to fourth grade, I was the only brown kid in my classes, and the class pictures always looked like lessons in *which one of these doesn't belong?*

In an attempt to curb the segregation of public schools, some cities bused a few Black kids into all-White schools in all-White neighborhoods. White kids were never bused to Black schools. Black mothers believed White schools were better resourced, cleaner, safer, and, well...White, so being bused to a place like that was considered a step up for a little

Black kid. To me, it didn't feel like a step up to be bullied and called "nigger" every day.

One thing the kids on my block got right, though, was that White kids were weaker and softer. They cried and they couldn't fight for shit. But they probably didn't need to be tough, because they got all the stuff they wanted. All the stuff I wanted, too. The latest toys, brand-new bikes, and the best snacks. Despite getting whatever they wanted, they could be as cruel and mean as the kids on my block, but in those early years it was the adults, the parents and teachers, who were the most harmful and hurtful. When I heard "nigger" it was almost always coming from the mouth of an adult.

On the first day of first grade, I was seated in the back of the class even though we were assigned seats by alphabetical order with A's at the front. Because my last name starts with D, I should have been near the front of the room, but for years my seat was always in the last row behind Weinberg and Yardley or Valentino and Yakowitz. At the beginning of a school year, the teacher, Miss White Whatshername, took one look at me and before even asking my name or assigning any other seats, sent me to the back of the room. She then arranged everyone else in alphabetical order. Next to me sat a redheaded freckled boy, and when everyone was in their seats, Miss Whatstername read all our names aloud and had the children say "here" as their name was called. When she got to the back row, she said, "Trevor Wilson," and the boy next to me raised his hand.

She stared at him for a long moment. Then she called out, "Patrick Francis Dougher," and I raised my hand.

Again, she stared long and hard. She shuffled some papers and looked up. She said, "Okay. We're going to do this again, and I don't want any funny business from you two. Now, which one of you is Trevor?"

My White classmate raised his hand.

The teacher slammed her book down, then pointed at me. "And I suppose you're Patrick Francis?" I nodded. "Okay! That's it!" she yelled.

Freckles started to cry. "I guess you two think this is funny! Both of you *up*! I will *not* be starting the school year off with this nonsense! Both of you to the principal's office, *now*!"

And together we marched to the principal's office. The teacher refused to believe there was a brown kid named Patrick Francis and a White kid named Trevor.

So many things about that school were awkward or painful because I was the sole Black kid. When we had to pair up and hold hands for lunch lineup and I happened to get a girl as a partner, I was quickly reshuffled so I was either next to a boy or next to no one. I was the kid with no partner and no hand to hold.

Most of my public school teachers were Jewish, and in second grade I had Mrs. Bernstein. She was young and perky and kept us entertained with stories and games. I was the token Black kid in her class, and she seemed to give me special attention because of it. I went from the back of the class in first grade to the first seat in the first row in second. I was movin' on up. Mrs. Bernstein was outwardly affectionate with me. When she called on me to answer a question, she called me her "little brown bubele."

During one school holiday, she took a trip to Israel and came back with a keffiyeh, the traditional Palestinian headscarf. She regaled the class with stories of Israel, then she gave me the special honor of going to the front of the class to model the keffiyeh. As she tied the scarf around my head, she said, "Oy, so cute!" I could feel myself blush. Then she said, "Now I want you to run to all the classrooms. Don't bother to knock on the doors, just burst in and say, 'I'm a *terrorist!*'"

When I did, the teachers laughed and patted me on my head. "Oh, that Mrs. Bernstein is certainly a crack-up!"

My mother was not amused.

Dreamland

FANTASY WAS MY first drug of choice. Before I even understood what it meant to be high, I was addicted to the high of my imagination. Fantasy is "Lucy in the Sky with Diamonds," "Strawberry Letter 23," and every Saturday morning kids' show theme song. Fantasy is swirl ice cream with rainbow sprinkles.

When I was only seven years old, I occupied myself, home alone, by going off in a dream world of my own creation. I'd crawl under the covers, shut my eyes tight, and block out reality. I think I must've seen the Beatles' *Yellow Submarine* when I was quite young. I didn't understand that animated movie, but it left an impression on me because my dreamland looked a lot like that world. Colorful, cartoon, psychedelic, and groovy. I could while away hours in that fantasyland, being the hero in my made-up adventures. It's where I escaped when I felt pain, shame, or disappointment. It was my happy place when I was sad.

I also really liked being dizzy. I never wanted to leave the fantasy world in my mind, and anytime I got dizzy, I didn't want the feeling to stop. Lucky for me, kids on my block in Bushwick had discovered the game "sleep," which involved breathing in and out as fast and deep as you could, basically making yourself hyperventilate for a minute or so. Then a kid, usually older and bigger, would hold you in a headlock and choke you out until you lost consciousness. They'd "put you to sleep." When I was put to sleep, I'd be out sometimes for as long as two or three minutes. During that sleep, I'd experience the trippiest kaleidoscopic dreams, and when I came to, I'd be visited with visions of angels and fairies.

I was the kid always begging to be put to sleep, even though when I saw other kids being put to sleep, it always looked like they'd died. Some kids had to be slapped around hard before they woke up.

No one wanted to play the game anymore after one little girl a couple of blocks from us never woke up. The kids on my block said she was all dressed up in a pink dress for her birthday party. They said she looked like a perfect little doll when the ambulance rushed her away.

I still begged to play "sleep." I just wanted to be...away.

First Communion

THE FIRST TIME I got drunk was at a Christmas Eve party.

I was six years old.

The party was at my dear Irish aunt's apartment in East Flatbush. The whole family was there, as well as friends and neighbors. Aunt Chris's apartment was packed and hot, and the adults drank, smoked, played cards, and made merry. They paid little attention to us kids. My brother and cousins and I ran around, ate goodies, and made up games, like holding hands and swinging each other round and round until both the swinger and "swingee" were so dizzy they couldn't stand. We called that one "spin fall." The only real attention we received was when we mistakenly got in some adult's way or made too much noise. "Children are to be seen and not heard!" they'd say. "Go play in the other room!"

As the party wore on and the adults started feeling good, my aunt, who was only maybe twenty-two, thought it might be a grand idea to line up all us kids at midnight and give us a sip of wine to celebrate the birth of Christ. As the other adults watched and laughed, she performed this act as a sort of mock Catholic Communion ceremony. She even made the sign of the cross over our foreheads as we stepped up to sip from her "chalice" of cheap sweet sangria.

She lined us up by age, and I was the youngest kid in the room, so I went last. I watched my older brother and cousins take their sips and grimace. They played along with my aunt and liked the attention, but I knew every one of us would have preferred Kool-Aid. My brother spat the wine out on the floor. "Sacrilege!" the adults joked.

My cousins and I had watched enough cartoons and slapstick movies to know whatever was in that bottle made people drunk, and drunks were funny and entertaining. After taking sips, my brother and cousins even staggered around and slurred their words, doing their best impressions of cartoon drunks, which got laughs from the adults. But before long, the other kids got bored with it and went back to romping around and roughhousing with each other.

Then it was my turn.

I knew adults *loved* wine and booze, and that it seemed to make them more fun, playful, and loud. They'd act silly and giddy. It made them act out of character. It was scary and exciting.

I stepped up, and my aunt, whom I absolutely adored, said some Latin-sounding words, made the sign of the cross, and held the glass to my lips. I don't remember how I felt about the taste of the wine, but I do remember being pleasantly surprised by the warm feeling that began to wash through my body. I had the tiniest sip, but I immediately felt the *power* and *glory* of it. In a flash, I understood why the adults loved this stuff so much. For me, it was love at first sip.

After my wine Communion ceremony, I went back to playing with the other kids, but I was distracted. I wanted more of the warm feeling, and I wanted it now. From the edge of the living room, I watched the adults closely. When they set down their drinks, there would be just a moment when they weren't paying attention, and I figured in the smoke-filled apartment with all the noise and commotion, they wouldn't notice me taking a little sip.

For the next hour or so, I sneaked sip after sip, then went back to play. And after every stolen sip, I felt a little happier. A little more powerful and a little more energetic. I didn't let the other kids know what I was doing for fear they'd tell on me. I knew this was wrong, but it felt so... right.

When the room started to spin a bit, I loved it. It was like standing still but being on a merry-go-round at the same time. I don't remember any Christmas stuff happening after I took that first sip. I'm sure we opened presents and maybe even sang carols, but none of that mattered to me.

I wanted more, and it was taking too much time and patience to wait for the adults to get distracted long enough for me to sneak another sip. I noticed an almost full bottle of wine unattended near the adults, who were, by this time, pretty drunk themselves. I managed to steal the bottle away and, without being noticed, hid myself in a hall closet, where I sat in the dark and finished it off, one gulp at a time. I was told that's where somebody found me. Unconscious and covered in vomit. Poisoned by alcohol. They rushed me to Kings County Hospital, where I had my stomach pumped.

I was told later if I hadn't been discovered as quickly as I was, I could have easily died from choking on my own vomit.

I spent most of Christmas Day in the hospital.

The following year, my aunt hosted another family Christmas Eve party. This time, she didn't give us kids wine. She didn't need to. At the age of seven, I was already an alcoholic. I managed to find another bottle of unattended wine and sneak it unnoticed back into the same closet from the previous year.

And that's where they found me again.

Give Thanks

WHEN I WAS seven years old, Mom, Dad, my brother Darik, and I went to have Thanksgiving with my aunt Carrie in the projects in Brownsville. It was the first and only time we went out as a family to celebrate the holiday.

All four of us piled into the building's rickety old elevator, holding trays of mashed potatoes and macaroni and cheese. It was cramped and hot. The elevator was dark, and its one dim lightbulb kept flickering on and off. The elevator smelled of piss, sweat, old food, and disinfectant. My aunt's apartment was only on the ninth floor, but it seemed like we were in that closed space for half an hour. As it slowly ascended, the elevator groaned, bumped, and shuddered like a dying animal. My dad said to my mom, "We need to get off this thing." At that moment, there was a loud wrenching sound and the elevator stopped with a thud! My mom pushed buttons, but it didn't help. Nothing moved. The elevator was perfectly still and we were perfectly stuck. Minutes that felt like hours ticked by as we waited for the elevator to move again. The air got even hotter and thicker in those close quarters. Then, as if to give a slow response to the buttons being pushed, the lights went out. My father said, "It's okay, stay calm. This kind of thing happens all the time." But the shaking in his voice betrayed his words. An emergency light went on, casting the elevator in an eerie red glow. Below the light was a white button. Mom pressed the white emergency button, but that only made the elevator heave and tip sideways. We were all thrown into a corner, and the food lurched out of our hands and splatted on the floor. My brother giggled and said, "We're gonna fall!" as if this was a fun-house ride. I began to cry because he was right—we *were* going to fall.

My dad kept looking up to the roof of the elevator, where there was an escape hatch. He tried to reach it by jumping in the sideways-leaning elevator, but he kept landing in the corner. Then, with a creaking sound straight out of a horror movie, the doors slowly opened halfway, revealing we were between floors. We saw two bowed legs, from the knees down. My aunt Carrie's legs.

"Hand out the chirren!" she shouted.

My dad picked me up and shoved me through that little gap. Next, my brother, then my mom, but when it was time for him to crawl out, he couldn't get a grip on the floor of the building to lift himself, and there was no one left to push him up. Then suddenly, with a loud metal, tearing screech, the elevator lurched even farther to the side.

My mom shouted, "Hurry, Frank! It's about to fall!"

Another loud tearing sound and the elevator sank down

another foot. I think that scared my dad to the point where he had a flash of fear-based adrenaline. He leaped up and out of the elevator just as the final cable snapped. The crash and boom of the elevator plummeting shook the whole building, and a thick black dust cloud rose out of the shaft.

The doors shut and my dad sank to his knees. My mom lifted him to his feet. We stood there as a family, filthy, all of us dusted with black soot. No one made a sound until my aunt Carrie broke the silence with one word: "Lord."

It was the best Thanksgiving of my seven-year-old life. We were dirty, shaken, and banged up, but we survived. I saw my mom and dad act like heroes.

My aunt's tiny apartment was warm the way only NYCHA project building apartments can get. Our cousins and uncles were all packed in, and the place smelled like fresh bread and cinnamon. There was so much love and joy in the room. For dinner, we had my aunt Carrie's famous fried chicken and collard greens. There was all the traditional Thanksgiving fare, including the best sweet potato pie ever made. It was the most delicious meal I'd ever eaten.

When it was time to go home, we had to walk down the dark, dank stairway that smelled like stale piss, fresh reefer, and old wine. There was another elevator running, but at the sight of it, my dad said, "I think we're better off taking the stairs."

When we finally reached the lobby, we saw the mangled remains of the elevator we'd narrowly escaped. There was yellow police tape closing it off. It was crushed as flat as a soda can that had been run over by a truck.

Fresh Air

THE FRESH AIR Fund was a popular program where usually well-meaning, well-to-do people "adopted" some poor inner-city kid like me and gave them a summer week in the country. When I was eight years old, my parents signed me up, and I was whisked away from my family and neighborhood and taken to a place for which I had no reference. I'd never left the city before, but here I was, being loaded into a Volkswagen van, and within two hours I was on a farm in upstate New York, where I was to live for the next seven days with complete strangers. White strangers.

My host was a swinging bachelor named Sonny, who looked like a movie star. I couldn't tell how he made his money, but something told me it was by doing something dubious. He'd take secretive calls throughout the day and excuse himself to "meet a friend, real quick" in the middle of the night. Whatever he did, he must've been successful at it, because his pad was swinging. Sonny was a dude of the times, hip and with-it. He was groovy with his tight bell-bottom jeans and big peace sign necklaces. I think he thought it would be a funky feather in his cap to have this cute little nappy-afroed ghetto boy to show off.

It was all stimulus overload for me. For the first time in my life, I walked barefoot on grass and didn't worry about stepping in dog shit or broken glass. I saw real farm animals. I could also *really* smell them, and I thought, *This is a new kind of stink*. So different from city stink and somehow... better. I was allowed to pet cows, horses, goats, and chickens. I dipped my hand into a pond and watched a little fish scoot away and a frog jump. It was groovy.

The first meal out of the city was too fresh, too rich, and too foreign for my system. Sonny picked dandelion greens from the pasture and made a salad. We had milk that had just come from the cows. I threw up.

For my entire stay, I saw no one who looked even remotely like me. Everyone looked like they'd stepped out of a scene in *The Brady Bunch* or *The Partridge Family*. Everywhere Sonny took me, people stopped and stared. All week long, kids and adults touched me without my permission. They'd pat my afro or rub my skin. I was a pet.

Sonny was quite the ladies' man, and he took me to meet his girlfriends, who fawned over me like I was a prized poodle: "Oh! He's so cute!" "Where did you get him?" "Where can I get one of those?" "Does he steal?"

Then he introduced me to his nieces and nephews, a bunch of kids who appeared to be my age or slightly older, and he left me with them in the bedroom of his oldest nephew, who must have been about twelve or thirteen. After they'd all had their fill of rubbing my skin (to see if the black came off) and playing in my hair ("Oh! It's just like sheep's wool!" "Are there bugs in it?"), and after the little girls were warned to stay away from me, I got to explore his room. He had a great collection of LPs, and I was blissfully playing record after record. Then came more of their commentary. It started with "We don't have any of *your* music here" and "We only have civilized music." Then "Why don't you dance for us? You people love to dance, right? Show us your dancing."

The oldest nephew spoke about me as if I wasn't there. "Niggers are mostly monkey," he told his siblings. "They play good drums and have good rhythm because they come from the jungle, where they weren't smart enough to have words like we do, so they used drums to talk. They play sports good because they're still mostly savage. Like animals. We saved them from the jungle and taught them how to be human."

His brothers and sisters listened to him as if they were learning something from an expert. They nodded as if they completely believed him.

The saddest thing was I believed him, too.

Then I had to endure something that always came up whenever I interacted with White boys—their curiosity about Black penises. The older nephew kept asking me to show it to them. "I bet it's big like a monkey's. All niggers have giant ones." "Is it the same color as the rest of you?" And the famous "I'll show you mine if you show me yours."

Somehow, I got out of that one.

The Fresh Air Fund exposed me to a world outside of mine. A world that was cleaner, healthier, and wealthier. A world that was ignorant and racist. A world that made me ever so happy to go home to my beloved Brooklyn.

Sunday Split

MY DAD WAS Irish Catholic.

My mom was Jehovah's Witness.

I was Confused.

When I was ten years old, my parents decided I was mature enough to choose which religion I would follow. And so a spiritual tug-of-war began for my young soul. They declared I would go with my dad to church one Sunday and with my mom to the Kingdom Hall the next, and so on, until I could make up my mind.

I couldn't make up my mind.

Catholic church with Dad had definite pros: I got to have one-on-one time with my dad, church service wasn't until 10 a.m., and it was only four blocks from home. And we didn't have to get dressed up like a lot of other Catholics because we went to the "folk service," which was led by a young, long-haired priest who played acoustic guitar and sang Beatles and Simon & Garfunkel songs. I liked those songs. The service was only forty-five minutes long, and thanks to all the folksy sing-alongs, it felt even shorter. I also liked the art in my dad's church. The statues and stained glass were awesome and scary. White Christ in all His glory, surrounded by His adoring apostles. Mother Mary, beautiful and aloof, and the emaciated Christ, crucified on the cross, looking like a holy hippie. I grooved on all the intricate patterns, details, and colors of the huge stained glass windows. I marveled at the high ceilings. I dug the costumes and pageantry of the priests, and the smell of the incense. The sacred ritual and solemn ceremony. I think I mostly liked that Dad bought me candy and chips on the way back home, rare treats.

There were some real cons, too. With the exception of the singing, I didn't understand anything that was happening. I didn't understand Latin. God in the Catholic Church felt distant, cryptic, and mysterious. *His* church felt spooky and morbid. Not many people attended the service, and the ones who did were White and spent a lot of time staring at Dad and me. Also, every depiction of God, the saints, and angels was White. And I learned that if you weren't baptized Catholic, you couldn't get into heaven and would burn forever in hell. It seemed a bit harsh.

Kingdom Hall with Mom also had some cool pros: I got to spend time with my mom, who I usually didn't see much during the week because she worked overnights, as an accounts clerk for Chase Manhattan Bank. The people at the Hall looked more like me, mostly shades of brown and black. I had crushes on some of the girls and friendly rivalries with some of the boys. The Witnesses were kind, sincere, and welcoming, which made it feel like community. The Bible and

God (Jehovah) were presented in a way I could understand, in plain English with simple explanations. The service was easy to follow. While I didn't necessarily find it enjoyable, it was mostly positive and pleasant.

But there were cons. The service started at 8 a.m. The Kingdom Hall was a couple of miles from our house, so we had to get up at 6 a.m. to be on time. We had to get dressed up, which meant every other Sunday I had to put on a jacket, dress pants, a nice shirt, and a tie. Ten-year-old me didn't love that. Then there was the length of the service: *two hours.* Halfway through, I wanted to choke myself with my tie. And the music! The hymns were terrible, rhythmless, and stale. You couldn't even so much as clap your hands or move in time, because there was no time. It was painful to be in a room of Black and brown people who had to stand stiffly and sing soulless dirges. There was also no real ritual or ceremony at the Kingdom Hall, and the room itself was just a plain wood-paneled box. It was all dry and unstimulating to my eyes and ears.

Like God in the Catholic Church, Jehovah was a jealous and vengeful god who was also loving and merciful. I couldn't quite figure *Him* out, and worst of all, Armageddon was coming, and if you weren't a baptized Jehovah's Witness, you were doomed for eternity. It seemed a bit harsh.

Thankfully, this religious ping-pong situation didn't go on for long. My dad ran out of steam after a few months and we stopped attending church altogether. I ended up going to the Kingdom Hall by default. I never got baptized, but for a couple of years I did take Bible studies and performed "field service," which meant yes, I was one of those annoying people who rang your bell early to offer you *Awake!, The Watchtower,* and eternal life in paradise.

I found Jehovah's Witnesses to be genuinely good and righteous people. But eventually, I drifted away from their belief system and their idea of one Almighty God that was okay with destroying His own creation, save a chosen few, if He wasn't worshipped, adored, and strictly obeyed the way He wanted. He seemed insecure and dangerous to the highest degree.

So at twelve years old, I split and started my own spiritual quest for a god that felt right to me. A colorless god that didn't judge and condemn. A god that didn't feel cold and distant, but one I could feel in my soul. A god I could feel in my body.

Pet Peeve

I WENT THROUGH a period when I was obsessed with reptiles and amphibians. I studied them, drew pictures of them, and spoke about them to no end. My brother Darik, who we called Dee by this time, got tired of hearing about snakes and iguanas, salamanders and newts, turtles and toads, and my absolute favorite — chameleons, which I loved most because they were just so magical and otherworldly. They could literally change colors! I dreamed about chameleons. How I wished I could have a chameleon of my own.

One day I was flipping through a comic book, looking at the ads for X-ray glasses, sea monkeys, and plastic toy soldiers, and I saw it: *Five Live Chameleons* for just ninety-nine cents! I could have my own chameleons, my own little reptile pets, and for less than a buck!

I dropped exactly ninety-nine cents' worth of jangling

dimes, quarters, and pennies into an envelope, sealed the lumpy bundle, wrote my return address as per the instructions, and mailed it off to a post office box somewhere in Florida.

And I waited.

And I checked the mail.

And I waited...

After a couple of months, it became clear to even eight-year-old me that I'd been scammed. There were no live chameleons coming from Florida.

I kind of forgot about it, but one day close to six months after I'd mailed off my envelope, a box arrived. It was the first official mail I'd ever received. This nondescript brown paper box — six inches square, beat-up, torn, and smashed — held my dream. I was overjoyed. Literally trembling with excitement.

With my heart thundering, I called my brother to watch the unveiling of the chameleons because he'd been making fun of me for months for actually thinking they were going to ever show up. I carefully placed the box on the living room table and gently as I could, pulled it open. A stale funk escaped. My brother laughed. Nothing happened and nothing moved. I looked inside to see shredded newspaper, and that was all. My brother laughed harder.

I was so disappointed, I started to throw away the whole pile of paper waste, but out of blind desperation and to shut my brother up, I emptied the box onto the table. Out came this clump of newsprint, and entwined in the newspaper confetti were chameleons. Four of them. Four perfectly fossilized crispy chameleons. They were so dry and brittle, they broke apart when they hit the table. My brother laughed so hard, a fat white booger flew out of his nose and landed next to a dead chameleon, which made him laugh even harder.

I felt so wronged. Not only did the chameleons come half a year after I ordered them, but they came mummified; plus, there were only four of them, though the ad had promised five. I was not happy.

Then something moved!

In the middle of the shredded newspaper, there was stirring. I pulled back the paper to see one skinny little lime-green chameleon. She was incredibly fast. She hopped out of the newsprint onto the middle of the table, took one look at my brother and me, and like a green streak, made for the window.

My mom always had a green thumb. She would get a plant, totally neglect it, and somehow it would still grow like it was in the Garden of Eden. Mom had a virtual jungle of plants in front of the living room window. They grew dense and lush, practically blocking out the light. That's where the chameleon jetted to. She leaped from the table into the jungle and was gone. My brother rolled on the floor with laughter.

For days, I searched for the chameleon in that thicket, but she blended in so well I couldn't find her.

My first attempt at having a pet of my own wasn't entirely successful, but the chameleon lived, and dare I say thrived, in that window jungle. For at least a year, I caught the quickest glimpse of her in my peripheral vision. Just a quick little movement in the plants, a flash of green. She looked healthy and happy in that natural environment, and I gave up trying to catch her. She was free. She was a feral chameleon. She was a maroon, living off the land, even though I could never figure out what she ate. My mom cleared that question up: "She's eating roaches, and she'll never starve."

We had roaches. Everyone did. The neighbors, my friends, the corner store. Roaches were a reality. A fact of life. We didn't like them, but we accepted them.

In fact, my first real pet was a roach named Burny.

Around the same time as the runaway chameleon incident, I'd gotten into the routine of waking up before everyone to have a bowl of cornflakes to start my day. That's how I met Burny.

As I munched away, he came out of hiding as roaches are wont to do when they sense the possibility of a meal, but unlike most roaches, which are sneaky and shy, Burny was bold and confident. He crawled out and stopped about a foot in front of my bowl and waited patiently. Like the family dog obediently waiting for a table scrap.

I looked for something to smash him with. The closest and most handy thing just so happened to be the whistling teakettle on the stove. A most efficient instrument of torture and death. I took the kettle from the flame and slammed it down on top of him, thinking he'd be both squashed and scalded, flattened and burned. He was a goner. This was about to be one dead-ass bold roach.

But no. *Not* dead. When I lifted the kettle, he was indeed squashed and burned, but he was still very much alive. His back legs were mangled, and the scalding had turned him white, but he was definitely still among the living and seemed of good cheer as he crawled away.

I felt too sorry for him to finish him off, and I reasoned it would be best to let him crawl back to his roach family and die at peace in their arms or legs or whatever.

How surprised was I when Burny appeared bright and early the next morning, just as bold and chipper as the day before! Still dragging his mangled legs and still burnt white, he waited patiently, a foot in front of my cereal bowl. I felt bad. I felt guilty. I had caused pain and suffering. The least I could do was give the little fucker a cornflake, and with that act, our friendship was cemented. From that day on, I called him Burny. I don't know what he called me.

Burny visited me every morning. Sometimes he'd make circles around my cereal bowl, dragging his pitifully useless legs behind him, but usually he just waited until I gave him a cornflake. I would talk to him, ask him how his day was, tell him whatever was on my mind, you know, shoot the breeze. "Good morning, Burny Burns! How was your night? Get any roach nookie? Oh! Damn, probably not, huh? You're all fucked up; sorry about that. Guess what? I think my crush Bernadette likes me! She kind of winked at me at recess, but maybe she just had something in her eye. What's that? Oh, you got jokes. Burny and Bernadette would make a good couple? Very funny."

Usually, Burny didn't say much. He was the strong, silent type. He would just concentrate on his cornflake. I didn't mind that Burny wasn't a big talker. I mostly just appreciated his company.

This special secret relationship went on for about a month until one morning, my brother stumbled in on us. I was telling Burny about what I wanted for Christmas when I heard, "*Please* tell me you're not talking to a roach, and *please* tell me you ain't feeding it!" He was looking for something to squash Burny with. "And what's *wrong* with it? Why are you hanging out with a busted-ass burnt, crispy roach?" He took off his slipper.

Burny was oblivious to the danger he was in. As was his way, he calmly continued blissfully eating his free breakfast. He probably thought life couldn't get any better. But here came my brother for the kill. He shoved me out the way, and just as he raised his slipper like a medieval sword, a lightning-fast green streak flashed across the table. She snatched up poor, unaware Burny and disappeared back into the window jungle.

That was the end of Burny and, in fact, the last time I saw the chameleon. She probably died after she ate Burny. She wasn't used to cooked food.

My brother laughed so hard he almost went into cardiac arrest.

A couple of years later, my dad brought home a little jet-black cat. He named the cat Satan. My mom wasn't too pleased with the choice, but she had to admit Dad's second choice was even worse. There was no way my mother was going to call out to the cat, "Heeere, Blackie! Come get your dinner, Blackie!"

Satan was a pretty regular cat, for the most part, as he grew from a kitten to adolescence. He ate, slept, licked himself, and occasionally knocked one of my dad's beer glasses off a table, but something happened to him when he hit puberty. Satan grew to be a big cat seemingly overnight. He was about the length and width of a medium-sized dog, but what really made him a handful was that Satan was horny as hell.

That cat humped the air. Cats have retractable dicks, but Satan's was always fully extended and ready for business. He sat in the kitchen window and meowed and complained, nonstop, all day. "YOOOOO let me out! I need some PUSSSSY!"

Mom used to admonish my dad. "See? That's what you get for bringing home a damn black cat and naming him

Satan! Keeping us up all night with his horny ass *cat*erwauling! It's a *cat*astrophe! That cat is all kinds of bad luck!"

About a year after we got Satan, we moved from our apartment in Bushwick to a house in Flatbush. The move made Satan even hornier. He was now an indoor cat desperate to get outside, where he could live to the fullest. Every day and night, he waited at the back door, patiently looking for a chance to escape. The neighbors on either side of us had cats. Female cats. Female cats that were always in heat. Satan suffered.

One of the benefits of the move was I finally got my own room. I was a ten-year-old geeky kid with glasses and a big ol' nappy afro, and my room was my fortress and private sanctuary. I kept the door closed at all times, which is why I could never understand how Satan managed to get in. Sometimes I'd wake up in the middle of the night to find him sitting on my chest, looking me in the eyes. I swear he looked like he was thinking lusty thoughts.

This phenomenon of waking up to Satan on my chest went on for a couple of months. Around that time, I'd often find in the morning that areas of my afro would be damp and sticky. I figured I'd been drooling at night and snotting on my pillow.

But then this happened.

One night I woke up with the need to pee. Still half asleep, I tried to lift myself off the bed, but I felt a heavy weight on my head. I couldn't get up! Coming fully awake, I reached above me to find out what was holding me down.

Satan was holding me down.

Satan was on my head.

Satan had his claws dug in.

Satan was meowing like crazy.

Satan was fucking the shit out of my nappy afro.

I yelled out! It was like waking into a nightmare. My afro was being cat raped, and I couldn't get him off! I squirmed, twisted, and pulled, but he wasn't letting go. Satan was riding my afro like a bucking bronco. Clamped on with his claws while humping and howling like a Halloween werewolf!

My brother's room was right next door. He burst in just in time to see Satan bust a nut in my 'fro.

My brother laughed so hard, he lost all his baby teeth.

Satan escaped a few weeks later. Someone left the back door open, and he bounced. We looked all over for him, but Satan was gone. He'd made a break for it, and now he wasn't about to let his nasty captors, especially those of us who didn't welcome his nocturnal affections, ever hold him back again.

A few months later, we started noticing all these little black kittens around the neighborhood. Dozens of them. Satan was alive and well and fucking as much and as many pussies as possible. My mom called these little black cats "Satan's Demons," and when she saw more than three of them together, she'd say they were "Satan's Minions."

One autumn morning, I was in the park about four blocks from our house when I saw a big black cat a short distance away. I was sure it was him. I called out, "Satan! Come, Satan! Come to me, Satan!" Two passing Jehovah's Witnesses shook their heads. "You're going the wrong way, son," they said, and handed me a couple *Watchtower* magazines.

Satan finally did saunter over about five feet from me, sat down, and curled his long black tail around his body. He just sat looking at me. I said, "Come on, Satan, you've had your fun. Let's go home." I could tell he knew who I was, but he kept tilting his head this way and that, like he was weighing his options. Finally, he stood up and swaggered away.

I couldn't figure out why he wouldn't come home with me. Then it hit me. I had cut my afro. As far as he was concerned, it was over between us.

After Satan, our family got another cat. She was a stray that called to me from a garbage can. A mutt of a cat, all mixed colors and mismatched eyes. I named her Bowie. When I found her, she was full-grown and, unbeknownst to me, pregnant. We'd had her about a month when she gave birth to a litter of the cutest little mixed golden kittens, all puffy fur and little whiskery faces and the tiniest of meow squeaks. My parents were not pleased, but it was impossible not to fall in love with these adorable little creatures.

I had a great-aunt on my mom's side named Delores Catherine, affectionately known to all as Aunt Cat. She was one of the sweetest, kindest, most loving human beings I'd ever met, and she was hands down the best cook in the family. Aunt Cat's fried chicken made sworn vegetarians cheat, and God's angels in heaven placed orders for her sweet potato pie. She got the nickname Cat partially because it was short for Catherine and partially because she loved cats.

As sweet as Aunt Cat was and as amazing as her cooking was, the thing that really stood out about her was her butt. Literally. *Stood out.* Aunt Cat's booty was the stuff of legends. It was huge. *Really* huge, but(t) what made her rump so unforgettable was it seemed to belong to another person. A much bigger, fatter person. Aunt Cat was short, less than five feet tall. Her top half was slight and small, she had tiny breasts and thin arms, and her legs were very skinny. But in between all that, *BOOM!* Hottentot times ten. An ass that defied the laws of gravity. If Aunt Cat weighed 150 pounds, easily 125 pounds of it was made up of that behind. She never seemed like she could control her caboose, like her rear end dictated her movements. That booty made all the decisions, and Aunt Cat, she just followed obediently. She was at the mercy of her hind parts. Her buttocks had a mind of its own.

We had a family gathering, and Aunt Cat came with the pie and chicken, so everybody was excited. When she saw all these kittens prancing around, she squealed and clapped her hands. The kittens romped and played freely around the house and were getting into and climbing up on everything. Aunt Cat scooped one up and took a seat on the couch.

Now, when Aunt Cat sat down, she usually stayed put because all that background baggage made it such a production to get back up, so she sat there on that couch for the whole party, blissfully playing with the kitten in her lap. It was when she got up to leave that we saw something that would scar us for life. When Aunt Cat had flumped down onto the couch hours earlier, she'd unknowingly sat on one of the kittens. The poor thing had been smashed flat by that ass. Dead as a doornail with a look of shock on its little face.

What made matters even worse was that Aunt Cat couldn't tell she had a dead, flat kitten attached to her posterior. Her big ass didn't even register the tiny disturbance. It was like throwing a stone into the ocean.

My mother laid her hand on Aunt Cat's shoulder and said softly, "There's something on the back of your dress."

Aunt Cat almost fainted.

My brother laughed so hard he actually died and resurrected three days later.

Once we got rid of the cats, we got a dog. A dumb dog named Dee Dee. Dee Dee was a birthday gift for my brother, whose initials are D. D. I don't think he wanted a dog. I don't think any of us wanted a dog, but we got a dog. A really dumb dog. Dee Dee was the name she was given at first, but we quickly rechristened her Dizzy (or Double Dumb) because there was something wrong with that dog. She was on the spectrum before anyone had heard of a spectrum. If a dog could have Asperger's syndrome, Dizzy would have been their poster dog. She simply didn't pick up on social cues. Now, don't get me wrong, she was the sweetest little dog ever. Totally lovable, just fucking dumb.

Dizzy ran headfirst into things and knocked herself out seemingly for sport. She chased her tail in a fast circle until she threw up, ate the vomit, then started all over again. Dizzy couldn't be trained to do anything. We'd say, "Dizzy, sit!," and Dizzy would shit. Maybe she was deaf and dumb. When I tried to walk her, she strained against the leash until she knocked herself out from lack of air. I think she liked it. Doggie autoerotic asphyxiation. She'd come to, then choke herself out again. Dizzy liked being dizzy.

And on top of that, she was fucking horny. She was the female canine version of Satan.

Dizzy would drag her pum-pum on the carpet with this look of stupid ecstasy on her face all day if we didn't stop her. Her head was pretty much always between her legs, licking away. Horny and dumb is not a good combination.

But maybe not so dumb, because somehow she managed to get some doggie dick. She got herself knocked up. We were never able to figure out when or how it happened, since she was always in the house, in the backyard with us, or getting walked and knocking herself out. Maybe it was Immaculate Doggie Conception.

She grew bigger and bigger with pregnancy, but no one was really paying attention because there were a lot of things happening in the house at the time. My brother got sent away to a rehab facility (my father should have gone with him because he was drinking around the clock), I was getting in fights almost daily with the Black kids in my school and the White kids in my neighborhood, and Mom was busy working a night shift at the World Trade Center and trying to hold it all together. Dizzy's pregnancy was low on the list of priorities.

On one snowy winter day, I was too sick to go to school. I had a fever and was weak and throwing up. Mom opened a can of chicken noodle soup and headed off to work, leaving me to fend for myself. I lay in bed feeling horrible. Dizzy waddled up next to me, cuddled with me, and watched over me like she knew I was sick. She wouldn't leave my side.

I must have fallen asleep, because I came to in time to see Dizzy peeing on my bedroom floor, and to make matters even more gross, she was licking up the pee as it came out of her. I shouted, "Dizzy, you nasty bitch, don't pee on my floor!" And then to add an even grosser level to the grossness, she started to shit!

Except it wasn't shit, because it moved. *On its own.*

Dizzy started to lick the mucky little blob beneath her, and I realized what was going on. She was giving birth. I was in awe, still grossed out but amazed. Then Dizzy did something completely unexpected. After she cleaned up the first blind, helpless creature, she grabbed the little thing in her mouth. I was horrified. I'd heard of this before, that sometimes a mother creature eats her babies. I didn't know what to do. I thought, is she so clueless that she thinks her puppies are food? I couldn't let her eat her puppy in front of me, but before I could tumble my sick, fevered ass out of bed to save a slimy little dog from becoming its crazy bitch of a mother's afternoon snack, Dizzy hopped up on the bed and ever so gently deposited the puppy in my lap.

What followed was one of the most beautiful and touching moments of my life. She repeated this five more times. Each time she had another puppy, she licked it clean, picked it up with her mouth, and, with extraordinary trust and love, deposited it in my lap. When she was done, exhausted and spent, she curled up next to me and slept.

I couldn't help but cry.

Tar Baby

MY FIRST JOB lasted a week. When I was twelve years old, my dad's friend Bill Gross sent me to be a gofer with his buddy's roofing company. I was told my job would be to run short errands, get the crew lunch, and maybe do some light sweeping and cleaning up at the end of the day. I was excited to get started, to earn money and be my own "man."

I showed up bright and early on Monday morning. The crew of six potbellied Irish and Italian guys were hungover and grouchy. They were rank with alcohol sweat, and they cursed with every other word. They sent me to get coffee and donuts first thing, and when I got back, they turned me right round for a beer run. It wasn't even 8 a.m. yet.

I kept introducing myself as Patrick, but apparently my name was Heyyou, as in "Heyyou, bring me another fucking beer" and "Heyyou, pick up that fucking bucket and bring it over there." I didn't mind. I tried to be useful and stay busy, sweeping and picking up after them even when they weren't telling me what to do. At noon they sent me over to Sal's Deli with a huge, intricate lunch order. "Heyyou, go get us tree fuckin' salami and American cheese heros, plenty of mustard, hold the lettuce and tomatoes, two fuckin' ham and Swiss on rye, extra pickles and coleslaw on the side, and a fuckin' bacon, lettuce, and tomato on pumpernickel, hold the lettuce and tomato, and douse in mayo. Get us a coupla bags of plain chips, none of that fancy fag shit, and grab us a coupla more six-packs of Bud." They didn't offer me anything. When I came back quickly and they saw I'd gotten all their orders right, they were pleased and, as usual, spoke about me like I wasn't standing right there. "This one is pretty fucking smart. They ain't usually so fucking smart," and "This one over here looks pretty fucking strong. They get strong young, these people. We should maybe give him some fucking nineties to haul after lunch."

The crew worked slowly and took frequent breaks before lunch. After lunch they moved even slower and took more breaks. They were lazy guys who moaned and complained about everything from the weather to politics to their sports teams. "Geez, dis fuckin' sun today, huh? Whatta we in fuckin' Africa?" And "Dem fuckin' Democrats are ruinin' dis fuckin' country, I tell youse, bunch of fuckin' tree-huggin' fags." And "What about dem fuckin' Mets, huh? Geezuz, dey couldn't win a fuckin' game against my kid's fuckin' peewee league team. Fuckin' bums."

We were working on the roof of a two-story residential house in Ditmas Park, and we got up and down from the roof using two rickety ladders propped against the side of the house. I'd spent a lot of time on our roof at home. It was one of the places I'd go to escape, to be alone and fantasize about being a hero in some far-off land. I wasn't afraid of heights. Although I'd never climbed a ladder as high as this one, I went up and down like a pro.

That afternoon, when I was on the roof trying to look busy, Bobby, the crew chief, shouted, "Heyyou! What are youse doing? Go down and bring me up a fucking ninety." A ninety was a five-gallon bucket of tar that weighed about sixty pounds. I never figured out why they called them nineties. I weighed maybe a hundred pounds soaking wet with a brick in each pocket, but I was eager to please these guys and scurried down and somehow managed to carry the bucket of tar that weighed almost as much as I did up two flights on a shaky ladder perched at a precarious angle. There was no safety harness, no ropes, not even a helmet. Once I managed to get the first ninety up onto the roof, hauling them up became my duty, along with running errands and sweeping.

All day long I heard them say things about me that seemed to be compliments, but they were always tinged with insult: "Of course he can fucking climb good. Like a fucking monkey, this kid."

They started calling me "Ninety Monkey." "Yo! Ninety Monkey, bring us up another bucket!"

But that was to my face. Behind my back, I heard "Ninety Nigger."

We ended the day at 6 p.m. I'd worked for twelve hours nonstop. I didn't have money to buy lunch, and none of those guys offered anything, so I'd worked without eating. I was parched and starving by the end of the day. As the guys were packing up, one of them called out, "Heyyou! Good job today. See you in the fucking morning!"

I walked the nearly two miles home, sweaty, filthy, and

thoroughly exhausted, but with my chest puffed out. A hardworking man.

The next couple of days were just like the first. I worked twelve hours nonstop, and they kept finding new things for me to do. By midweek, I was laying down tar right alongside them. I wasn't very good at it, and I ended up with more tar on me than on the roof, so I got a new nickname. "Tar Baby! Smile so's we can fucking see ya!" They thought that was a riot.

We finished the roof by Thursday, so the guys spent most of Friday lounging around and sending me on beer and sandwich runs and having me clean their tools all day.

At 6 p.m., Bobby pulled me aside and said, "All right, Tar Baby, you fuckin' worked hard this week and these fuckin' guys like you. We got another job next week." He wrote down an address. "See you here six a.m. sharp on Monday."

He handed me my week's pay in a crumpled envelope. I had worked sixty hard, dirty, dangerous hours, but at least now I'd have enough money to buy a bike. On the long walk home, I stopped to look in the envelope.

Two dirty twenty-dollar bills stuck together with tar.

The Cemetery

IN EAST FLATBUSH, we lived right around the corner from Holy Cross Cemetery, the second-largest cemetery in Brooklyn. I went to P. S. 181, which was about a mile from my house. I had just started fifth grade. My walk to school took me along the south side of the cemetery. It was usually a solitary journey. Few cars passed and very rarely did I see other people. I loved the morning walk. I'd leave early, when it was still a little dark and the streets were empty and dead quiet. It was my personal fantasy time. I created adventures to play out as I walked. I was a hero soldier one morning, clearing the streets of snipers and hidden enemies; another morning I might be a cool spy on the run from assassins, or a famous detective, looking for elusive clues to solve a case of murder.

Every morning, I left the house thinking, *What will be my story today?*, and as I walked, I looked around for something to spark my imagination. One morning, I looked down and noticed a large drop of rust-colored paint on the sidewalk. Nothing particularly special about it except that every few steps there was another drop, and then another and another. As I turned the corner to walk along the side of the cemetery, the drops continued. They disappeared for half a block or so, then returned even bigger and more splattered. I imagined someone carrying a dripping can of paint.

Along the cemetery's dirt path, the drops became more like a steady stream, smaller drops, closer together. I realized it wasn't paint. It was definitely blood. It looked like whatever was bleeding had started running. The blood mixed with the dirt. I remembered rumors that Haitians were sacrificing animals by the cemetery in voodoo rituals, and I told myself this must be the blood of a goat that got away. It couldn't be a chicken. The drops were too big, and there were too many of them.

As the dirt path ended at the concrete, the drops abruptly stopped. Nothing for one block, two blocks, three blocks. The trail went cold. My detective mind couldn't work it out. Had I imagined all that blood? I risked being late for school and backtracked to where I last saw a drop. Yes, it was there in the dirt on the cemetery path. Did someone scoop up the goat? Did it run into the cemetery? Did it somehow just suddenly stop bleeding on its own?

I walked on, scanning the ground. After four blocks of no more drops, I stepped right in the middle of a puddle. Not rusty red but a deep, rich red. A big thick puddle of blood. It was as if the goat had fallen on that spot and bled heavily for a long time. I quickly stepped out of the pool of blood and turned around to examine the puddle. In the middle of it were crumpled tissues and what looked like a torn T-shirt, soaked red.

It wasn't a goat.

I headed toward the corner of the block. I could see in the gutter a white sheet. Clearly the outline of a body under it. There were bloody sneaker prints that turned into drag marks from the puddle to the corner. He'd made it about half a block more. Someone had covered him where he fell for the last time.

I stood alone looking at the sheet-covered body of the anonymous dead man. It was eerily quiet. His hand stuck out from under the sheet. It looked like he was reaching out for help. His fingers slightly curled. His palm had a perfect red dot in the middle.

Stigmata.

I retraced my steps after school, and there was no body under a sheet, no bloody drag marks, no sneaker prints, and no pool of blood.

Erased.

No drops of rusty red on the concrete. I began to believe I had dreamed the whole thing. I felt dizzy and spooked. But when I got to the cemetery, mixed in the dirt were the faintest drops of rusty red.

One morning about a month later, right before Halloween, I was sick with a bad stomach. My mom made me go to school anyway, but as soon as I got there, I threw up in the hallway. The school sent me home right away. My parents were at work, and Dee was at rehab, so I usually came home to an empty house. I always knew I'd be the first one home, so every day, I made sure to take a house key with me to school. On this dark, gray, windy, rainy autumn morning, I headed home alone feeling sick and tired. The streets were quieter and emptier than usual, and they had that ominous, creepy feeling you only get around Halloween.

I didn't see another soul as I walked along the side of the cemetery, but after a couple blocks, I felt I wasn't alone. I glanced quickly over my shoulder and saw a big man walking about half a block behind me. He had on a long trench coat and a hat pulled low, covering his face. I felt a chill and sensed something wasn't right. I sped up my walk, but after a couple blocks, I looked back and saw he'd sped up, too, and now was even closer. I thought maybe I should slow down and try to look like I was distracted by something and let him pass. But when I slowed down, he did, too, except he'd inched even closer to me.

I knew I was in trouble.

At this point I was only about a block from my house, and I decided to make a dash for it. I thought if I ran as fast as I could, maybe I could get to my door before he could catch me. I ran faster than I'd ever run, faster than I'd dreamed I could. I didn't even bother to look back to see if the guy was chasing me.

I made it to the driveway between our house and the next-door neighbors' and fumbled in my pockets for my key. Then I realized something that stopped my breath and nearly made my already sick stomach sink to my feet. *I'd left my key at school!*

I thought, *I'll sprint to the neighbors' house, pound on the door, and they'll let me in to safety.*

I was about to dash to the neighbors', but thankfully I stopped to peek out from the corner of our house first, and there he was. Trench Coat was standing at the head of the driveway, looking around. He hadn't seen me, and it looked like he wasn't sure if he'd picked the right driveway. I had to make a move. I had to get to someplace where he wouldn't see me.

We had a tiny wooden tool shack at the back of the yard, and I made a run for it and, as quietly as I could, climbed on top, as I had done so many times before. I lay flat. From there, I could see the driveway, my yard, and the back of my house. I waited and watched and tried to breathe as little as I could. It seemed like I was lying there for an hour.

My stomach was rumbling and making gurgling noises, and I prayed it would stop. I also prayed the man would give up looking for me, that he'd turn around and get out of my neighborhood. I prayed he *would not* come down the driveway.

My prayers weren't answered.

Without lifting my head, I could see the enormous man step from the driveway and into our backyard. He was huge, tall and broad. He looked like a skyscraper. I still couldn't see his face, but I could see his huge hands: giant, hard-looking White hands. He stood silently, looking around in all directions. Then he walked up to our back door and tried the knob. He violently yanked on it, then backed up and looked in our windows. Then he tried the door again, pushing and pulling it, rattling it like he expected it to give up and let him into our house.

My stomach rumbled and growled, and I was sure he could hear it, that and the booming of my heart. I held my breath and watched him slink around the house, looking for his way in.

He peeked into the windows again and even tried to push them open. Then, suddenly, he stopped trying, looked all around the yard one more time, and lumbered back down the driveway. I watched him walk away, took a deep breath, rolled over onto my back, and for a few silent minutes thanked God. Then I rolled back over so I could climb down, but just as I was about to start to slide down to the ground, there he was again! He was back! He'd quietly slunk back up the driveway and was now standing right in front of the shed, no more than three feet from me. I was looking right down at the top of his hat, an old sweat-stained fedora. I could smell the stale, moldy stink coming from his crumpled gray wool overcoat. He smelled like old, unwashed clothes.

If he'd looked up, he would've seen me, but instead, he opened the creaking shed door and looked in. He just stood there, staring into the shed. He was so close to me, I could have easily reached out and touched the top of his head. He could have just as easily reached up and snatched me down with one of his giant hands.

He slowly shut the door, then walked all around the shed. I could hear every thump of his heavy shoes. I thought it was over for me. I was sure he'd hear my terrified breaths.

But after a few seconds, he turned and walked back down the driveway, and this time I didn't stop watching him go. I watched and breathed.

Gone.

This time, he was gone. I waited ten more minutes, then let myself down and hustled to my neighbors' and asked for the spare key. I didn't tell them what had happened. I didn't tell my parents or anyone else. I tried to forget about it. I let myself in and tried to start in on my homework, but I couldn't concentrate. What had just happened? I asked myself. Did I imagine it all?

A day or so later, right after Halloween, my mom said she didn't want me walking by myself to and from school anymore. She said, "Walk with your friend George, and don't walk by the cemetery." She didn't explain why, and it wasn't until I got to school and heard what everyone was talking about that I understood.

The day before, the body of a boy about my age was found just four blocks from my house.

By the cemetery. The boy had been strangled to death.

The killer was still at large. They were looking for a big White man wearing a trench coat.

Enter the Dragon

I CAN'T FIGHT for shit. This statement isn't theory. It's based on evidence. I've had many fights, and I've lost the majority of them. I've ended up with broken ribs, broken fingers, bloody noses, busted lips, headaches that wouldn't go away for days, ripped clothes, broken glasses, and swollen, black, bloody eyes. One time in sixth grade, I came very close to losing an eye, and that was during a fight I was actually winning. I think it was precisely because I was winning that the dude I was fighting decided to pull out a 007 knife and go for my eye. By the grace of God and good reflexes, just as he lunged to stab me, I managed to turn my head just enough so he missed my eye by half an inch and instead plunged his knife into my cheekbone. Blood spurted out so quickly he panicked, dropped his knife, and ran. I kept the knife for many years, and I still have the scar. When I look at it, I'm reminded of just how close I came that day to losing an eye.

I grew up in a time and place where fighting was mandatory. You fought to survive. Although I wasn't a great fighter, I had a couple of things going in my favor. For one, I was too dumb to realize I couldn't fight, or maybe I was just optimistic about it. Like I was playing the odds. "If I got my ass kicked the last three times, it only makes sense I'm gonna come out on top this time!" This line of reasoning didn't really work.

I didn't mind fighting, even with my losing record. Again, it wasn't because I was a masochist or particularly tough—quite the opposite, actually. It was more because I was stubborn and tenacious and had a high threshold for pain. I also had a quick, volatile temper, and simply didn't know when to back down.

But the main thing I had going for me was I took a beating with style. I could be getting my ass kicked, but I looked good while it was happening. I danced to the rhythm of the blows with the grace of a ballerina. I was well practiced in the choreography of receiving a whupping. Looking the part was definitely a saving grace. I never cried and I never surrendered. I managed to lose and still look cool.

It helped that I had older brothers and cousins who beat me up on the daily. Big, strong older brothers and cousins. I didn't have to leave home for an ass-kicking—it was readily available at all hours and easy to access. As a result, I was never intimidated or scared of anybody my age or even several years older. How could they possibly beat my ass worse than my muscle-bound older brothers did?

Karate and kung fu were becoming a thing in New York by the time I was ten years old. There was that corny TV show

Kung Fu, with this stiff, awkward White guy making believe he was Chinese. We only tolerated the show for the rare moments when actual Chinese people were on it, or when the corny White guy had flashbacks to his time at Shaolin.

All the neighborhood kids were grateful when Channel 5 started showing real Chinese kung fu movies on Saturday afternoons. Movies with titles like *Five Fingers of Death* and *The Man with the Golden Arm*. The streets would be perfectly quiet from noon to 2 p.m. every Saturday, then, like clockwork, all these kids would come busting out of their houses ready to try out the fantastical moves they'd just watched. Imitating the kung fu masters, we kicked and chopped one another while flying off the hoods of cars. Sticks became swords, mop handles fighting poles, and our pajamas were our kung fu outfits.

Channel 5 only had about six kung fu movies, which it played in rotation. They all pretty much had the same theme: the student avenging the master who'd been deceived and murdered, or the underdog who gets beat up, finds an old master, and in a pretty predictable montage learns kung fu, then goes back to kick everybody's ass. We loved these movies, but none of the actors really stood out, and although we were all inspired by the poor-underdog-getting-revenge-on-his-oppressors theme, there wasn't really one hero we could identify with.

Until Bruce Lee!

There was a kid who lived up the block from us, Wendell, and he was a martial arts fanatic. He was four years older than me, which practically made him an adult in my eyes. He lived and breathed kung fu, and he was actually a talented martial artist. He was already a brown belt in Shotokan karate. Wendell discovered Bruce Lee before everyone else in the neighborhood and had built a shrine to him in a corner of his basement. Wendell had ventured out to Forty-Second Street and seen Bruce Lee movies like *Fist of Fury*! He even went to Chinatown by himself and brought back all these great Bruce Lee posters and real kung fu gear.

The first time Wendell invited me to see his shrine, it was like a religious experience. He spoke of how this guy was the master, the greatest ever. Undefeatable and cool as hell. Wendell conducted a Bruce Lee sermon and preached about this new martial arts messiah. I looked at the bigger-than-life posters and fell in love. This was a kung fu Jesus. Handsome, suave, and badass. I devoutly studied those posters. Bruce in still action, stylishly dispatching his enemies with the grace of a ballet dancer and the cool of Muhammad Ali. I had found my first real hero.

And then my hero died.

I was devastated, yet Bruce Lee's death only made him more of a Christlike figure. He'd come to earth to bless us with badass and anoint us in kick-ass. Having done his earthly work, he had gone back to the heavenly dojo. He went from hero to god. Then, a month later, by the grace of the Bruce Lee god or maybe even the real God, we were given *the movie*.

Enter the Dragon came out.

It was like the resurrection.

Overnight, everybody was talking about Bruce Lee and how *Enter the Dragon* was the coolest, meanest, and most dangerous kung fu flick ever. The movie poster showed a shirtless Bruce, front and center, holding up nunchucks, looking hard and tough. Directly behind Bruce was a suave-looking, handsome Black man with a big afro and sideburns, his hands outstretched in a karate pose. It was Jim Kelly, a Black man in a kung fu movie! There was a hero fighting with our god, and the hero looked like *us*. It filled us Black kids with pride. Bruce Lee fighting alongside Jim Kelly only cemented his legend in our minds and hearts. He saw us. Bruce was down with us.

My greatest dream, my biggest hope, my grandest desire, was to see *Enter the Dragon*. The movie was playing in only four theaters in New York City and only for a limited time. But even if I could somehow have gotten my parents to cough up the three dollars to pay for a ticket and let me go, which wasn't going to happen, the movie was rated R. I was too young to get in.

Wendell, being older, had managed to see the movie. Like ten times. Afterward, he went into Chinatown and bought every *Enter the Dragon* poster he could get. He took down all his other Bruce Lee posters and put up the new ones. The Bruce Lee shrine became an *Enter the Dragon* shrine. The posters captured moments from the movie: Bruce with the iconic three bleeding cuts across his tight abs and down his cheek. Bruce in his catlike defensive poses. Bruce punching, kicking, and flying. Superhuman superhero Bruce Lee.

I stopped by Wendell's daily to worship at the shrine of Lee. I was as devout as any Catholic, as any Buddhist, any Orthodox Jew. Wendell regaled me with stories and details from the movie, and I never tired of hearing the plot twists. I especially wanted to hear how Bruce and Jim Kelly teamed up and fought side by side to take down the bad guys. It turned out to be something that never actually happens in the movie, but Wendell freely embellished and added details to please his audience.

Wendell's retellings were as close as I was going to get to

actually seeing the movie, and I made the most of it. It was entertaining, and my imagination exploded as I filled in the gaps by picturing the still images on the posters coming to life. Wendell and I acted out the scenes. I imitated the poses, the cool Bruce Lee stare and his swagger, his fierce and imposing attitude. I posed shirtless in front of my bedroom mirror, three stripes of ketchup carefully drawn down my cheek and across my scrawny stomach. Even though I'd never seen Bruce Lee actually move, I was sure I was getting good at imitating him.

Whenever I was practicing my ass-kicking execution, I was usually thinking of the Murphys, probably the last White family still living in the neighborhood. They were notorious. There were about thirteen of them, ranging from twenty-one years old down to toddler, boys and girls, all redheaded and all tough, mean, and racist. When we first moved to the neighborhood, it was the Murphys who chased us out of the park, calling us every kind of nigger and monkey. It was the Murphys who rode by on their bikes and threw bottles and spat on us. The Murphys chased us with bats and spray-painted *Niggers Must Die* in front of our house.

As the neighborhood changed and more African Americans and West Indians moved in, I saw the Murphys less and less. They stayed quiet as they went about their business, but I could still sense their hate. I had a festering resentment toward the Murphys and particularly Mikey, the one who was closest to my age. That bastard had spat in my face a year before *Enter the Dragon* came out, and whenever I imagined myself destroying an enemy in a cool Bruce Lee style, it was that ugly Mikey Murphy I pictured.

One morning on the way to school, I saw a flash of red hair a block ahead of me. To my mind, I was Bruce Lee incarnate, and I was ready to get my righteous revenge. I caught up with the Murphy and tapped him on the shoulder.

Hard...

"You remember me?!" I said with a menacing slowness.

The Murphy looked me up and down and coolly said, "No," then kept walking.

I tapped him again. Harder. "Well, you should, 'cause you spit in my face, and now I'm gonna fuck you up!"

Again, the Murphy looked me up and down. He was cool and calm. Too cool and calm. He was also about two years older than me and quite a bit bigger. But Bruce Lee ain't scared of nobody.

In a calm voice, the Murphy said, "Look, kid, I don't know you, and I don't remember spitting on you, but if I did, I'm sorry, okay?"

I wasn't expecting an apology. "Nah! Not good enough. You disrespected me and my family." Wendell had told me that Bruce said those words all smooth and deadly before he got his revenge on the evil Han. "I'm gonna bust your ass, but I'm late for school. Meet me right here at three o'clock if you ain't a pussy."

The Murphy let out a kind of exasperated sigh. "You sure you wanna do this, kid?"

That should have warned me.

I had the butterfly stomach all day anticipating the fight, but every time I caught a glimpse of my reflection, I stopped and struck a perfect Bruce Lee pose. I couldn't concentrate on my schoolwork as I played out the fight in my head, over and over. It was going to be just as I'd imagined. Me as Bruce Lee, easily and smoothly dispatching a bully.

A few of the older kids had started to wear kung fu

slippers to school. They were cheap black slip-ons all the Chinese kung fu guys wore in the movies. Of course, Bruce looked the coolest in them. Somehow, I managed to convince a kid to trade shoes with me for the day even though his slippers were way too big. I stuffed paper in the front of them. Every time I looked down at my feet, I knew victory would be mine.

The Murphy was waiting for me when I got to the spot at three o'clock. He was sitting on the sidewalk, scratching the ground with a stick and looking bored. He asked again, "You sure you wanna do this, kid?"

I didn't speak. Bruce wouldn't have spoken. I unbuttoned my shirt all cool-like and flung it off to reveal my brother's way-too-big old, stained wifebeater. I had purposely worn this because Bruce wore them, so they were badass. Of course, Bruce's wifebeater was new, clean, and actually fit him. Bruce also had real muscles, but those were minor details.

I knew I was looking hard as I struck the most beautiful and perfectly executed *Enter the Dragon* pose. I was impressed with myself. I looked bad.

The Murphy suppressed a yawn. Then, one more time, "You sure you wanna do this, kid?"

I answered his question with an air kick, just as the *Enter the Dragon* posters had taught me. I imagined the fight would go down with a beautifully executed, lightning-fast Bruce Lee kick to the Murphy's chin, and then two quick punches to finish him off.

In reality, the kick was slow. It was also easily a yard from his face. This was disappointing enough, but what made it worse was my oversized borrowed kung fu slipper flew off and careened right past the Murphy's head.

"You wanna go put your slipper back on?" the Murphy said.

I eased back into the perfect combat pose I'd practiced a hundred times before. I would've made Bruce Lee himself proud! Anyone watching would've thought, *That poor White boy is in big trouble! The nappy-headed one with the missing shoe is a master!*

Then the Murphy punched me in the nose.

Hard...

It hurt, bled, and blurred my vision a bit, but it didn't lessen my resolve for righteous revenge. I thumbed my nose the cool Bruce Lee way Wendell had shown me and swung deep with my leg low. This was a classic Bruce move from a poster. The idea was to sweep the legs out from under an opponent. I did a perfect 360-degree circle.

Somehow, in executing this move, I lost my other slipper, and as badass as I knew my deep sweep looked, I was nowhere near the Murphy. I missed him by a mile but I thought he must be intimidated by my skill level. How could he not be? I looked just like the poster!

When I stood up after the execution of this spectacular sweep, I saw the Murphy looking at me confused. Aha! Clearly I had baffled him with my technique.

He punched me in the nose again.

This time, my glasses went flying.

The Murphy simply shook his head and walked away, leaving me standing there nappy-headed, bloody-nosed, half blind, and shoeless. The underdog in need of a master and a good training montage.

A few months later, *Enter the Dragon* was rereleased. Just as my fifth-grade year drew to a close, the word went out that Bruce was back. This time, the movie was showing exclusively on Forty Deuce and there were only late-night shows. I had to figure out how to see it!

I saved money. I plotted, schemed, and coerced. I begged, pleaded, and demanded. And one sweltering summer night, my dream came true.

My cousins Michael and Milton, aka Bandit and Rock, came over to spend the night. For weeks, I'd bugged them about my plan to finally see the most important movie ever made, and tonight was the night we would execute it. In those days, my mom worked the 8 p.m. to 3 a.m. shift at the newly built World Trade Center, and my dad came home from work around 7 p.m. and usually drank himself unconscious by no later than 10 p.m. This gave Dee, Bandit, Rock, and me about a five-hour window to get to Forty Deuce, somehow get into the theater (we were all underage, barely teenagers), watch the movie, and get back before Moms got home.

None of us had ever been to Forty-Second Street. We'd heard rumors and warnings about how wild and dangerous the "Deuce" was, but nothing prepared us for what we experienced that night. Bandit and Rock had brought some skinny loose joints, which we smoked between train cars on the way to the city. We emerged from the underground as high as the Empire State Building and as excited for the adventure ahead as only pubescent boys can be. We stepped smack into the middle of Babylon, of Sodom and Gomorrah, in all its decadent glory.

The sights, sounds, smells, action, people, transactions, and energy of Forty-Second Street were overwhelming. Complete sensory overload. In our maybe half hour of roaming around Times Square, I witnessed and experienced many firsts. It was the first time I saw someone giving and getting oral sex, the first time I saw a junkie shoot up, and the first time I smelled a peculiar odor that reminded me of burnt plastic but that I would find out years later was the burning of freebase cocaine. Pimps in full pimp gear; prostitutes who ran the range of looking super sexy to super sick, and some who were obviously men dressed as women; slick-talking, three-card monte players; men walking hand in hand and kissing; hustlers of all types; and guys even our inexperienced eyes could tell were dangerous. Stickup kids roamed like packs of wolves, and drugs were openly offered for sale. I'll never forget the dude with the little plastic packets of a tan substance in his palm calling out, "I got that shit that killed Bruce Lee!" The freakiest and funniest thing we saw was a gnarly old dwarf shitting between two parked cars.

We were tripping out, but as wild and dangerous as the Deuce was, we blended right in. Four Black boys all under fourteen walking this strip after midnight on a weeknight didn't even merit a second look.

The marquee read *Bruce Lee in* Enter the Dragon *and Sonny Chiba in* The Street Fighter. Sonny Chiba was number two on the martial arts hits list. He was to karate what Bruce was to kung fu, and the argument was always who would have won if Bruce and Sonny had had a showdown. Sonny was bad, no doubt, so bad he even earned the distinction of having people refer to marijuana by his last name. We no longer smoked pot or reefer. We smoked cheeba.

I wouldn't have minded seeing *Street Fighter,* but I prayed for two things as we stood in line: *Please, please, please let us not be turned away because we're too young* and *Please let it be* Enter the Dragon *showing tonight!*

Turned out sometimes prayers are answered. The disinterested, worn-out-looking booth operator took our money without even bothering to look up. We entered the theater to watch an R-rated movie and stepped into a dark, crowded, noisy, dank cheeba-and-cigarette-smoke-filled room that could have come straight from an R-rated movie.

We stood in the back, trying to let our eyes adjust to the dark and the smoke. There seemed to be seats near the front, so we started down the aisle, and as we looked left to right, something became clear even in the darkness. One side seemed to be made up of almost all Puerto Ricans with a few Black faces sprinkled in, and the other side was exactly the opposite: almost all Black with a few Latin-looking dudes scattered about. We caught cold, staring eyes as we descended. Then I heard from my left, the Black side, "Mighty, mighty Tomahawks!"

The right side immediately responded, "Skulls, Skulls, Savage Skulls!"

Then, after a moment, "Civilians!" We'd been identified and classified. We didn't belong to either side. We had unknowingly walked into a theater filled to capacity with two of the city's largest and most notorious gangs, the Tomahawks from Brooklyn and the Savage Skulls from the Bronx. Both of these powerful gangs had traveled from the safety of their turf, their home boroughs, to Manhattan to pay homage to the master. I truly believe the only thing that stopped an epic rumble that day was their mutual reverence for Bruce Lee.

We chose four seats at the front and slumped down in them as low as we could go and sat there with our mouths shut.

The air was electric with tension and testosterone. Comments and insults flew back and forth across the aisle. Snapping and ranking and some pretty funny jokes being cracked on the opposing gang. Things were getting really loud and raucous, and the back-and-forth between the gangs was starting to edge toward serious, but then the movie started.

I was starting to worry I was going to miss the movie because of the shouting and chatter, but then perfectly, as if on cue, a fantastic and hilarious thing happened. The opening scene began to roll. Bruce was dressed only in what looked like black underwear and was fighting a heavy-set guy dressed the same, but I couldn't hear the movie because the insults and general noise from the audience had reached a crescendo. Then suddenly, a little kid in the theater, probably no older than six or seven and dressed like a mini Savage Skull, stood up on his chair and yelled in a voice so deep and heavy it could have belonged to a three-hundred-pound professional wrestler, "Everybody shut the fuck up—Bruce Lee is on!"

Both sides broke up laughing, and with that, all the tension broke. The theater got quiet as church. There was a reverence. There was respect.

Bruce Lee was on the screen.

I don't think I've ever been so fully absorbed, engaged, and present as I was sitting in that theater taking in every move, every nuance, and every bit of the essence of what was happening on-screen. Here was Bruce Lee, actually moving in front of my eyes, and it was glorious! All those still images on Wendell's posters I'd studied and fantasized about for months had come to life, and it was even better than I had imagined.

I was in heaven.

Bruce was our god, and Jim Kelly was his only begotten son. During the movie, the only time noise erupted from the audience was when Jim Kelly was killed. "See?! That's that bullshit! Why they kill the brother and let the corny-ass White boy live?!" In that moment, those notorious, powerful gangs became united as one.

I sat in awe. I studied the screen. I was transfixed, filled to the brim. It was truly a religious experience. Ecstasy.

When the movie was over, the audience whooped and hollered. I was spent. My brother and cousins jumped up and down and threw punches and kicks at each other, but I was still and remained silent. I'd been steeped in the tea of Lee and was infused with his spirit. I'd been reborn and reincarnated. The Dragon had entered my soul.

For the rest of the summer, I practiced what I'd seen on the big screen. Every day, I did one hundred push-ups, determined to get buff and ripped like Bruce. I bounced on my toes like Bruce, kicked and threw punches like Bruce. I made Bruce Lee cat sounds. I even got the Bruce Lee stance, stare, and attitude down to a T.

I was Bruce Lee.

And I plotted the revenge of my revenge on the Murphy.

On a morning during the first week back to school, I spotted the distinctive red head a couple of blocks in front of me. This was the moment I'd worked and practiced for all summer. I was ready.

I tapped the Murphy on his shoulder.

Hard...

"You remember me?!" I said. I didn't even wait for him to answer. I smoothly stepped back into a perfect Bruce Lee stance, thumbed my nose, and motioned for the Murphy to "come hither" for his well-deserved ass whooping. I looked good and knew Bruce himself would have been proud.

I was calm and confident. I was cool and in control. I had studied the master. I had embodied the master.

I was the master!

I let out a catlike Bruce Lee growl as I made my move.

The Murphy punched me in the nose.

Hard…

Front Line

IN SEVENTH GRADE, I started going to school in the Marine Park section of Brooklyn. Like in Ridgewood, the schools were better resourced, cleaner, and more modern than those in my zone, but for those of us who were bused, the schools were definitely not safer.

Marine Park was one of the last neighborhoods in Brooklyn the Whites were holding on to. For. Dear. Life. It was mostly Italian, Irish, and Jewish. I went to school with the children of cops, firemen, shop owners, and low-level gangsters.

The Jewish kids were probably the least racist, meaning they were racist but were probably not going to beat me up because of it. They also tended to be smarter and more liberal, so if any White kid was going to side with you, it was most likely a Jewish White kid. The Irish kids, distinguishable by their tough hippie jean jackets with the Grateful Dead, the Who, Led Zeppelin, and Disco Sucks patches, were clearly super racist. They were always on the front line of any of the mob attacks the bused kids endured. Irish kids were usually the kids of cops or city workers and didn't interact with us at all. On their own, they were weak punks, but in packs, they were like vicious dogs. The Italian kids may have been the most interesting racists of all, because they were so much like us in so many ways. They were clearly the alpha White kids of the school, and they ran the halls like the Mob ran their neighborhood. If a Black kid passed a bunch of them on the street, they'd shout stuff like "Go back to Africa, ya fuckin' monkey!" But at the same time, they were in awe of us. Between the Italians and the Blacks, every day was a competition for who was the most badass, macho, and cool. While the Irish and most of the Jews listened to rock and wore dusty jeans and kept their hair long, the Italians listened to what we listened to, disco and funk, and they danced like we did, doing pale versions of the hustle and the freak. They attempted to mimic our style and swag. Italians had the short hair and wore the dress pants, the velour tracksuits, and the clean new sneakers. They were athletic and prided themselves on being tough. They were so similar to us, yet they hated us the most. I often wondered, did they hate us out of pure envy because they knew they'd never be cool inside, never cool in their blood, no matter how many pairs of Pumas and Jordache jeans they owned, no matter how many Earth, Wind & Fire and Chic songs they knew by heart?

Every time I heard a fight had broken out in our school between a Black and a White, I could bet the White was an Italian. The other thing about the Italians was the girls. Like the guys, they sort of styled themselves after us. They did their nails and hair and wore the same kind of jewelry and outfits as the Black girls. And they were cute! They flirted with us mercilessly. But only when no Italian guys were around.

Then there were the Puerto Ricans, the biggest code switchers of all. They bused in with us, and all the way to school they were "down with the niggas," but as soon as we got to school, all of a sudden they were Italian or Black-hating Ricans. Then, at 3 p.m. and back on the bus where nobody else could see them, they were magically "niggas" again.

The Whites didn't get along with each other, either. The Irish and Italians didn't like the Jews, because they were Jews. The Jews didn't trust the goyim. The Irish didn't like the Italians, because they were practically niggers, and the Italians didn't like the Irish, because they were low-life drunks and druggies. But hating Blacks was one thing they could agree on, and if ever there was any kind of altercation involving a Black kid and any kind of White kid, they'd join forces like they'd made a sworn pact to defend Whiteness at all costs.

We Black kids who bused in were lucky if there were three of us in a class of thirty, but we held our own. We had to. And we knew we were tougher and badder than even the baddest Italian.

Except for this kid Dominic.

Dominic was a terror. He'd been a muscle builder since preschool. He was as big and strong as a construction worker, and he was *mean*. He made no secret of how much he hated "niggers," and even the hardest hard rocks in the school avoided him. But here's the thing about Dominic: He was practically Black himself. His family must have been from the most southern tip of Sicily, where the swarthiest Italians come from, because Dominic had full features, a wide, flat nose and full lips. He was only a shade lighter than me, and his hair was almost as curly as mine. To top it off, he dressed almost exactly like a Black kid, and he prided himself on how good a dancer he was. He'd be hanging out in front of the school on Monday mornings with his little boom box, blasting whatever disco song was popular at the time and showing off his moves like he'd watched *Soul Train* on repeat all weekend.

If there was a race fight at school, Dominic was on the front line of it. He regularly picked fights with the toughest Black guys—"Hey, moolie! Did I fuckin' catch you staring at Francesca in the cafeteria at lunch? You're fuckin' dead at three o'clock, you fuckin' mutt!"—then he usually beat them up.

The handball courts in the schoolyard were as segregated as everywhere else in the school. The wall had a White side and a Black side. You simply did not cross that boundary, but there was an unspoken understanding that if a Black ball went over to the White side, someone would throw it back and vice versa. This practice was called "ball back," and it kept a fragile peace.

One day I sat on the benches across from the handball courts, watching the Italians play a heated game on their side, while Black girls played on their side. One of the Black girls hit the ball over the wall, and they waited for it to come flying back, but it never came.

A Black girl named Michelle called out, "Could y'all ball back, puleeeze?"

Dominic's distinct baritone voice answered, "You can kiss that ball goodbye! No more ball back for niggers!" Laughter rose from his side of the wall.

Michelle was a heavy, dark-skinned girl. She had a sharp

tongue and wasn't scared of anyone. She talked back to school security guards, teachers, bus drivers, anybody. Michelle didn't take no shit and Michelle didn't give a shit! I guess the day Dominic wouldn't send the ball back was the day she'd had enough of being called a nigger, the day she'd had her fill of Dominic's macho racist shit. Alone, she strolled over to the White side and picked up the ball. This in itself was an almost unthinkable act, but what happened next forever tipped the balance of power in the schoolyard.

Michelle smacked Dominic.

In front of all his macho buddies and all his little groupies, Michelle swung her arm back like she was calling down Jesus and all the angels from heaven and launched her palm so hard across Dominic's face, you could probably hear the slap a block away. It sounded like a big tree branch cracking in two after being struck by lightning. It was the smackdown of legends. It was a smack that reduced the big muscled, badass Italian to a sniveling little boy.

That smack was straight-up disrespectful.

It was the smack that ended an era.

Michelle left Dominic, the notorious nigger hater, standing there tearing up like a little boy who had wet his pants in public. She picked up the ball, slow-strutted back to the Black side of the wall, and commenced playing as if nothing out of the ordinary had just happened. "Now, where was we?" she calmly said, as if she hadn't just shown herself to be the baddest-ass human of any sex or race in the history of the world. The pride I felt that day cannot be put into words.

Dominic didn't return to school for almost two weeks, and when he did, you could still see the print of Michelle's hand on the side of his face. He had changed. He got quiet and humble, held his head down in the hallway, and when he did speak, the baritone was missing from his voice. He even made friends with some of the Black kids, which was shocking in itself, but the most mind-blowing thing of all was that by the end of the school year, he was dating Michelle's best friend, a girl even darker brown than Michelle.

While I was at Marine Park Junior High School, we seemed to have what we called a "riot" at least once a week. Usually, a fight would break out between a Black kid and a White kid, or a Black boy would talk to a White girl and the Whites would use it as an excuse to chase us to the bus stop and out of their neighborhood. There'd be maybe twenty of us being chased by a crowd of a hundred bat-wielding Whites from the nearby high school and surrounding neighborhood. And it wasn't just other kids chasing us; there were grown-ass men with bats chasing twelve-year-olds. Some kids got caught and really banged up, too. Busted heads and black eyes. Mysteriously, the cops were never around.

Still, in the middle of all this hostility and violence, I managed to make a few friends among my White classmates. In fact, for a short while, there was a little group of us who would go out together at lunchtime to explore "the creek." That was what we called the little saltwater marsh inlet across a big open field from our school. I was the only Black kid bold enough to venture so far away from school, where we risked getting caught and harassed by older kids, but going with my White friends made me feel safe. We called ourselves the Creek Crew.

I loved the adventure of dashing across the field and heading into the wild marsh. We weren't supposed to be there. It was considered trespassing, and that made it even more exciting. Exploring the beach and all the things that washed up, the fiddler and horseshoe crabs, the clams buried in the sand, and the mussels clustered under rocks. I loved the salty, rich smell of the air, and the sight of the tall seagrass blowing in the breeze. There were a lot of exotic-looking seabirds that flocked there, and I'd marvel at their colors and distinctive calls. It was a magical place for a city kid.

One day after exploring the creek, we had some extra time before we had to be back to school, so we decided to sit for a while in the big field. The five of us sat in a circle, and I sat with my back toward the creek. We were joking and telling stories when, one by one, my friends started making excuses to leave. When there were just two of us left, my friend said, "I need to pee. I'm going back to school, but you stay here." I thought it meant he'd be coming back for me. He didn't come back.

As I watched him hustle toward the field, I felt something heavy and hard slam down on my shoulder.

I whipped my head around and saw *the Hook*.

The Hook was a local legend. Kids told tales of this big bad older Irish kid who hated Black people more than anything. He had a prosthetic arm with a big sharp hook where his hand should have been. The story was that the Hook had caught a Black man breaking into his house and they'd fought. The Black man pinned him down and cut off his hand. That's why the Hook hated Blacks so much.

Now the Hook was going to take it out on me, and terror shot through my body. He was big as a grown-up, and he loomed over me with his heavy hook weighing on my shoulder and a bat in his hand. He had three other White boys with him: one who was about my size that I didn't recognize, another kid from our school who I used to see around, and a stoner kid who smoked cigarettes in the bathroom and always cut class.

The Hook dug his hook into my shoulder. I felt it nearly piercing my skin. "A nigger broke into my house last night. I think it was you!"

"What?! No! It wasn't me! I swear!"

They all laughed. They sounded like a group of drunken pirates.

"What are you doing here, nigger?" the Hook asked.

"I was hanging out with my friends for lunch. The bell is about to ring. I got to go back!"

"You ain't going nowhere, nigger! You thought we wouldn't catch you? You fucking nigger!"

More laughter and side comments. "Look how scared the little monkey is!" "Cry for your mommy, nigger. She ain't coming to save you. She's busy spending her welfare check!"

I kind of sheepishly laughed along, trying to make out like this was all just fun and games. A friendly hazing. "I'm sorry. I just want to go back to school."

"I'll tell you what," the Hook replied. "I'll be fair. You're too small for me to fight, so you can fight Eddie here, and if you win, we'll let you go." They all thought that was the funniest thing.

Now, I wasn't stupid. I knew there was no way out of this. This Eddie kid was about my size, and I knew I could probably beat him, but I also knew if I started winning, they'd all jump me. I also knew if I refused to fight Eddie, they'd jump me. I was going to get my ass beat either way.

"What's it gonna be, nigger?!"

I was desperate. I blurted out, "My name is Patrick Francis! I'm half Irish!" As soon as the words left my mouth, I knew it was a huge mistake.

Those boys pounced on me. They beat me to the ground, punching, kicking, and hitting me on the back, arms, and legs with the bat. The Hook ripped my clothes and gouged deep, bloody scratches into my skin as he dragged me through the grass.

The body does something merciful when it's taking a prolonged beating. It shuts down the pain center in the brain. I still felt the blows. I knew I was being badly beaten, but I went numb. It was as if I was outside of my body. Like I was watching some other kid getting the shit beaten out of him.

I don't know how long they beat me, but when the beating stopped, I lay on the ground, looking up into the sky, as one by one, they stepped over me and spat in my face. The Hook was last. "Nigger, don't you *ever* call yourself Irish again!"

It was their laughter as they walked away that awakened the pain center in my brain. I picked myself up and hobbled back to school, although I could barely walk from the bat blows to my legs. My clothes were ripped and shredded and covered in mud. My face dripped with blood and spit, and already I could feel my cheeks and lips and forehead starting to swell. My knees, hands, and elbows bled, blood mixed with mud. My flesh was scraped off from being dragged. Despite how I must have looked, the security guards didn't stop me when I entered the school. In the halls, no one said a word to me. I made it to my seat in class.

When my teacher, Mrs. Eisenberg, saw me, she screamed, "Oh! My God, Patrick! What happened?"

The whole class turned to look at me. Everyone except the Creek Crew. They just stared straight ahead.

Fallen Boy

JOSE AND PETE-O were initially my older brother Dee's friends, but they soon adopted me and made me their mini mascot. Pete-o's name was actually Pedro, but my brother could never get it right, so he just called him Pete-o, and it stuck. They were tough Puerto Rican kids three years older than me, which would've made them about fifteen or so.

Jose was an aspiring graffiti writer, a master bike mechanic, and an accomplished bike thief. He was also into weight lifting. Jose was diesel and proud of his muscles, and the girls loved him. He brought a set of weights over to our backyard and taught me how to lift in between showing me how to shorten a chain, change a fork, tighten spokes, fix a flat, and adjust brakes. He also taught me how to combine the best bike parts from several stolen bikes to make my own unique creation. We created what we called "Frankensteins."

Jose helped me steal a bike from my friend Chris who lived around the corner. Chris had left his brand-new bike unattended in front of his house. I swooped in, scooped it up, and hustled it to my backyard for Jose and me to disassemble.

We'd taken Chris's bike apart and mixed the pieces with other parts lying around my backyard when Chris showed up with his father. They wanted to know if I'd taken the bike, and they started poking around. My father witnessed the whole thing from the kitchen window, where he'd been sitting. He came out half drunk, and with great theatrical flair said, "How *dare* you imply that my son stole your bike!" and told them to leave immediately. He did it with a smirk on his face. I think he knew I stole that bike.

Pete-o was Jose's cousin. He was taller, thinner, and quieter than Jose. Underneath, he was gentle and nice, but he came across as menacing. Pete-o liked bikes, but his main love was graffiti. This was when "writing" was just beginning to emerge as an urban art form. Pete-o was super talented, and his tag, *Dizzo*, was everywhere. He kept a drippy homemade marker created from a school chalk eraser, India ink, and electrical tape on him at all times. He called it his "mop." Pete-o was the first kid from our neighborhood to bomb a whole train — tagged up an entire train from front to last car.

One afternoon, after visiting my uncle Charlie in East New York, I got on the J train at the Broadway Junction stop and sat in a corner seat. I looked down at the empty seat next to me and saw that someone had left a sketchbook. It was one of those black-bound, hardcover books artists use. I knew what it was immediately because my uncle Charlie had several of them filled with his doodles and nude drawings of my aunt Eula. I picked up the book and stashed it in my bag.

When I got home later, I leafed through it. There were no blank pages—it was completely filled, but it didn't contain the artsy sketches and drawings I'd expected; instead, every page was covered with graffiti tags. It was like this graffiti writer had used the book to work out styles and ideas, and then passed the book to other writers. There were many different types of tags and bubble writings throughout the book, but it was clear it belonged to one writer in particular. This guy Dondi had filled most of the pages, but he certainly had a lot of friends in the graffiti world. His book had tags from dudes named Daze, Crash, Zepher, and many others. Apparently, these kinds of shared sketchbooks were part of writers' culture. It was a graffiti writer's codex and bible.

The next time I saw Pete-o, I mentioned I'd found a sketchbook on the train filled with tags, and he asked to check it out. He didn't say anything as he flipped through the pages, but when he was finished, he nonchalantly asked if he could borrow it. I never saw the book again.

These names would become legendary as the architects and originators of brand-new fonts and styles. The contributors to that sketchbook were the founding fathers and pioneers of an art form that would go on to influence movements throughout the world.

I felt cool, grown, and protected whenever I hung out with Jose and Pete-o. It was a hood honor to be seen in their company. One summer Saturday, Jose swung by on his magical fifteen-speed, all-chrome, tricked-out chopper bike he'd made entirely from stolen parts. It had a front shock absorber, mirrors on the handlebars, and an extra-long sissy bar. It was a big pimpin' bike, and he took it out only on special occasions. On this day, he said, "C'mon, jump on your bike. We're gonna meet Pete-o by Vanderveer. There's a jam today!"

The idea of going to the Vanderveer projects sent ice down my back. Vanderveer was notorious for gangsters, hard rocks, and stickup kids. It's where people got robbed and beaten up. It's where people were thrown off the roof and stabbed in the staircase. Most folks rode an extra stop on the bus to avoid having to walk through its courtyards. Vanderveer was to be avoided at all costs.

Sensing my hesitancy, Jose said, "Don't worry. I got you! Me and Pete-o ain't gonna let nothing happen to our little man. It's gonna be a jam!"

Vanderveer's schoolyard park was packed. We could hear the music blocks before we got there. Like graffiti, DJs with two turntables and a mixer, and an MC with a microphone going through an echo chamber were the new thing happening in Black and brown neighborhoods all over the city.

We met up with Pete-o and posted up on our bikes, watching the crowd do the freak. I felt secure and safe sandwiched between my Puerto Rican friends with their perfect afros and crisp new white Converse sneakers. (As a rule, Black kids wore Pro-Keds, Pumas, and Adidas, while Puerto Ricans mostly rocked white Cons. It was an unspoken understanding.)

Jose and Pete-o seemed to know everybody. They nodded,

shook hands, and talked shit to the girls. The jams were thumping from giant speakers built inside huge homemade boxes, the MC was saying smooth, clever shit, the dudes were looking cool and hard in Kangols and gabardines, and the fly girls were pretty and sexy in shorts and jellies. The air smelled of Newport cigarettes, cheap cologne, and testosterone. Skinny loose joints of cheeba were passed around, along with quarts of Ol' E. The buzz, the music, the fine honeys—the whole scene was perfect, making me forget where I was.

Suddenly, I felt the crowd shift. People started pushing past us, initially in what felt like slow motion and then in a harried, crushing panic.

It was the first time I'd ever heard actual gunshots.

Four cracks. Thinner and higher-pitched than I would have expected. There was also an odd burnt-sulfur smell in the air.

The crowd rolled over us and passed like a wave, leaving the three of us on our bikes exposed. Where just a blink ago there had been a hundred dancing bodies, now there was just one, lying face up in a growing pool of blood. He was only a few yards from where we sat on our bikes. The teenager was outstretched like he was trying to make snow angels on the hot tar. His eyes were wide open, looking surprised and confused and as if he was staring into the sun. A single tear ran down his cheek. His mouth was wide open, and his teeth were red with blood. His legs quivered. One of his Pumas lay next to him. He had a hole in his tube sock, revealing a big toe.

The record scratched and the music went silent. For one moment, there was perfect stillness. No one moved toward the fallen boy.

With his hand opening and closing, it was as if he was

trying to grab and hold on to something. Beckoning someone. Then, in a sudden jolt, his whole body twitched and shook, and his hand clenched into a tight fist.

I thought he might get up. I thought he was going to sit up and put his sneaker back on.

He didn't.

Godbody I

GRAFFITI WRITING WAS everywhere. It was literally the writing on the walls that beaconed the birth of the hip-hop era. Trains were covered inside and out with graffiti. Tags, throw-ups, and wild style. Urban hieroglyphics. It was a normal part of the landscape. We took it for granted that trains and blank walls were now to be decorated with bold vandalism.

I was never much of a "writer." I tried for about six months to make a name for myself, but I just wasn't very good or dedicated. I wrote *Warz* (short for Warzone) as my tag. I tagged everywhere I went and started to think I was developing a rep, too, until I noticed real writers were tagging over *Warz* with the word *Toy*. It was the worst insult in the graffiti world. I got the hint.

A similar thing happened when I tried breakdancing. I

wasn't bad. I just wasn't good. Both writing and dancing were taken seriously by the emerging culture, and it was highly competitive, so if you weren't good, or "fakin' the funk," you could get your ass kicked, or worse. My uprock was never down, and my breakdancing was broken. When I tried to rap, people said, "Wrap it up." My shit was corny. My B-boy was more like a C- or D-boy. Still, I appreciated, respected, and admired those who could really write, dance, and rap.

DJs with two turntables, mixers, crates of records, and giant cabinets of speakers seemed to pop up overnight. With them came MCs, or masters of ceremony, who grabbed the mic to rap smooth and slick shit that kept the crowd moving. They fascinated me. They were our inner-city griots, street poets, speaking their rhythmic rhyming phrases with pimp cool. They were at block parties, basement jams, and schoolyard throw-downs. They rhymed and led call-and-response chants: "Raise your hands in the air, and wave them like you just don't care, and if you feeling good and looking fly, let me hear you say, 'Oh, yeah!'"

The crowd would respond, "Oh, yeah!"

And you don't stop.

I thought it was hip and cool. The MCs would often drop empowering messages, like some street code that was spiritual and profound. It reminded me of the way the cool, hard Ausar Auset brothers from Bushwick, with their white robes, turbans, pierced noses, and combat boots, used to speak, or how the Nation of Islam brothers in their crisp suits and bow ties rapped. Strong, wise, and militant.

"Love Is the Message" by MFSB is the forever New York City block party jam of jams. I was at a block party in Bed-Stuy when the DJ played the anthem and extended the breakdown section by seamlessly mixing it back and forth between two records. The MC grabbed the mic and began singing in harmony with the strings, "Study your lessons 'cause the Black man is ALLAH! Allah is GOD, Allah Allah Allah is God! Study your lessons!"

I asked my cousin Rock what it all meant. He said, "Oh! That's that Five Percent shit."

Reggie and Roland were two notorious hard rocks I considered my friends back in middle school. They were way ahead of me in street knowledge. They came from the projects and from families with far-reaching reputations as hustlers and gangsters. When we came back from summer break going into seventh grade, Reggie was no longer Reggie and Roland was no longer Roland. They were to be addressed as Freedom Allah and Justice Born. They had become Gods. They were now Five Percenters and part of the Nation of Gods and Earths. "Peace, God" replaced "What up?" as the universal greeting, and Five Percent became the culture and religion of the street.

Freedom and Justice taught me the basic tenets of the Five Percent doctrine and schooled me about the *Supreme 120 Lessons*. I never claimed to be God or Five Percent, but it became an important rite of passage to have knowledge, wisdom, and understanding of Supreme Mathematics and the Supreme Alphabet.

Five Percent language worked its way into street culture and then into what would become hip-hop culture. It was how we spoke. It was magnetic and poetic. "Word!"—meaning you agree with something—came from "Word is bond." Getting together to bullshit transformed into "building in a cipher." Our girlfriends were now our Earths, and our moms were our Old Earths. Your homeboy was now your sun.

I loved the tough poetry of the Five Percent flow and its

emphasis on self-knowledge and empowerment, but I could never really wrap my head around considering myself an "original Asiatic Black man, the maker, the owner, the cream of the planet Earth, the father of civilization, and God of the universe." Somehow, referring to myself as "God" felt blasphemous and impossible until I heard an older Five Percenter telling a story.

"So knowledge this, God! Now y'all know I can walk anywhere in Medina [Brooklyn] and not have to worry because everybody knows me here, but sun bus it! I had to break north to Mecca [Harlem] to check on my Old Earth. Now you know them Eighty-Fivers [uninitiated] on St. Nick are savage. Uncivilized, sun! Them niggas shifty and sheisty. I was starting to get shook but then I remembered I'm Godbody. Ain't nobody can touch me, sun! Word life!"

The word *Godbody* resonated with me. I pulled the storyteller aside to ask him about it, and he broke it down like this: "Now, when I say I'm God, I'm not talking about that One God, the old man on a throne in the sky that rules over heaven and hell. See, I have knowledge of self and my divine nature. I am God made manifest in human form. I *embody* God, and that's why I am Godbody, and so are you." His lesson that day was the beginning of a change in me. Before that day, I had viewed the idea of a God outside of myself, but he started me on a path to discover the God within.

The Basement

THE BASEMENT OF our family home in East Flatbush was the most important space in my life. When we moved from Bushwick to the new house, the basement was unfinished, so one of the first things my parents did was have it paneled with cheap fake wood, which was all the rage. They had the floor tiled and the ceiling dropped. Seventies working-class chic.

Although I had my own room, the basement is where you'd almost always find me. It was my safe place and hideout. It was my lair and personal fantasyland. When I saved up and got my first cheap little stereo at twelve years old, instead of setting it up in my bedroom, I took it down to the basement, where I put on whole concerts by myself, making believe I was a famous rock star performing to adoring stadium crowds.

The basement was where I first felt a sense of autonomy and independence. In fact, it became a place of many important firsts for me. It was where I first tried weed with my brother and cousins. It was where I created my first paintings and learned to play the drums. The basement was where I first experimented with psychedelics and cocaine, and where I first threw up from drinking too much of my father's wine. It became my personal library, gym, art and music studio, and sex den.

I lost my virginity to a petite and pretty half-Chinese, half-Jamaican girl named Charmaine on the pullout couch down there. I hardly knew Charmaine. We never even came close to dating. I was fourteen years old and beginning my freshman year of high school. I was in the cafeteria when she walked up to me and said, "I'm coming home with you today." She got on the bus with me after school without a word, and walked the half mile from the bus stop with me without a word. Charmaine followed me downstairs, where she unceremoniously undressed herself and then me. She got on top of me without a word. When we finished, I walked her to the bus stop without a word. In fact, we never spoke again after that day. I returned to the basement and sat on the couch feeling empty and used. Charmaine was the first of many sexual encounters that took place in the basement. That basement was where my son was conceived six years later.

Soon after my father died, I dropped out of high school, tore down the cheap wood paneling, and ripped up the tiled floor. I wanted the basement to look how I felt inside: raw, exposed, and shattered.

When my mom came home from work and saw the demolition and wreckage, she banished me to the basement. "You created it. Now you live in it." She had an old mini stove and dilapidated refrigerator installed, then locked the door between the basement and the upper floors and took away my keys to the front door.

And so began my life of fending for myself.

I was fine with it. I fancied myself a "Rasta punk rocker," so the raw unfinished basement fit my aesthetic. Now, at seventeen years old, I had a roof over my head, but I was left to my own devices. I had to feed and clothe myself and find money for basic necessities. What little money I had from part-time hustles usually went to getting and staying high, so I was often hungry. I became the guy who "spontaneously" showed up at friends' houses at dinnertime, hoping to be invited to a meal.

Out of sheer hunger and desperation, I started dumpster diving for food. One night when I was coming home late from a party, flat broke, high, and hungry, I passed the Key Food on Brooklyn Avenue. I noticed the dumpsters behind the store were overflowing with damaged produce and day-old bread. I filled my knapsack.

From then on, I'd wait until the store closed and the block quieted down, then, like a giant rat (which I was in active competition with), I'd go rummaging for any fruit or vegetable that looked even marginally edible. I was a strict vegetarian, and I wasn't interested in the meat products, so I left all that for the other rats. For many months, I lived on stale bread and damaged produce. I learned to make healthy, tasty meals with castoffs.

Then I started breaking into houses. The first house I robbed was my next-door neighbors'. Jimmy and Jean had moved in with their two daughters a couple of years earlier, and they were pretty well-off. Jimmy owned a big liquor store on Nostrand Avenue. He seemed to have a new car every few months, and he often bragged about how much money he made. They had all the latest in stereo equipment, and their house was well stocked with liquor. They had boozy barbecue parties every weekend in their backyard.

    I met a rising star in Black activism and politics at one of their backyard parties. He was sitting there with his greasy James Brown hairdo and fat belly, looking smug and half drunk, when I came over with my girlfriend, Felicia, hoping to get some food and drinks. We said hello to everyone, but I didn't feel particularly welcome, so before long, we politely excused ourselves. Back in my basement, Felicia told me the activist had keyed in on her. She really was quite beautiful and sexy. She was also seventeen. She said the activist took her hand, whispered in her ear, and slapped her on the ass.

    "Whispered what?" I wanted to know.

    "That nasty, fat old man asked if he could eat my pussy."

Breaking into a next-door neighbor's house is dangerous and foolish for obvious reasons, but breaking into Jimmy's was especially insane. Being the owner of a popular liquor store in the 1980s meant Jimmy was a constant target for getting stuck up, so he always carried a gun and openly flashed it. In fact, he readily bragged about his personal arsenal and how many people he'd shot already. The first time I ever saw and held an Uzi was when Jimmy proudly put it in my hands. "Niggas tried to stick up the store yesterday," he said. "I shot one of them with this bad boy here. Feel it, boy! That's death you're holding."

    Jimmy was also the first person I knew to own pit bulls. This was a decade before they became the hip-hop and "ghetto dog" of choice. His pit bulls were killers. He fed them raw meat doused in hot sauce and sprinkled with gunpowder to keep them mean. He also beat them mercilessly.

In other words, breaking into Jimmy's house meant I had a very probable chance of being either shot or ripped to pieces. I didn't give a fuck.

I let myself in through a basement window, with the family and the dogs sleeping one floor above. I cleaned him out. He had about three hundred dollars in cash lying around. I took that, his new stereo, a gold watch, and about ten bottles of liquor. Making two trips, I even cleaned out his mini fridge.

By 6 a.m., when he came knocking on my back door, I was pleasantly full of his ice cream and potato salad, and delightfully drunk on his Hennessy. He was holding a 9mm by his side. He said, "Some nigga broke in my house last night. When I find him, I'm gonna kill him." He looked at me suspiciously. I had been setting up his stereo when he knocked. I had his gold watch in my pocket and his Hennessy on my breath.

I said, "What?! Somebody had the nerve to rob you? Let's go find them motherfuckers!"

That summer, I broke into and robbed six more houses in the neighborhood. Always hauling my loot back to the basement. I was a basement-living, dumpster-diving, one-man crime wave.

Broken

IT WAS THE last day of summer break, and even though I was looking forward to starting eighth grade, I was trying to get the most out of the day. I was by the cemetery around the corner from my house, doing bike tricks with some other neighborhood kids and trying to impress Waynetta, the girl next door. I had a mad crush on Waynetta, but she rarely showed me any attention, which is another reason I was giving it my all that day. She actually clapped when I rode with no hands and one foot on the handlebars, so I decided I'd really impress her by doing a one-handed wheelie, something I'd never tried before. It was a bad idea. I barely had the front wheel off the ground when I lost control. The bike fell over, I twisted and contorted, and my leg snapped in two. A complete break of the tibia and fibula. Everyone heard and saw the snap. It sounded like a piece of heavy wood being cracked in two.

I limped to a car and sat on the hood. The break was midway between my knee and ankle. Waynetta ran over to help, but she was giggling when she said, "I think you gonna need stiches!" She playfully lifted my leg, holding it up below my knee and above the break. My leg drooped down as if a new knee had been created. It was surreal. I fainted.

Because of the severity of the break and because I was still growing, I was put in a cast up to my waist, and I had to take the year off from school, the year I was going to turn thirteen, the entry into my teens, the "bar mitzvah" year. The last year before high school, one of the most vital periods in developing a social identity. Because of the accident, I spent this important formative year basically alone.

I was assigned a tutor who came three times a week for an hour. He was a kindly little old Jewish man who used most of the time to tell me stories from his life and his escape from the Holocaust. I looked forward to his visits—not so much for his instruction, but for his stories and company.

My older brother was in rehab. Before then, he and I had gotten high together often, but I never thought he was out of control enough to land him in rehab. He was a troubled teen, but not really an addict. I thought it was my dad who needed rehab. He was the one who came home from work half drunk every night and proceeded to drink himself fully drunk before passing out. My mom worked nights. She slept most of the day and left for work in the late afternoon. Often, she'd come home in the early morning to find my dad in a deep, drunken sleep in front of the TV, a full ashtray by his side.

Mostly out of loneliness and boredom, I read nearly every book in the house. We had a couple of disorganized book cabinets on the porch that housed everything from trashy romance novels to Shakespeare. I read without discrimination. In fact, without knowing it, that year I read every book that would be required reading in high school. I also spent hours drawing and writing poems. I devoured my dad's record collection, and his collection of *Penthouse* and *Hustler* magazines. My fantasy world flourished.

At this point, my dad had switched to drinking wine. Before this time, he'd gone for beer and gin when he got home from work, but now he was buying sweet red wine by the gallon. I'd wait for him to fall out, usually only an hour or two after he came home, then pour myself a big glass, root through his ashtray for his filter-less Pall Mall butts, select which LPs I was going to listen to, and hobble on my crutches down to the basement, where my cheap stereo and headphones were. I broke open the cigarette butts and rolled the tobacco into two or three full cigarettes. Then I spent the next few hours being carried away by Santana, Miles Davis, Sly and the Family Stone, Dave Brubeck, or Jimi Hendrix. Like my dad, I got drunk every night.

Rose-Colored Glasses

DURING THAT YEAR I was out of school and in a cast up to my waist, my nice Jewish tutor did his best, but my real tutelage came from Michael Cappiello.

Michael was one of the last White kids left in the neighborhood. He seemed like a grown-up to me, knowledgeable and worldly, even though he was only five years older than me, and he gave me attention at a time when no one else did. Hippie Mike was my friend, teacher, guru, counselor, and coach. A couple of times a week, I grabbed my crutches and made my way up the block to hang out with him. Michael turned me on to some great music. Pink Floyd, the Beatles, the Who, Cream, and Led Zeppelin, and although our neighborhood had become predominantly West Indian by this point, Michael was also the first to play Bob Marley and the Wailers for me.

He was a natural character, brimming with charm, charisma, and humor. Hippie-handsome. He kind of fashioned himself after a young Eric Clapton, whom he really resembled. We smoked weed in his basement while he told me wild stories from his active imagination sparked by his love for *Star Wars* and *Heavy Metal* magazine. He was wildly entertaining and equally kind.

One day, I hobbled over to his basement on a freezing morning. Michael had made us hot chocolate, and he covered my exposed foot with a blanket. Then he lit a bowl of weed and handed me an awkwardly wrapped package. Taking a deep pull off the pipe, he said, "Here, kid. I been digging your little doodles. You got talent. Try this out and let your imagination go wild!"

Inside was a watercolor set, paintbrushes, a set of colored pencils, and a pad of art paper. I don't think he realized the profound impact that simple gesture of generosity had on me, and the lasting impact it would have on my life. I'd always been attracted to art, and I showed some natural talent for it, but I'd never received any real encouragement, or even acknowledgment, from my parents. By giving me those basic art supplies, Michael was telling me he saw me at time when I felt especially invisible.

I knew Mike was genuine and sincere, even though his tutelage came through a hippie's rose-colored glasses. He taught me the whole hippie aesthetic and philosophy of love, peace, and unity. As Mike explained it, hippies didn't see race and believed all people were one groovy family. I was hooked. I was a little broken-legged, nappy-afroed, weed-smoking, wine-sipping hippie at thirteen years old, and I loved my cool, hippie "big brother" more than anything.

Mike came to my door one afternoon, and I could tell

something special was happening, because he was decked out in his hippest of hippie finery—his favorite faded and patched bell-bottoms, his *keep on truckin'* square-toed worn leather boots, and his best and brightest tight tie-dyed T-shirt. His long hair was out in all its glory, and he'd wrapped a bandana around his forehead like a groovy shaman. He said, "C'mon, maaaaan! We're going to party!" Behind him was an old Volkswagen minivan full of freaks. It was a scene straight out of Haight-Ashbury circa 1967.

I somehow managed to get into the van with my cast and crutches. His friends welcomed me with hugs and handshakes, then somebody gave me a little handful of magic mushrooms and a bowl of weed. We drove for what felt like only a minute, but when we stopped, I looked up and realized we were actually across Brooklyn in Bensonhurst. That should have been my warning. Bensonhurst had the reputation of being no-man's-land for Blacks. It was known for its racist mobs of Irish and Italians, but as we got out of the van, Mike said, "Don't worry, it's cool. You're with me, and my friends are gonna love you. You're with me." I felt safe with Michael. I knew he wouldn't let anything bad happen to me.

We made it up to Mike's friend's flat, and a pretty hippie chick greeted me warmly at the door. She had long, straight blond hair and big blue eyes. Her cheek kiss and tight hug left me smelling like patchouli. The decor was exactly as I imagined a hippie place to be, all Indian paisley prints, plush pillows, and psychedelic posters. There were maybe ten people there. I was the youngest person by at least five years and the only person of color, which gave me a foreboding feeling in my gut, but because these were hippies, I rationalized I was safe. I couldn't move easily with the cast on my leg, so Mike set a cushion on the floor for me to sit on. Incense burned, and my favorite Floyd, Stones, Cream, and Hendrix played.

The mushrooms kicked in and made everything feel super profound, and the weed being passed around felt like a communal blessing. People danced and got into deep, esoteric conversations, and a sweet hippie couple decorated my cast with Magic Marker rainbows and flowers. This was the hippie bliss Mike had described. I felt connected and appreciated. I felt a beautiful, loving glow. I felt like I belonged.

After a couple of hours of tuning in and dropping out, a new group of hippies joined our commune. It was our hostess's boyfriend and his friends. The energy shifted almost immediately. The music changed from Hendrix and War to Lynyrd Skynyrd and the Allman Brothers. These guys looked like hippies with their long hair and faded denim, but there was something different about them. I could tell from the minute they saw a Black kid at the party, they weren't pleased about it.

As the evening progressed, the newcomers made snide, passive-aggressive remarks. "Hey, *soul brother*, sorry we don't have any disco music for you to boogie to. Ha ha! I'm just kidding!"

"Hey, *bro*! I bet you're starting to get the munchies. Should we send out for fried chicken?"

It was all said in a playful way, but even in my stoned state, I was picking up the vibes.

The new group started going in and out of one of the bedrooms. Through the open doorway, I saw a Confederate flag on the bedroom wall. When one of the hippies came out rubbing his nose, Mike whispered, "Coke."

Before long, the conversation got more intense and greasier, and a dark, aggressive energy invaded the space. One of the redneck hippies shouted across the room, "So, like, hey! Like, what are you even doing here, man? Trying to score a White girl?"

Another hippie, one of the original ones who had been cool with me an hour prior, piped in. "Yeah, like, you just been, like, smoking everybody's weed and, like, sitting there looking all sketchy."

I didn't know what to say.

A couple of the other cool hippies joined in with harsh, biting comments directed at me. They laughed, but none of it was funny.

Mike had gone into some other room, which made me feel like a vulnerable target. I didn't even really know where I was. Bensonhurst might as well have been another country. A hostile country.

Suddenly, Mike came out of the bedroom, followed by the hostess and her boyfriend. Mike helped me up because, apparently, they wanted me out immediately. Mike whispered, "Don't worry—I got you. It's cool, but we got to go now!"

I got to my feet with Mike's help and swung on my crutches to the door. Across my chest I carried a small Indian shoulder bag Mike had given me. It was my magic hippie shaman bag, and I always wore it with pride whenever I hung out with Mike. It was my "stash" bag, where I kept a pad and pencils, a pipe and matches, groovy rose-colored sunglasses, and whatever book I was reading at the time.

As we got to the door, the hostess pushed hard on my chest. "Where do you think you're going with my stuff? You're not leaving until you empty the bag!"

Mike protested weakly. It was weird to see him so timid.

She said to him, "It's your fault for bringing a thieving nigger into my house!"

Her boyfriend yanked the bag over my head and dumped the contents on the floor. Nothing stolen.

One of the guys said, "Check his pockets!" He held me roughly and shoved his hands into my pockets, pulling them inside out. When he didn't find anything, he knocked the crutches from my hand and pushed me down. Then he turned around, stormed into the bedroom, and slammed the door.

I lay on the floor and started to cry. I couldn't get up on my own, and no one moved to help me. Mike gathered my things and finally got me to my feet. None of the hippies would even look at me.

We got downstairs, and the hippie hostess came hustling down after us. She looked at us like she was about to apologize. Then she said, "Hey, man! Sorry it had to go down like that, but you know all niggers steal, and you're a nigger, so... you shouldn't have come here."

When I got home that evening, I noticed the groovy rose-colored hippie sunglasses I had in my shoulder bag had been crushed.

Gizmo and Gadget

WHEN I STARTED my freshman year of high school, I was a noticeably different kid. After spending a year alone, I felt no need to be part of any cliques or in-groups. I had my own style. I was mostly quiet and observant, and when I did speak, I wasn't interested in gossip and small talk. Most classes bored me. I'd already read all the books my peers would be expected to read in their coming four years, and I'd done it for fun.

While most of the kids were just starting to experiment with drinking, smoking cigarettes, and weed, I was already an old head. In my racially segregated school, I communicated as easily with the White kids as I did with the Black ones. I was tough, but I didn't roll with the hard rocks. I smoked, but I didn't hang out with the stoners. I was good at sports, but I didn't join any teams or run with the jocks. I was smart but not a nerd. I was all those things and none of them, and I think it was my indifference to being popular that made me popular.

I stopped going to class. I went to school but hung out alone in empty back staircases, reading, writing poetry, sketching, and fantasizing that I was a rock star. I sold weed and fooled around with girls. I had no interest in grades or diplomas, and many days I simply cut school altogether and roamed the streets and parks.

Gizmo and Gadget were the most notorious neighborhood gangstas at the time. They were the prototype for what rappers in the '90s would later refer to. When Onyx, Biggie, or Wu-Tang talked about "bad boys," they were describing Gizmo and Gadget. They were Brooklyn legends at a time when Brooklyn was at its grimiest and most dangerous.

When I'd been in middle school, kids spoke about Gizmo and Gadget the way middle school kids talk about everything, all exaggeration and hearsay, making them into local superheroes and trying to top one another with what they knew.

"I heard from my cousin who lives in the same building as Gadget that him and Gizmo robbed a bank in the city and then came back to the projects with bags of cash and just handed it out!"

"Yeah, well, I heard from my big brother who went to school with Gizmo's girlfriend that him and Gadget threw a dude off the roof last week, and the cops were too scared to even do anything, even though everybody saw them do it."

There were so many rumors and stories going around about Gizmo and Gadget, no one really knew what was true. What I did know for sure about them was they came from out of the Vanderveer projects. *No one* questioned their supremacy in that neighborhood. They were the founding members and leaders of the Decepticons, a ruthless gang responsible for all kinds of terrorism. A gang at the forefront of the crack era.

The Decepticons were a new kind of street gang in Brooklyn, very different from their predecessors, like the Tomahawks or the Jolly Stompers. First, the Decepticons didn't fly colors or wear gang paraphernalia, and they didn't "rumble" with other gangs. Because they didn't make a big show of numbers and were basically anonymous, it was impossible to know who was connected to the gang, and that was their strength; because of it, they ruled quietly and deadly. They were also different from their predecessors in that the majority of them were first-generation West Indian, mostly Jamaican. They were more like the Mafia than a typical street gang, more about money and power than turf, and like the Mafia, the Decepticons murdered their rivals. They ushered in the gun era. You didn't get beaten up by Decepticons. You went missing.

Harlem had the Supreme Team. Brooklyn had the Decepticons.

The first time I saw Gizmo and Gadget was a couple of days before the last day of seventh grade. Kids were nervous because the school was distributing the school rings for those lucky enough to afford one, and the word was out that hard rocks from Erasmus Hall High School were going to swoop down at 3 p.m. and go on a robbing spree.

Everything was quiet until we reached the bus stop. Then the word went up: "It's Gizmo and Gadget and them! It's Gizmo and Gadget!" Sure enough, I looked up to see these legends turn the corner. It was like we were being descended upon by gods in matching starched Lee denim and crisp new Pumas.

I had an image in my mind of how they would look. In my imagination, they were both big and tall with that kind of hard, lean muscular physique, like hungry wolves. Dark-skinned and handsome in a sinister kind of way. In my mind, they dressed in the height of Brooklyn hard rock fashion: mock necks, gabardines, Kangols, and fresh sneakers. I pictured them as kind of interchangeable, like they looked so much alike you could mix them up.

I got most of it wrong.

Gizmo was in fact tall and dark-skinned, but he wasn't thin. He was big and muscular, but he wasn't any kind of handsome. His features were coarse, and his skin was pockmarked. He was just plain scary-looking. Gadget was no kind of tall. He was short and squat, and he was caramel-colored, with sort of a baby face and hair that was nappy like it was one or two days from becoming dreadlocked.

The one thing I did get right was they both dressed sharp. Gadget tended to look more like a Kingston rude boy than a Brooklyn hard rock, but they both wore lots of gold, and each rocked a gold tooth. Gizmo wore a large diamond stud earring, and Gadget had gold rings on each of his fingers.

Here they were in the flesh, walking with the iconic flat-footed, hard rock bop. Almost like they were moving to a rhythm. Behind them were three or four other notorious thugs from Vanderveer. I recognized Fat Cat and Bam Bam, mini street legends in their own right.

We kids froze in a combination of awe and fear. It was almost like an honor to be robbed by Gizmo and Gadget. They waded into us middle schoolers, taking what they wanted at will. Most of the kids just handed over their rings and stood there crying. A couple had to be yoked up in order to let go of their rings, and one or two got a bloody nose, but it was Gerald Jean Francois who became our hero that day.

Some of the kids who gave up their rings were the bullies and bad boys of our middle school. Kids like Roland and Reggie were baby gangsters, but even those guys didn't try to fight back. It was Gerald, the Haitian kid who wore church shoes to gym class, the only kid who wore a tie and smiled in class photos. Gerald, the kid who kept a little Bible in his book bag. Gerald, the kid who actually *had* a book bag. It was this little nerd who fought back. He was *not* letting go of his ring.

Gizmo and Gadget had Gerald between them, and they were taking turns hitting him in the head and chest so hard you could hear the impact. Gerald's nose was bleeding, and he was spitting blood. They pushed him down and his head hit the concrete hard. They held him in a yoke, and his knees scraped the ground and bled. It was brutal. Gerald curled up in a fetal position, and Gizmo kept kicking him until Gadget finally pulled him off. Then Gadget did something that surprised everybody. He lifted Gerald up gently and smiled at him. He even brushed him off a little before he let him go.

Gerald came to school the next day. He never missed school. His eye was black and swollen, his lips were split, a patch of his hair was cut out for stitches, and he was limping, *but* he was wearing his ring! When I asked him why he took such a beating for that stupid ring, he smiled and said, "You think *that* was a bad beating? That's nothing compared to what my mom would have done if I came home without the ring she paid for."

* * *

Gossip, rumors, and stories about Gizmo and Gadget continued to grow, as did their status as Brooklyn gangster legends. At the height of the Decepticons' influence, they were rumored to be making thousands of dollars a day moving cocaine and crack.

One morning in my freshman year, I decided to skip school like I had done so many days before. I walked to Foster Park, about ten blocks from the Vanderveer projects, which was considered neutral ground. It was more of a family park than a "hangout" spot. It was maybe 8 a.m., and the park was basically empty. Everybody was at school or work. I strolled to find a bench to chill on, and I wasn't really paying attention to where I was going. I heard "Peace, God," the universal greeting at the time.

"Peace," I responded automatically. Then I registered where the greeting had come from. First, I saw the hands. Gold rings on every finger. Then the crisp, clean Pumas in deep royal maroon, a color I'd never seen before in any sneaker. Then I looked up and saw the baby face and the gold-toothed smile. Gadget was sitting alone. I was so surprised that I wasn't even scared.

He asked, "You smoke?"

I nodded.

He motioned for me to sit on his bench. Then he passed me a fat joint and a lighter. I lit up. I didn't have the slightest idea of what to say or do, so I just sat quietly.

When I went to pass him the joint he said, "Nah, that's all you, sun." He lit his own, and then started speaking in hushed tones to me. He talked about how he missed his mother and his family back in Jamaica. "I been here too long, sun. This country cold and dirty. It made me cold and dirty. Back home, I was different." He talked about a girl he'd been seeing. He told me she was pregnant. "I got mad women, but I ain't got one woman, you feel me? They like what I be giving them, money and jewelry, but they don't like me." He talked about feeling like no one understood him. He said he was tired. He said he regretted many things he'd done. "Sometimes I be doing shit, and it ain't really me. It's like something gets inside of me, and I can't control that shit. It ain't me, God. It's like a devil inside of me. Sometimes I be scared of my own self." He coughed at one point and blew his nose. I knew it was to hide his crying.

I listened, nodded, said nothing.

He talked until he finished his joint. Then he stood up and walked away.

I sat there for a while, thinking I'd just had an impromptu therapy session with a murderer. Wondering if it put my life in danger. Deciding I didn't care if it did.

I sat there until I finished my joint. Then I got up and walked away.

Ray Ray's Reparations

IN THE EARLY '80s, I was one of the very few Black kids in Brooklyn who not only listened to punk rock and new wave music but also dressed the part. I took my fair share of abuse for this. I think most of the people in my neighborhood simply had no point of reference for a nappy-headed Black kid in ripped and torn skinny jeans and holey T-shirts held together with safety pins. I wore old-man baggy, wrinkled suits and big army boots at a time when most Black kids were wearing fresh coordinated polyester outfits with sharp creases. I'd switched up my style a year or so earlier, after I heard the Sex Pistols and the Clash. The messages in the lyrics of their songs and their look crystallized what I was feeling: rebellious rage, teenage angst, and a desire to be boldly different. Before then, I'd been like everybody else, all sharp creases, gabardines, and Kangols. Ever since the change, most of my hard rock and bad boy dreadlock friends regarded me with confusion or disdain. "Yo! Fuck happened to you? You be looking like a whodunit. A mystery mess." I got called freak, weirdo, madman, and faggot on the daily, all of which I took with pride.

Although I took verbal beatings and got plenty of strange looks, no one ever tried to step to me physically. Maybe I looked too crazy, or maybe despite looking like a complete outcast, I still managed to walk with a swag. I had confidence.

When MTV hit the air, the neighborhood dudes started to catch on a little. "Oh! You on that weirdo White boy new punk wave rock shit!" I did most of my shopping at the Salvation Army in Brooklyn, where you could still get an original '60s suit for a couple of bucks. It's where I found my favorite fuzzy mohair sweater for about fifty cents. I was rocking it one time, and Dexter, the neighborhood hard rock comedian, called me a "Muppet on drugs." Damn, I loved that sweater!

Occasionally, if I managed to come up on some money, I'd go to Trash and Vaudeville or Manic Panic on St. Mark's Place in the East Village for some freaky shit from England, like creeper shoes and bondage pants, but more often I was getting my chains and studs from local pet shops for a fraction of the price.

I was one of the rare kids from my hood who ventured to the city to hang out, so by the time I was seventeen I'd already been to all the iconic clubs. I slid into the Mudd Club and chilled next to Basquiat before he was Basquiat. I scooped up chicks from New Jersey at Danceteria and the Peppermint Lounge. I hung out hard at CBGB.

I liked CBGB the best. I had a way of talking my way in, so I rarely paid. The place was my kind of gritty and tough. It was cramped, dark, and dirty. The filthy bathrooms were covered in scrawls and had no doors. It wasn't for the faint of heart, but I saw some great bands there. Loud, fast punk bands. Bad Brains and Minor Threat blew me away with their speed and precision, as well as their messages of righteous rebellion, but it was bands like Agnostic Front, Reagan Youth, Warzone, and Kraut that really set the scene. Those bands were mostly made up of street kids who hung around the Lower East Side. Not always the most talented, but all heart.

Between CBGB and A7 on Avenue A, there was a whole multiculti, grimy hardcore punk rock scene happening. Being a part of it meant not recognizing it was happening. It was organic.

One night I left A7 half drunk and followed a crew to a loft party somewhere nearby, where there was this terrible punk band playing all awkward and out of tune. They sucked musically, but they didn't take themselves seriously. They cracked self-deprecating jokes between songs, and I enjoyed their slapstick. I slam danced in front of the improvised stage and accidentally smacked the shit out of a girl behind me with my wild, swinging arms. I busted her nose pretty badly. There was a bit of a fuss when her boyfriend tried to stick his chest out. "Hey, buddy, you hit my girl!"

I said, "Nah, man, *she* hit my hand with her nose. She needs to apologize!"

The band kept playing, and it all blew over soon enough, bloody nose and all. It turned out the band was the Beastie Boys. I'm pretty sure it was their first gig.

* * *

One fall afternoon, I was about to jump the Q train at Newkirk Avenue, heading to CBGB to catch a hardcore matinee show, when I heard, "Ay, yo! That's you? Waddup, kid?!" I turned to see my dude Ray Ray, aka Cut 'Em Up, strolling up with his infamous flat-footed (so your sneakers don't crease) homeboy stride. I knew Ray from round my way, and I was always happy to see him for several reasons, one being we went way back and had done our share of dirt together, stole a bit and sold some weed. It gave us a bond and a history. I trusted him. Secondly, Ray had a well-deserved rep. He was a real hard rock, a thug before they were being called thugs. Nobody fucked with Ray, and if I was running with Ray, nobody fucked with me. Third thing that made me happy to see Ray was he always had weed and was never stingy with it. Most of the time, he was selling treys, nickels, and loose joints, but he never hesitated to light up anywhere, anytime. If I ran into Ray, I was guaranteed to get high, and I was always down for that. Lastly and most importantly, I genuinely liked him. He was bold, smart, and funny, and as bad as he was, I knew he had a good heart.

He went simply by Ray Ray when we first met. I think it was a combination of things that eventually earned him the nickname Cut 'Em Up. We joked and play fought a lot, but after he got sent away to Spofford Juvenile Detention Center in the Bronx for doing some stickups, things changed, including his nickname. After a year in Spofford, Ray showed up again, still funny and upbeat, but with a kind of darkness to him. He also came back with a fresh scar that ran down the side of his face, the result of a razor blade fight. It took a long time to heal, and even when Ray was laughing, he looked dangerous. Now Ray was "cut up."

He'd always been good with his hands. Fast, strong, and

skilled at jailhousing, the name for the type of street boxing that originated at Rikers Island. Jailhouse rock, or 52 blocks, was like a combination of kung fu hand blocks picked up from '70s martial arts movies and actual boxing techniques. It looked like a kind of stylish dance, but when done right, jailhouse was quite effective for offense and defense. I've seen quite a few niggas knocked out jailhousing, and Ray was responsible for many of those KOs. Ray was quick to play box with anyone, but when he got back from juvie, he was less playful with the boxing and more serious about carrying a knife. A 007 knife, to be precise.

These knives were very popular at the time. Cheap, easy to get, and deadly. A 007 was a collapsible knife with a wooden handle and a rawhide string that wrapped around your hand to keep it from slipping or being snatched during a knife fight. It came in a variety of sizes, from a three-inch to an eight-inch blade. Ray carried the eight-inch, and it seemed he didn't go anywhere without that knife. After a while, he got a reputation for using it. A rumor went around saying he'd cut up and stabbed several people.

Either of those things, the scar or the knife, could have earned him the nickname Cut 'Em Up, but there was something else.

Ray was the first kid on our block to get two turntables and a mixer. Years before the term *hip-hop* was coined, DJing and MCing had been a thing in our neighborhood, but only a few people were doing it. Then it seemed like overnight, everybody was a DJ or MC. To be a DJ, you needed money or some other means to get the necessary equipment and records and space to set up and practice. I'm pretty sure Ray Ray got his DJ setup by "other means." Along with the turntables and mixer, he acquired some giant-ass speakers and two copies of "Freedom" by Grandmaster Flash & the Furious Five. As far as I knew, he never had any other records. He would blast the song over and over for hours, mixing, scratching, and "cutting" it back and forth between turntables. He started calling himself Cool DJ Cut 'Em Up Ray Ray, which eventually got shortened to Cut 'Em Up Ray, and then just Cut 'Em Up.

On that afternoon, there I was, standing outside the train station dressed in my old torn T-shirt, ripped and dirty tight black jeans, worn army boots, and a flannel shirt tied around my waist. Cut 'Em Up playfully looked me up and down. "Yo! What happened to you, kid?!" He questioned my crazy look kind of out of duty, but it was more of a tease than a real question. "Yo! Where you going looking like a bum-ass reject?"

I told him where I was headed. Told him how wild CBGB was and how crazy these White boys acted when those loud, fast bands played.

He said, "Let me ask you something. Do them White boys smoke weed?"

I knew exactly what Ray was thinking.

Customers.

Next thing I knew, Cut 'Em Up and I were on the Q train, passing a joint back and forth and cracking jokes on all the other riders. We must have looked like an odd couple. There was bum-ass reject me, and there was Cut 'Em Up in the impeccable height of B-boy fashion: blue Kangol (tilted to the side); Cazal glasses (minus lenses); a blue nylon T-shirt; a gold-link box medallion around his neck; a sharp-creased, two-piece Lee jeans set; and straight-out-the-box blue Puma Clydes with fat laces. He was clean, crisp, and new, and I was dirty, ripped, and old.

When we got to the city, I could tell Cut 'Em Up was out of his element. He stuck close to me and stared around in wonder at even the simplest things—the tall buildings, men walking hand in hand, the diversity. He was like a wide-eyed tourist in his own city. He kept saying, "Yo! I'm buggin'! It's wild out here!" It occurred to me he never really traveled much beyond our neighborhood, even to other parts of Brooklyn, let alone Manhattan. Going over the bridge was an adventure for Ray Ray.

At CBGB, the doormen gave him weird looks. He was so clearly out of place. Just being Black made us a major minority, but at least I dressed the part and kind of blended in. Cut 'Em Up stood out like the goth kid at a church picnic. He knew it, too, and it made him overcompensate. His B-boy stance got extra B-boy, and he kept his arms so tightly crossed around his chest, it looked like he was trying to hug himself to death. He stayed at my side like an obedient puppy and said, over and over, like a mantra, "Yo! This shit is bugged out, kid! This shit is bugged out."

Eventually, some skinhead White kid approached him and asked if he had any weed. I mean, after all, a B-boy at a CBGB hardcore matinee could only be there for one reason, right?

"Dude, you holdin'?" the skinhead said.

Ray Ray looked at me, then back at the skinhead, and said, "Yeah, man, I'm holding. Holding these nuts!" as he cupped himself.

Within minutes, Cut 'Em Up looked like he was standing on the trading floor of the New York Stock Exchange. White boys surrounded him, holding up their cash trying to score a bag or a joint. Cut 'Em Up's gold tooth glistened as he smiled his biggest "make money, money, money!" smile. He sold out just as a band took the stage. A local three-piece hardcore band I'd seen before. The packed crowd began to push and shove. The sound from the stage was deafeningly loud. I looked over at my man, expecting him to be ready to leave, but he was still smiling, even with his fingers in his ears.

Then the mosh pit started in front of the stage, and I stepped back as far as I could to avoid the flailing arms and swinging fists. Slam dancing is a melee. It always seemed to me like White dudes having tantrums and taking out their angst on one another, but I enjoyed the energy and spectacle. Soon dudes were throwing each other around, banging and crashing into one another. It looked like a brawl from an old Western. I tried to pull Cut 'Em Up back from the melee, but he wasn't moving. He stood there with his mouth open in absolute awe. The first song was over in about two minutes, and during the brief pause of relative quiet, he shouted, "Yo! What the fuck is they doing?!"

I yelled back, "Slam dancing!"

He looked at me with a scrunched forehead. "That's *dancing*?!"

One or two more quick songs later and the mosh pit was really swinging. Then, without warning, Cool DJ Cut 'Em Up Ray Ray dove in!

In seconds, he was enveloped by the crowd, and I lost sight of him, but I felt a shift in the pit. The energy seemed to go up a notch. A song or two later, Ray parted the crowd like Moses and the Red Sea and emerged to hand me his 007, Kangol, and Cazals. He stripped off his jacket, chain, and T-shirt, and waded back in, wearing a smile like a kid opening presents on Christmas morning. It was the happiest I'd ever seen him! There was my man from round the way in the middle of the mosh pit at a CBGB hardcore matinee doing serious bodily damage.

Cut 'Em Up was cutting up! Throwing White boys left and right like a tornado. He was slamming, pushing, punching, kicking, stomping, and tossing anybody he could get his hands on. Ray was on a search and destroy mission. He was shirtless and sweating like a slave in the sun, and all the while, the gold tooth glistened and the scar on the side of his face stretched with joy as he manhandled them White boys. When the band finished playing, Ray stood alone like he was in the middle of ground zero, then he turned in a full circle to survey the wreckage he'd caused. He'd definitely earned respect in the pit.

Cut 'Em Up Ray may have never gotten his forty acres and a mule, but he sure as hell got some reparations that afternoon.

Gangsters I

WHEN I WAS growing up, it was always said there was no such thing as the Mafia. It was always said with a wink. At Marine Park Junior High School, there was a kid named Vinnie Cuccia, who was a regular terror. He was this skinny little blond kid who used to fuck with everybody. He cursed out teachers, smoked cigarettes in the hallway, always had a billfold of cash, and came and went in and out of classrooms as he pleased. The security guards gave him a pass, and the teachers all kissed his ass. Even the hard rocks and homeboys stayed out of his way. Vinnie dressed sharp for a White boy—no jeans. He stayed crisp in coordinated tracksuits. He had the gold chain with the horn on it, and the pinkie ring. All the girls loved Vinnie (even the Black girls), and he was always shadowed by his goon, Big Tony. Vinnie was a gangster in training.

When I turned fifteen, my friend Chris, one of the last Italian kids left in East Flatbush, got me a job at the Glenwood flea market on weekends. The flea market was actually a warehouse filled with makeshift booths of merchandise that had "fallen off the back of a truck." This was in the disco and classic rock era, when the Mafia was running things in New York City.

Chris and I worked for a Jewish Vietnam vet named Andy Allenberg, who sold refurbished stereos, electronics, records, and head supplies (pipes, rolling papers, scales, etc.). Next to us was a booth that sold discount leather jackets and fur coats. On the other side, a booth that sold cartons of cigarettes and bottles of liquor under the counter. It was all super shady.

Andy was a sweet guy, but he was also a junkie with a gambling problem who owed money to loan sharks. Every Sunday right before we closed up, he'd give me an envelope full of twenty-dollar bills, then dash out, saying he had to "be somewhere." Fifteen minutes later, two guys would show up. *Big* guys, with hands like hams.

The shorter of the two always did all the talking. "Hey, kid! Where's your boss, eh?" They seemed to be laughing at an inside joke. "Did he leave us anything?" I'd hand over the envelope, and they'd usually peel me off a twenty-dollar bill, slap me not too gently across the cheeks, and say, "Here ya go, kid! Buy your girlfriend something nice." In 1978, twenty dollars for a fifteen-year-old was *a lot* of money, so I was happy to be the go-between.

One time, the flea market got broken into and robbed. It was a case of gangsters robbing gangsters for stuff that had been stolen in the first place. Chris and I got there early to open up, saw the place had been ransacked, and immediately realized it was a golden opportunity. It was a giant place with a lot of booths, and there was still a lot of stuff left that the thieves hadn't taken. We climbed over the partition into the booth next to Andy's and filled four huge Hefty bags with mink coats and leather jackets. Then we went down the aisles stuffing bags with designer jeans, cartons of cigarettes, and bottles of booze. To remove suspicion, we even robbed our own booth, taking a couple boom boxes and stereos. We moved fast and hid the haul in the dumpster behind the warehouse before the other vendors showed up. When they did start to arrive at the flea market, there was general confusion, pulling of hair and gnashing of teeth among the vendors, but there also was a sense of resignation. They seemed to know the people who had robbed them were beyond retribution. Nobody called the cops.

Later that night, Chris and I went back to collect what we'd stashed. It took us three trips to get it all to my basement. We'd scored big-time! We figured we'd stolen a few thousand dollars' worth of merchandise.

We got away with stealing from gangsters, but we'd been really stupid to do it. Some other people weren't so lucky. About a month after the break-in, the two "nice guys" who used to collect the money from Andy were found executed on the abandoned train tracks behind Brooklyn College. The guy who owned the mink and leather booth next to us mysteriously disappeared, and we heard the guy who sold the cigarettes and booze suddenly "moved to Florida." The booths started closing one by one, and about a month after those murders, the Glenwood flea market closed for good.

I saw Andy one last time, a couple of months after the flea market closed. He stopped by my house and asked me to come sit in his van with him. He was a mess, smoking joint after joint. Had two burning at the same time. He was sweating, shaking. The war and his addictions had fucked him up. At that point, my own addictions to alcohol and drugs were just beginning, and I saw Andy as a cautionary tale, one that, unfortunately, I took no heed of. When I got into his van that day, I saw he'd packed it with what looked like everything he owned. And he'd lost a ton of weight. He kept asking me if I'd heard anything, if I knew anything. He kind of implied I'd had something to do with the robbery.

Sometime later, Andy had an "accident." He was found with half his head blown off. There is no gangsters' paradise.

A Monkey Can't Sell Bananas

I AM AN addict.

Marijuana was *A Love Supreme* by John Coltrane, "Singing Winds, Crying Beasts" by Santana, and every reggae song recorded before 1990. Marijuana was Tater Tots and a blueberry-banana smoothie. It was that mellow friend who just wanted to hang out and give you an unsolicited shoulder massage. It meant no harm.

I don't remember the first time I smoked weed, but it was probably with my brother and cousins, and probably when I was about eleven or twelve years old. My brother was three years older than me, and by then he was already selling weed. One time, he hid his stash under the couch cushion, and our dumb dog Dizzy found it and ate what was about an ounce of primo bud. That poor dog was ripped out of her mind for days. She laughed at her own doggie jokes, barked at nothing, spun around in circles, and jumped in paranoia. I think it was seeing the dog like that that made me want to try it.

I loved it right away. I loved the hazy, warm rush to my head from the first puff, and the feeling of relaxed numbness it gave me with every puff after. I smoked whenever I could and found like-minded kids to hang out with. By sixth grade, I'd gravitated to the stoners, the faux-hippie kids in the Grateful Dead tie-dyed T-shirts. My White friends Josh and Greg always seemed to have weed to spare, and it was good weed; that's when I learned a friend with weed is a friend indeed. I got a reputation as a mooch, but I didn't care what people called me as long as I could get high.

I loved the ritual of weed. With my brothers, cousins, and Black friends, it was pulling out the album cover to strain and clean the herb from stems and seeds. Our reefer, or cheeba, came in treys and nickels, little manila envelopes that cost three and five dollars. We'd gather our quarters and dollars and chip in to get a bag from a barely disguised storefront. It was poor-quality herb, dry and full of stems and seeds that gave us headaches. We usually smoked skinny joints rolled in Bambú or E-Z Wider papers. "Puff, puff, and pass" in a cipher often accompanied by quart bottles of Olde English or Colt 45 malt liquor. We told jokes and tall tales. The weed made the jokes funnier and the tales taller. Sometimes conversations would get heavy and deep, and the weed helped to get us vulnerable. We'd play fight or look for some adventure to get into. Buggin' out. With my Black friends, getting high was a very communal act, and being high together bonded us. I didn't get high with people I didn't like or trust. Unless they had weed, of course.

Smoking with White kids was different. They usually had high-quality stuff. Sticky buds of sinsemilla or Thai stick that came in plastic ziplock bags. There was usually more of it, too. Smoking with White folks had a different rhythm. Not better or worse, just different. With Black kids, I smoked exclusively joints, but with White guys I smoked pipes and bongs, as well as joints. There was still the ritual of rolling, but also of packing the pipe or bong, and although the weed was passed around, it never felt as communal to me when the White guys were involved. We were most likely going to listen to music and drift off in our own hazy bubbles.

Getting high always seemed to have a spiritual component for me. My friends and I might be cracking jokes and talking shit, or just chilling and listening to music, but I still felt the beneficent spirit of the herb. Somehow, smoking gave me an awareness that I wasn't alone and there was a mystical higher power all around me.

When I smoked with my Rastafarian friends, that spiritual vibration was most apparent. To Rastafarians, herb was the "healing of the nation" and was to be used to reach "Ites," which means spiritual heights. It is a holy sacrament and a gift from the Most High (a name for God I always found to be ironic). The holy herb was believed to be found growing on the grave of King Solomon and was ordained to heighten wisdom, awareness, and connection to spirit.

We smoked ganja, or kali, in baseball bat–shaped spliffs rolled in paper, a corn husk, or fronto, which was whole tobacco leaf. Spliffs were rarely passed. Each man rolled and smoked his own, but it was done together, ceremoniously. We sometimes smoked in a chalice or chillum that was passed around, and this kind of smoking always felt the most sacred to me. True Rastafarians made smoking a ritual. Often, we read Bible passages as we smoked. Then we'd reason and build. "Jah! Rastafari!" my friend Jabari would proclaim, letting out a thick plume of smoke. "Brethren, I and I are like the tree planted by the rivers of water. Rooted to stand firm in Babylon, seen?" to which we would reply, in unison, "Rastafari!" Then one of us might quote a scripture to further the stream of thought.

Two devout Rastas, Ras Enoch and Ras Ephrim, who ran a recording studio situated above a Burger King on Flatbush Avenue, were so holy they rolled their spliffs using pages from the King James Bible. They said their plan was to "smoke the whole Bible." When I came to know and hang out with them, they were already up to the psalms.

I had the honor to smoke with the one Peter Tosh on several occasions. I absolutely revered Peter for his music and righteous spiritual militancy. Peter Tosh was my hero. He held court and entertained by sharing stories and philosophies. Mostly, he made me laugh. At the time, I was working at a video store on the Upper West Side. Tosh randomly wandered into the store one day, rented a bunch of vampire movies, and left me a spliff as a tip. After that, Peter began to drop in almost daily to spend time and peruse the movie selections. We became friends. One time, he ran out of herb, so I gave him all I had: a nickel bag, which he promptly rolled into a single spliff. The next day, he took off for Jamaica. About a month later, he strolled into the shop and plopped a big ziplock bag of herb on the counter, along with a bag of mangoes he'd picked himself from his land back home. He smiled and said, "I didn't forget the I." There were probably two ounces of premium bud in that ziplock bag. It felt like I had been anointed. I called the weed my "Tosh" and smoked it with great reverence.

If I could have continued to smoke herb in the way I believe it was intended—as a spiritual exercise, the way the Rastafarians used it—I would've happily done so, but I am an addict. Some say marijuana isn't addictive, but anything can be addictive if you have an addictive personality. They also say weed is a gateway drug. I think it's a gateway only for those who were heading through the gate anyway. I'm one of those unfortunates.

I was an unsuccessful weed dealer for a short time, unsuccessful for the same reason a monkey can't sell bananas. I got my start as a freshman at James Madison High School. Clarence, one of the school's security guards, noticed I got along with both the White and the Black kids and saw it as an opportunity to make some money. At the start of a week, Clarence gave me a bundle of pre-rolled skinny joints, then told me where and when it was safe to sell in the school. He knew the schedules and locations of the other security guards, and he would slide me in. He encouraged me to cut classes to be more available to move the joints, and I gladly complied. I worked the hallways and back stairways and both the Black and White sides of the bleachers, and I usually sold out by midweek and would have to re-up with another bundle of loose joints from Clarence.

On Sunday evenings, he'd stop by my house to collect his money. I was selling about fifty joints a week at a dollar a pop, and my pay was a joint for every five I sold. The arrangement kept me high, but I didn't like the idea of working for anyone, Clarence in particular. I never trusted him and I didn't like him. Even though I agreed to sell joints for him, I thought it was pretty sleazy of him to have a kid sell his weed in school. I quit after a couple of months. Clarence threatened to bust me by letting the dean know I'd been selling weed. He said, "If you quit now, I'm gonna get you kicked out of school for selling weed!"

"And if you do that," I said, "I'll have you fired and arrested for giving me the weed to sell, stupid!"

Back when I still worked for Andy at the flea market, I was often left alone in his booth for hours at a time. Eventually, he gave me the keys and stopped showing up at all. Andy was always disheveled and confused, and he was extremely disorganized. The booth doubled as his storage spot, and there was all kinds of stuff under the counters and tucked everywhere. On a slow Sunday, I was bored and started cleaning and organizing the booth, when I found buried under the counter and covered with dust and miscellaneous crap a big Hefty garbage bag.

It was a little less than a pound of weed, and by that point, I'd had enough experience to know simply by sight and smell that it was exceptionally good weed.

It was a little dry but definitely top-notch. Based on the thick layer of dust on the bag and the dryness of the bud, I guessed it had been tucked away for at least a year. Andy must have forgotten about it.

I didn't take the whole bag at once. I tried an experiment first. With Andy gone almost all the time, I figured I could sneak a bit of the weed and gauge over a couple of weeks if he noticed any missing. I reached in and grabbed a generous handful, then tucked the bag back where I'd found it. My friends and I stayed high as fuck that week. And the following week. The bag hadn't moved, which told me Andy hadn't noticed.

I took the Hefty bag home with me. I dropped out of high school, kept the part-time flea market gig, and went into the weed-selling business full-time. I bagged it up, rolled it up, and parceled it out. Ounces, halves, quarters, nickel bags, and loose joints. I spent my days and nights in the East Village at clubs, in Tompkins Square Park, and on street corners, peddling my product. Two or three months went by in a blur. I didn't make any money to speak of because I smoked my profits. I was high the entire time, which was ultimately my goal.

Over the years, I tried a few more times to sell herb, even though I realized from early on that to make it as a weed dealer, you can't smoke your product.

I'm a monkey with a banana.

I am an addict.

Godbody II

MY NEIGHBORHOOD OF East Flatbush was almost completely West Indian. The first time I saw a real-life Rastafarian was on Flatbush Avenue, somewhere around 1976. He was riding a bike down the busy street, pedaling with one foot and steering the handlebars with the other while reading the Bible and smoking a spliff! He was a young man, tall, thin, and dark, with a little scruff of hair on his chin that reminded me of a billy goat. He was cool, dressed in army fatigues and Clarks desert boots, but it was his hair that sealed the deal for me. What little I knew of Rastas then revolved around the mystery of their majestic manes of dreadlocked hair. Most of his was tucked into a huge red, yellow, and green knit hat, but a few strands broke free and went all the way down his back. He had a royal presence and reminded me of a lion. I wanted to be exactly like him.

If His Imperial Majesty Haile Selassie I Ras-Tafari-the King of Kings and Lord of Lords, the Conquering Lion from the tribe of Judah, and the elect of God was the living incarnation of Jah (Jehovah), then Bob Marley was His prophet, His Muhammad, His messenger. It was through Bob Marley's music and lyrics that "I and I" first began to feel and know Rastafarianism. I would gain a "higher height" of "overstanding" about the "groundations," the principles and tenets of Rasta, over time, but Marley was the entry and ambassador. Bob was my primary teacher.

The first two spiritual movements that attracted me did so through music, language, and style. The other connection was the emphasis on Black pride and culture. The Five Percent Nation of Gods and Earths and the Rastafarians represented righteous rebellion against the old colonial mindset. The wicked ten percent that controlled government and big business of the Five Percent doctrine equaled the "Babylon" of the Rastas' doctrine.

On my seventeenth birthday, my Jamaican girlfriend, Felicia, gave me one of the most important gifts of my life. A drum set.

I spent hours, days, weeks, months, and years teaching myself how to play. I locked myself in my basement and played along with my reggae musical heroes for whole days at a time. I practiced religiously. It got so that there wasn't any Burning Spear, Black Uhuru, or Steel Pulse "riddim" I couldn't play beat for beat. While my peers were at school, hanging out, or partying and doing the things normal teenagers do, I was alone in my basement, smoking my herb, letting my hair grow and knot, and playing drums. As my skill level improved and deepened, so did my immersion into Rastafari.

In the summer of 1979, my best friend, Keith, and I formed a reggae band. We argued endlessly over what to name our group, but finally landed on Soul Jahs. The other four members in the band were young Rastafarians we gathered from the neighborhood. For the entire summer, we met every day and rehearsed in my basement, and it was more than just learning to play reggae; it was learning how to live as a Rasta. We ate from a communal pot of ital stew, which everyone contributed to. Only fresh vegetables and spices. Free of salt or any animal product. We gathered and smoked the holy sacrament, passing spliff or chalice in a reverent and ritualistic way. We prayed into the smoke as we read passages from the Bible and sat and reasoned. This was similar in many ways to Five Percenters "building in a cipher." Speaking on matters of knowledge, wisdom, and overstanding. Listening to Rasta philosophy as related by the brethren in our group was like hearing the *Supreme 120 Lessons* spoken with a Jamaican accent and through a cloud of ganja smoke.

These Rastas, who became my spiritual guides, often proclaimed themselves to be "Selassie I," God himself. They put Jah in front of their names the same way the Five Percenters often put Allah in their names. I'd studied the lessons of the Five Percent and had a deep connection and respect for them, and now it was the same with Rastafari. I lived in accordance with its doctrine, spoke its language, and played its music, yet I wouldn't proclaim I was Selassie or call myself Jah. In both cases, I was in it but not of it, and I wore those religions like a loose garment. I "overstood" and agreed with the philosophy, but calling myself by the name of God just didn't sit right with me.

Perhaps my greatest Rasta lesson came a couple of years later in an unexpected and unpretentious way from a brethren named Ras Ashanti. He was one wicked reggae bass player, and I always looked forward to working with him. I knew our bass and drums were going to lock tighter than Alcatraz, and he always had such a positive spiritual presence. It was pretty much impossible to get upset when Ras Ashanti's vibration was present.

We were working long hours, rehearsing in a Lower East Side recording studio, when we took a much-needed break. Ras Ashanti excused himself. He was gone for some time, and I found him in the studio's kitchen with a spliff dangling from his mouth, barely visible in his dense dreadlocked beard. He was smiling and washing everyone's dishes. He had cleaned the whole kitchen and was boiling some root tea to share. We were alone, and I felt compelled to ask, "Ashanti, how is it you stay positive all the time? How do you stay spreading love?"

He was thoughtful for a moment before he spoke. "Brethren, I and I is a representative of His Majesty. I and I walk with Jah in my heart I-ternally. My heaven is on earth, and it is here and now. So I and I behave accordingly. Love, brethren. Now, let me ask the I something. If this moment is heaven, what does that make the I?" He took a draw and passed me the spliff, smiling with a gleam in his eye as he answered his own question. "That makes the I God! The bond of Rastafari is the bond of God. 'I and I' means God is within all man."

I was deeply moved by the simplicity and eloquence of his explanation. I felt the God within me stir.

Native Gun

THE YEAR MUHAMMAD Ali fought his last fight, Bob Marley died, and AIDS was identified, I turned eighteen. It was also when Bandit stashed a gun in the basement apartment. It was a .22. Small but deadly. Once I knew the pistol was within my reach, it was all I could think about.

Bandit had stopped using his given name, Michael, by the time he was thirteen or so. At first, he went by Trey, his graffiti tag. Trey soon morphed into Trey-Ski, and then into Trey-Ski the Bandit, and, finally, just Bandit. He was only two years older than me in age, but a lifetime older in experience.

My two older brothers and I shared the same mother, but we had different fathers. Bandit looked most like our mom. He was dark and handsome with chiseled features, whereas Dee and I were lighter-skinned, like our fathers. Bandit was charming and charismatic. The ladies loved him, and he loved them right back.

Bandit came to be as the result of rape. My mom was only eighteen years old when it happened. She couldn't bear to raise him, but she didn't want to put him up for adoption. Bandit was raised by my great-aunt Agnes, and up until we were in our teens, we thought we were cousins.

By the time Bandit left the gun in the basement, he'd already been in and out of Spofford Juvenile Detention Center and Rikers Island. He'd been a warlord in the Tomahawks and a low-level pimp. I guess he was a gangster, although he never really spoke about any of the nefarious shit he did. He didn't have to. His reputation was huge in Bed-Stuy and Brownsville.

On the streets, he was known as Bandit, but for me he was just Pork Chop, my older brother who was raised as my cousin. He stayed with us for a while after my great-aunt finally kicked him out, having gotten tired of all the trouble he was constantly getting in. He earned the family nickname Pork Chop because one day he defied Mom's strict orders, and out of sheer hunger and courage, fried and ate the last pork chop in the freezer. Consequences be damned! The only problem was, once he set the pork chop to frying, he went outside to play with Dee and me and forgot about it until black smoke started billowing out the kitchen window. We ran in to find the pork chop reduced to a spot in the pan about the size, texture, and color of a charcoal briquette. Bandit said, "Fuck it! If I'm going to get a beating for this damn pork chop, I'm gonna eat it!" He slathered it in ketchup and ate the piece of charcoal.

It wasn't more than a week after Bandit left the pistol that

I had it out. He had tried to hide it, tucked it under the couch in a nondescript paper bag, but I knew he stashed things in the house, cash and weed most often, so I would root around after he left, hoping to score a couple of dollars or some smoke. When I pulled it out, I felt an immediate sense of power. I didn't really know what to do with it. I had no real idea how to hold it, let alone shoot it, but for about a month, I carried it tucked in my waistband like I saw the Jamaican rude boys in my neighborhood do.

At that time in my life, I was wild and unpredictable and full of contradictions. On one hand, I strived to be righteous and spiritual; on the other, I wanted to be respected in the neighborhood as a bad boy. I was pretty much high all the time and had a quick and bad temper. I was angry and hungry a lot of the time, and I protected my fragile sense of manhood at all costs. I did petty crimes, like breaking into houses and selling weed, but I couldn't get into robbing and sticking up people like my cousin Rock and some of the dudes I ran with did. For some reason, my conscience wouldn't allow me to go that far. I fought, but I was never really the one to go looking for beef. Yet for the month or so that I walked the streets with the .22 tucked in my pants, I hoped somebody would look at me halfway wrong. I was volatile, a deadly combination of an overabundance of testosterone, teenage angst, and the ignorance that manifests as a feeling of invincibility and a lack of understanding of consequences that only a young man with a gun can feel. Basically, I didn't give a fuck, and "I wished a nigga would."

Knowing I had the pistol on me changed how I felt about myself and my world. I was aware every second that I had the power of life and death under my shirt. I felt dangerous, and I felt bold and bad. I was just waiting to be set off. Wanting and looking for an excuse to pull that gun out. The drive was strong. The desire intense.

What might have saved me was something my uncle Danny, himself a local legend, had told me years before: "If you pull out a knife or a gun, you *better* be ready to use it." I thought about that often, and perhaps it was my salvation. Yet still, situations I would have normally ignored now became potential opportunities to pull out my gun. When I carried the gun, I was constantly aware of it. I was powerful in a way I hadn't ever experienced. Walking around secretly armed was both exciting and intoxicating, especially as a teenager, when I was already naturally full of fear, doubt, and aggression.

I was lucky nothing really explosive happened while I had the gun. I lifted my shirt a couple of times, bad-boy style, to make somebody step back, but I never pulled, pointed, or shot it. I think I would have eventually, though, if Bandit hadn't come back for the .22, maybe six weeks after he had left it. The longer I carried the gun, the bolder I became. It was only a matter of time before I would have felt compelled to fire it. Fortunately, when he showed up, I'd already tucked it back where he'd left it. He pulled the gun out from under the couch, held it, turned it around in his hands, and looked at me for a long time. I think he knew I'd been carrying it, but he didn't say anything. He just lifted his shirt, tucked the gun in his waistband, and started to tell me a joke about who made the best pork chops in Brooklyn. He unknowingly, or perhaps knowingly, saved me that day.

It was less than two months later that I had another interaction with a gun, but this time it was quite deadly. This was a time when Jamaican rude boys were moving to Brooklyn in droves. Taking over. It seemed like all the killers and hard men in Kingston and Tivoli Gardens had decided to move to East Flatbush at the same time. The Vanderveer projects were one of their destinations. The projects that had once been predominantly African American were now like little Kingston.

My brother Dee practically lived in Vanderveer. He was a low-level drug dealer then, mostly selling weed and occasionally making a coke deal here and there, but he never made any real money. Basically, he sold just enough to stay high himself and to be able to afford Chinese food for dinner. I guess this ran in the family. Dee had a spot in front of a building near the Nostrand Avenue entrance, which meant you could pretty much always find him there conducting business. He had the same spot for years, and although there were plenty of other dealers in the projects, no one ever disputed his right to the corner. It was a point of pride for both of us that he "owned" that spot.

One late afternoon, I found myself out of weed and walked over to check with my brother. He was always good for a bag or two. After all, what was the use of having an older brother who sold weed if I couldn't get a couple bags on credit every now and then?

There was Dee in front of his regular spot. He was happy to see me. I think he liked my company. We joked and threw punches for a while before he smoothly and covertly passed me a couple of nickel bags. I didn't even have to ask. I was about to leave when we heard a distinctly Jamaican voice say, "Move from here, bwoy! Ah me run dis now!"

Dee and I turned at the same time to see a thin, nappy-headed, dark-skinned dude pulling up on us. He was speaking directly to Dee, ignoring me. "Me nah wan see ya face 'ere again, bwoy! Gwaan!"

To my shock, Dee replied, "Come on, Pat, let's go." I couldn't understand what was happening. Dee wasn't exactly a gangster, but he was no punk, and I never knew him to back down from a fight. I once saw him fight this kid and his brother at the same time and kick their asses. When their father came out to break it up, Dee fucked him up, too.

I was foolishly stubborn, running on blind pride. "Nah! Fuck that. I ain't going nowhere! Fuck this kid! Fuck he think this is?"

The Jamaican just stared at me, and Dee said in a tone more serious than I was used to from him, "Come on, *let's go*," and started walking.

But I didn't follow him. I turned to the Jamaican and said, "Ay, yo! Fuck you, yo! I ain't going nowhere!"

"Oh! So ya nah wan move, eh? Wait right here. I comin' forward!"

"Yeah, you come on back! Fuck is you gonna do, pussy?"

He turned around and walked across the small courtyard between buildings. Dee had already moved and was halfway down the block. He yelled back to me, "Come on! Is you crazy?!"

I must have been. Even someone with the most basic of street smarts knows you don't wait for somebody when they say, "Wait right here. I'm coming back."

I think it was just starting to dawn on me that I was being stupid when I heard the first shot. The Jamaican was walking back across the courtyard with a trademark yardman stride, firing shots in the air as he approached. I have to say, it was one of the hardest and coolest things I had ever seen in my life. People scattered as he let off another couple of shots, but I stood there like I somehow knew nothing was going to happen to me. I was stuck in place, marveling at the spectacle of what I was witnessing. I felt an odd kind of defiance. I think the fact that I was still standing there, that I hadn't run when he approached, somehow impressed the Jamaican. When he finally got within an arm's distance, he looked in my eyes and said, in a low, almost respectful voice, "Oh, so you is a *real* bad man, eh?"

Then he lifted the gun and pressed it to my forehead. That's when everything started moving in slow motion. It was such a strange feeling. I wasn't scared. I wasn't shook. I wasn't anything. I wasn't even really there. It was like I was watching the whole scene play out from a distance, like a spectator.

I saw his finger squeeze the trigger, and I didn't even close my eyes. I saw the barrel turn and I heard the click of an empty chamber. The Jamaican pulled the gun back from my forehead and looked in my eyes. Then he held the gun to the side of my head, right next to my ear, and squeezed again. Jamaican roulette. This time, it fired. Loud and hot. The sound nearly deafened me, and the heat singed the side of my face. My ears rang.

I stood in shock. I hadn't moved an inch. The Jamaican stepped back from me and shook his head. He said, "Me coulda *kill* you, nigga!" Then he turned around and walked away.

Dee came cautiously toward me. He looked around and motioned me to him. I met him halfway, and we headed toward home. He didn't say anything until we were blocks away. "Stupid ass! If I *ever* tell you to move, you move, you hear me?"

I said, "Huh?!"

* * *

One of the major contradictions of my life at the time was that although I was running the streets like a feral dog, hustling, doing petty crimes, and imagining myself as a bad boy, I was also a part-time babysitter.

My aunt Chris's second marriage was to a New York City Police Department gold shield detective named Ed O'Reilly. They had a son right away, my cousin EJ. When EJ got to be a toddler, Chris went back to work. I was about nineteen years old and living a few blocks away from them, and Chris asked if I'd babysit a couple evenings a week. It meant dinner and a little money for me, plus I really loved my aunt and my little cousin. We used to have a ball together. I'd babysit from 4 p.m. to about 9 p.m. and put him to bed around 7 p.m. I'd kill the last couple of hours watching TV or listening to music, sometimes helping myself to a shot or two from their liquor cabinet. It was a cool arrangement for a while.

After I'd been doing this gig for a year or so, I got bored and started rooting around in Ed's closet. I don't think I was looking for anything in particular. I was just bored. I found a case hidden way in the back of the closet. The case contained a gun. A big, shiny, old-school pistol. It was a standard service revolver, the kind they used to issue to NYPD cops.

I took the box to the bathroom and locked the door. I took the gun out. It was big, heavy, and cold. It was loaded, and I felt the power of holding it surge through me. I thought about borrowing it for a day or two, just until the next time I babysat. I remembered what it felt like to walk around with Bandit's little .22, and this gun was a monster compared to that one. I looked at myself in the mirror, holding the gun. I posed with it, feeling sexy and powerful. I pointed it at myself in the mirror and did an impression of Robert De Niro from *Taxi Driver.*

I put my finger on the trigger and placed the gun to my forehead. I pressed the barrel right between my eyes, then put the tiniest bit of pressure on the trigger. I said to the mirror, "Me coulda *kill* you, nigga!"

Turn Styles

ONE SUMMER DAY in 1983, I jumped the turnstile for the F train at Carroll Street. I was flat broke, as usual, and was headed to the city to get paid. I was twenty years old and worked in a video rental store for a coked-up madman named Jack, who made employees come to his loft apartment in SoHo to collect their pay. He would literally make everyone beg for what he owed them. He not only made me come to him at some random hour, he had a sadistic little game to punish me if I was late.

He introduced his policy my first week on the job. "Okay, so you want your pay for the week. Come to my loft on Thursday at exactly 12:35 p.m. I'm gonna dock five dollars off your pay for every minute you're late."

I was getting paid five dollars an hour.

It was his coke-brained power trip. When I showed up

that first week, he was in bed with a teacup full of coke and a big Black transgender hooker. He slowly doled out my pay in crumpled single dollar bills.

One time, he invited me to dinner at his other apartment on the Upper West Side. I really didn't want to go, but he was holding my money. Dinner was a platter of bloody-rare filet mignon and a bottle of wine. That was it, just meat and wine. The platter was served to us by the same muscular, six-foot-three trans woman in a see-through teddy. It was such a bizarre scene.

By the time of this particular turnstile-jumping afternoon, I'd been working for Jack for a few months and knew what to expect when I got there. As soon as I jumped and walked down the stairs, I saw the cop who had been hiding behind a column. I knew I was busted. He was coming toward me, and I was going to get a ticket, but I was just hoping it wouldn't take too long. I couldn't be late, couldn't afford to have my pay docked.

The cop said, "I saw you jump. Stand right here and give me your ID."

I didn't argue, but as I handed him my ID, I said, "Come on, man! Can we make this fast? I got to be in the city!" I guess he didn't like that. He told me to turn around and put my hands behind my back.

I said, "For what? Man, just give me the ticket and let me be on my way." The next thing I knew, I was handcuffed to a gate by the turnstile.

The cop stepped back, and I looked at him for the first time. He was short and shaped like a potato. He was the kind of guy who could work out every day of his life and he'd still be shaped like a potato. I read the name on his shirt, then looked up at him. Officer Mancuso had bad skin and bad teeth. We were about the same age, and he reminded me of some of the Italian kids I went to school with at Marine Park, the same look, the same accent and attitude.

"You think you're so cool, huh? Telling *me* to hurry up? I bet you're used to getting things your way, huh? You think you're 'the man,' huh?" He was using a mocking "Black" voice.

I could tell Officer Mancuso was the kid who didn't make the team, didn't get the girl, and didn't get to hang out with the cool kids.

"Hey, I don't know why you got me in cuffs, but can you *please* just write my ticket and let me go?"

Mancuso looked both ways. The only person around was the token-booth operator, and she couldn't see us from where she was sitting. He took another step back and pulled out his gun. He held it level to my chest for a moment, then he stepped forward and placed the barrel between my eyes. "Say something smart now. Come on! You're so cool! Say something cool now." He lowered the gun to my heart. "Come on, I dare you to say something."

Just then, another cop arrived, an older-looking, taller guy, probably a senior officer. He saw what was happening. He said something quietly to Mancuso, who holstered his weapon and followed him to the far corner of the platform. The other cop was talking down to Mancuso in hushed tones. Mancuso held his head down and a minute later disappeared down the stairs.

The older cop came over to me, undid the cuffs, and handed me back my ID. "Go on. Your train is coming. Nothing happening here."

* * *

Twenty years later, nothing had changed. I was coming home from a recording session in Greenpoint. It was about 2 a.m. on a weeknight, and the G train was empty. I had the whole car to myself and had settled in to read a book on Zen Buddhism. I stretched my leg across the seat in front of me, making sure not to let my boots touch the seat. I'd always thought putting one's feet on a public seat was inconsiderate, even in an empty car. I was deep into my reading when after several stops, a young cop got on. I looked up, nodded to him, and continued reading. After about three more stops, I felt a presence standing over me and looked up to see the cop staring down.

"What's up, Officer?" I asked.

"Get up! You're getting off at the next stop!"

The thing was, the next stop was Jay Street. My stop. I *was* getting off. I was genuinely surprised. "Hey! Yeah! I *am* getting off! How did you know?"

The cop took a step back and with a deadly serious tone said, "Don't be smart! I told you to get up!" He had his hand on his holster, and I realized this was no joke. I got up. He told me to stand by the door with my hands where he could see them. I was confused, but I complied.

The cop stood in front of me. "You think you're cool, huh?"

I thought of the incident with Officer Mancuso so many years before. Same precarious situation. The only difference was this cop was Hispanic. I read his nameplate.

Officer Garcia said, "You saw me get on the car, but you think you're so cool you didn't even bother to take your leg from across the seat? You think you're so cool you can just disrespect me?"

"Officer, I did see you, and I acknowledged you. The

train was empty, so I didn't think having my leg across the seat was a problem. I meant no disrespect."

"Oh! You *knew* what you were doing. I gave you a chance for three stops, but you think you're so cool."

"So, this is about me thinking I'm cool? You're making me get off the train because I think I'm cool?"

I should've kept silent. His face got uglier. Then he stepped back, looked both ways, and pulled his gun. He pointed the pistol at my chest. "Say something smart now. Come on! You're so cool! Say something cool now."

There was something much scarier to me about this encounter than the one with Mancuso. Garcia was shaking. His face was contorting. He was mumbling. He looked like he genuinely hated me. He looked like he really wanted to shoot me. I stayed silent. Put my head down. Waited.

Garcia held his gun on me until the train pulled into the Jay Street station. He holstered it only when the train came to a full stop. There was a group of six cops waiting for us on the platform. I didn't even realize Garcia had radioed ahead. I stepped out of the train and was surrounded and harshly frisked by two big cops. They went through my knapsack. In it was a sketchbook, the Zen Buddhism book I had been reading, and a banana.

People walking by looked at me like I'd committed a murder.

The cops didn't cuff me but held my arms tightly as they took me upstairs to the small police outpost at the Jay Street station.

"What's he here for?" the desk sergeant asked Garcia.

"He had his feet up on the seat," Garcia said.

The sergeant stared at him for a long moment, then told

me to sit down on the bench. Garcia walked away without looking at me again.

I sat there for over two hours. No one asked me for my ID, and no one said anything to me. There was a shift change. When the new desk sergeant came in, he had some quiet words with the exiting sergeant. I sat for another half hour before he looked over at me and said, "What are you doing here? Get going."

As I walked the five blocks home from the subway, it began to rain. I'm not ashamed to admit I cried.

Speck & Scrapps

I WENT TO James Madison High School in the Kings Highway section of Brooklyn. Bernie Sanders, Ruth Bader Ginsburg, and Carole King are some of the distinguished alumni. Although the school was racially pretty mixed, with the influx of us "bused-in kids," it was still very segregated. It was unspoken, but the White entrance was at the front of the school and the Black one was at the back. Even the bathrooms had unspoken but understood segregation.

Probably the most glaringly visual example of the segregation was division of the bleachers between White and Black sides. Kids hung out on the bleachers at lunch and between classes, and you *never* saw a Black kid on the White side or a White kid on the Black side. Period. So it was strange one morning when I cut class and went to our bleachers to smoke a joint and saw a lone White kid sitting at the very top on the Black side. He was blond-haired and blue-eyed and wore vintage army fatigues. That was odd enough, but what made the situation almost unbelievable was he had a JVC boom box (the kind you got robbed for!) and was playing some hard dub reggae. Unimaginable in 1980s Brooklyn. This White kid was smoking a joint and bobbing his head to *Scientist Meets the Roots Radics* on cassette. It was like some kind of audiovisual hallucination. I thought I must've been tripping. I left him there and went around the corner to smoke, thinking it must have been a mirage. A glitch in the matrix.

The next day, I cut class again at the same time, and again, the White kid was sitting alone, smoking at the top of the Black bleachers and this time listening to rap music. This was before it was even called hip-hop, and *no* White kids were listening to it. It was too much. I had to figure out what was going on. I approached the kid with the universal pothead greeting.

"Yo! Let me get a hit off that?" I asked. I had weed of my own, but I wanted to see what he'd say.

"No" was his answer. Flat and fearless, and from that moment, a friendship was born.

Burt Speck was one of the oddest people I'd ever met, but we immediately bonded over our shared interests in music, weed, and vintage army clothes. We had the same kind of misfit outcast energy. Speck hung out by himself. He told me he was sitting on the Black side not to make a statement but because "it's closer to the school. Why should I walk all the way over to the other side?" Simple, pragmatic, and logical.

He spoke with a deep monotone in a heavy Brooklyn Jewish accent. I liked his sharp wit and dry, sarcastic humor.

Speck was the first White kid I'd met who genuinely made me think he didn't see color. What he saw were opportunities to get over. The other thing we strongly had in common was the "hustle mentality." Speck was always looking for ways to make a buck, and I soon learned he was notoriously cheap.

One day after school, about a month after we'd met, he invited me to his house in the Jewish neighborhood off of Kings Highway. There I met his old bubbe. She was a Holocaust survivor and had lost her mind from the trauma. She had two long pigtails down her back that had long ago petrified into dreadlocks. She also had a pretty impressive beard. Now that I think about it, maybe his bubbe was actually his grandfather.

She called me something in Yiddish, which I found out later was the equivalent of "my little monkey."

We had a simple lunch of some toast and tea that afternoon, and when I was leaving, he looked up like he was calculating and said, "That'll be three dollars." He was dead serious. He wouldn't let me leave until I paid something toward the meager lunch. I *Blacked* him down to two-fiddy.

Only a couple of months later, during the Christmas school break, a blizzard fell and basically shut down the city. I got a call from Speck at 3 a.m. He explained there had been a fire in the Gap store a few blocks from his crib. The fire had burned the front of the store, but he noticed the back was basically untouched and there was only a chain on weak wood holding the back door closed. "You wanna make some money?" He knew I did.

Speck told me to meet him at his crib as soon as I could get there. He had a plan.

It took me over an hour, and I was nearly frozen by the time I got to his house. Speck was ready and waiting with two big supermarket carts, flashlights, industrial-sized garbage bags, and crowbars. We slipped and slid our way to the Gap on icy, empty streets. Speck was right. Breaking in was easy as butter. The back door opened into the stockroom. It was dark and foreboding in there. We slipped as we stepped over the blackened, charred remains of the fire that had burned the front of the store. We turned on our flashlights and directed them to the walls.

We'd hit denim gold.

There were stacks and stacks and racks and racks of Levi's and Lee jeans. The only problem was they'd all been doused by the fire hoses and were frozen solid. We began chiseling the jeans out and loading up our bags and carts. The jeans were caked in ice and smelled of smoke but otherwise perfect.

We made trip after trip in the deep snow from the Gap to Speck's house and back, and by the time the sun came up, we'd basically cleaned out the whole store. It was important that we finished and I got out of the neighborhood before it got too light because a Black kid on Kings Highway would have drawn all kinds of suspicion, at the very least.

By the time we were done, we had at least two hundred pairs of jeans, as well as several big bags filled with jackets, shirts, belts, and accessories. It was a *huge score*, and we agreed to sell them all and split the money, fifty-fifty.

As I was leaving, completely frozen, exhausted and filthy, reeking of smoke and soot, Speck said, "Here, take two pairs of jeans for now. We'll split it all up later."

Those jeans were about all I could carry at the time, but I was totally psyched at the prospect of what this major score would reap. We were going to be rich!

For the rest of the Christmas break, Speck went MIA. He

didn't answer his phone or return my messages. I must've called him fifty times over the course of that week. When we got back to school in the New Year, I looked everywhere for him, but he had gone ghost. No Speck at any of our usual hangouts. The strange thing was, people reported Speck sightings all over the school, but somehow I always missed him. The other strange thing was a lot of the White kids were wearing brand-new Levi's, and oddly enough, when I passed them in the hall, I smelled the faint scent of smoke. Then I noticed the Black kids were wearing new, smoke-smelling Lee jeans. (That was the breakdown back then; even the jeans and cigarettes were segregated. White kids wore Levi's and smoked Marlboros, and Black kids rocked Lees and smoked Newports.) Once I figured out what was happening, I was out for blood. But I wanted my money first.

I finally caught up with Speck on the "neutral" back staircase, where he was standing next to a big bag of jeans. There was literally a line of kids queued up to get to him. He was selling jeans for fifteen dollars each. He had the nerve to call it a "fire sale." When he saw me in the line, he gave me a sheepish smile.

"I've been looking all over for you! I got something for you!" Speck reached in his bag and handed me two more pairs of jeans. Before he let go of them, he looked up and mumbled some numbers.

Calculating.

"Okay, for you, gimme twenty-five dollars."

Speck was special.

I got my first apartment at twenty-two years old. It was on Smith Street in the Carroll Gardens section of Brooklyn. It was a one-bedroom railroad apartment my roommate and I somehow managed to make work as a two-bedroom. "Making it work" meant I had a mattress on the floor in a room I called my bedroom, a room that was actually supposed to be the living room. It was the room everyone walked through when they entered or exited the apartment and had to walk through to get to the bathroom and kitchen. In a nutshell, I had no privacy. I wondered how I let myself get talked into taking that room, but then I'd remind myself who my roommate was, and it removed all wonder.

I met Scrapper (aka Lord Scrapps) through mutual friends in the ska / rude-boy scene. In those days, I played drums in a popular band called the Boilers in that little subgenre world, and it immediately gave me status. Scrapper and I first met in the East Village, me a Black dude from East Flatbush and him a White dude from East London — a world apart yet incredibly similar. We hit it off immediately and recognized right away that despite our different cultures, we had far more in common than not.

We both grew up in West Indian neighborhoods, and we both grew up hard and tough and without much money. We were both misfits who liked music, style, women, drink, and drugs. Scrapper and I both got jobs at a video rental store in SoHo, a spot where it seemed all the "faces" on the ska scene worked at some point or another. We were both in need of a place to live, and I found us the spot in Brooklyn. Five hundred dollars a month, split fifty-fifty. We put down first and last months' rent in cash (a whopping thousand dollars!), and I signed the lease on my own since Scrapper was in the States illegally and couldn't use his name on any official documents. The ink wasn't even dry on the lease before Scrapper quit the video store job, but not before he organized a mini heist. We appropriated a truckload of antiques that Jack the sleazy owner had stored in the side room of the store. We furnished the apartment with those stolen antiques.

We were both clever and good with words, but Scrapper was far better, much more skilled at the smooth con than I. I'm not sure exactly how he talked me into the fucked-up bedroom situation, but I'm sure it started with "Well," then a pause. Even though I hadn't known him that long, I was already hip to some of his game, and his "Well" was infamous. I had already seen him talk women into his bed, bartenders into forgetting his tab, and hard guys into loaning him just a couple more dollars. It always began with that four-letter word, followed by a pause. If you heard "Well" come out of Scrapper's mouth, you could be sure what was coming next was going to be some beautifully brilliant bullshit.

Scrapps was deceptively tough. He didn't really look like a fighter, but he was definitely not soft. He was a good-looking geezer, tall and fit. He'd gotten bashed across the jaw with a baseball bat back in England, which left his neck permanently stiff and his lower jaw twisted to the left, but he was still a good-looking guy. Basically, he had the look of a smooth criminal and a proper villain.

He probably would have described himself as more of a "Jack the Lad" type, with his quick wit and charm, but he was pretty ruthless. Scrapper was a guy determined to get rich by the most nefarious means and the least work possible. I think that's what I recognized in him and what made me most comfortable with him. Despite his thick Cockney accent, he was basically like every hustler I grew up with in Brooklyn, including my brothers. Scrapps, like Speck, was always looking for the way to get over, for the hustle, the quick buck. He was the one White dude I never hesitated to let hang with me in a room full of Black gangsters and dreads, partly because he never pretended to be anyone but himself and partly because he had a slick style and swag that came from growing up with bad-boy yardies in Brixton. As blond and blue-eyed as he was, his mindset was no different than that of the Black American thugs in my circle.

The apartment we shared was a block from the projects. It was the beginning of the crack era, and ours was a pretty dangerous neighborhood, even for me, but not once did I think twice about Scrapper's safety. He knew how to walk.

Another thing we unfortunately had in common was being flat broke most of the time. When our first New Year's Eve in the new apartment rolled around, we found ourselves basically penniless, totally "skint," and busted. As a matter of fact, Scrapps was worse than just broke, since he was in debt to me for three months' worth of his half of the rent. We'd been in the apartment for only three months.

I'd been dating a beautiful young lady named Glenda for a few months. She was excited to spend our first New Year's Eve together, but I told her to make other plans. I had no money to take her out. Scrapps and I were counting out cigarettes and scraping resin from old weed pipes when I went through some coat pockets and came up with just enough money to buy two quarts of beer. It was only about 9 p.m. We decided we'd drink one right away and save the other for midnight. Since I'd found the change, it was only right that Scrapps make the run for the beer.

The bodega was three blocks away and wasn't a big trek, even though it had snowed pretty hard earlier, so when he took a long time to return, I started wondering. It occurred to me it wouldn't be totally out of character for him to take the little bit of change and hop the train to the city, where his prospects for scamming drinks and talking himself into a New Year's Eve party were considerably higher, but to my relief I heard the downstairs door bang open and a moment later Scrapper's Cockney calling up, "Oi! Give us a hand, me old son!" There, in the doorway, he stood, red-faced and out of breath, with a proud smile plastered across his mug. "Can you fakkin' believe some cunt frew this beauty out?"

He was standing next to a giant-ass foosball table he'd found and dragged for three blocks. To his credit, the table looked brand-new and like it could be worth something. Still, I wasn't overly impressed. "Fuck you wanna do with that?" I asked.

"What? This is our entertainment for the night! Help get it up the stairs, then!"

We dragged it into his room. Apparently, foosball was a big thing in British pub culture, and Scrapps was overjoyed because this was a "professional" table. "I've always wanted one of these!" he said. "Can you believe this beauty was sitting as pretty as you like on the cobbles?"

I could believe it.

"When I spotted it, I dragged it to our door, then went to call Squire to come over and play, and the good news is he's got a bit of weed as well!"

Okay, so foosball wasn't so bad, I guess. Squire was a friend of his from back in Brixton. A Black British rude boy who always struck me as a quieter, sneakier version of Scrapper. I liked him well enough, I just didn't fully trust him. Something about the quiet, calculating way he looked at me made me feel like he was always sizing me up.

While we waited for Squire, we started playing. I'd played foosball a few times before. There was a cheap old table in my after-school rec room in middle school. My West Indian friends liked it best because it was based on "football," which I knew as soccer.

We drank both quarts in anticipation of Squire's weed. I was appreciating the distraction of the foosball table, but every time Scrapper scored a goal on my side, the ball would get stuck, and we'd have to lift the table and lean it to the side for the ball to get free.

Squire finally showed up with a couple of spliffs, three Guinness stouts, and a pack of Player's cigarettes. It wasn't a dream New Year's Eve, but it was definitely an improvement on what we'd planned earlier. We smoked and played foosball, and when I got sick of the ball getting stuck, I called a time-out to figure out what the obstruction was. I stuck my arm into the table as far as it would go and rooted around. Sure enough, there was something wedged in there that I managed to pull out. It was a hard green plastic-wrapped bundle about the size and shape of a small brick. I set it aside, and we played a couple more games. Then Scrapper got curious about the little bundle and decided to investigate. He had a little collection of knives, and he used one to slice open the package. A bit of white powder escaped. My first thought was it was rat poison, and I said as much, but Scrapps wasn't convinced. Then he did something I wouldn't have dreamed of doing. He tasted the powder.

He stood there motionless, and I could see all kinds of emotions play across his face. I was concerned. I thought maybe this fool had poisoned himself, but then he said in a low, serious yet dreamy voice, "Cocaine. It's fakkin' cocaine! It's fakkin' pure cocaine and all!"

A quarter of a kilo of pure, uncut cocaine.

Squire was immediately upset, thinking we'd staged it all. He kept saying, "You lot are taking the piss! Fuckin' hell!

Youse are taking me for a right mug, innit? What are youse playing at, then?"

It took us a minute to talk him down and assure him we weren't "playing at" anything. We were just as surprised as he was. It was a fakkin' New Year's miracle!

We tried to figure out how this could've possibly come to be, and we came up with two plausible possibilities. Where we lived on Smith Street was the unspoken but well understood dividing line between the Black and brown project buildings on one side and the old-school Italian Mafia on the other. This was the time when cocaine was flooding the streets, and we reasoned that either Scrapps had stumbled on and disrupted a planned pickup/drop-off, or somebody was in trouble and needed to stash the coke quick, and the foosball table was just in the right place at the right time. Either way, we were sure whoever the coke belonged to would be looking for it...like, *really* looking for it. A quarter kilo of cocaine in the mid-'80s could have gone for as much as fifteen thousand dollars.

I was adamant about not doing coke. I knew if I started, I wouldn't be able to stop, and I'd already seen what it did to two of my uncles. It had turned them dark. I saw it rob them of their talents and families. Scrapper and Squire didn't share my reservations. Within minutes, lines were drawn up and phone calls were made. Then suddenly, Squire, who'd cried broke and destitute prior to us finding the coke, "discovered" a whole ounce of weed in his pocket and enough money to set us up with drinks. They invited their friend Alexandria, another British expat, over, and the party commenced. By midnight, as we rang in the New Year, I was drunk and high, but nothing close to Scrapper, Squire, and Alex. They snorted line after line, and it didn't seem to make the slightest dent in the package. I crashed out at about 2 a.m. and left them to it. When I came to the next morning, they were sitting together on Scrapper's flat futon, glassy-eyed and frozen-faced. Coked out of their minds.

In the following days, Scrapps and I made a plan to get rid of the coke and make as much money as we could. My request was totally modest. I wanted only $1,500, one-tenth of what the package was worth, and that amount included the $750 he owed me for back rent.

Scrapper assured me he "knew a guy" who for a modest fee could cut the blow for us and sell it in eight balls. He said he trusted this dude and that it was the best way for us to get rid of the package quickly with minimal chance of getting busted. We met with the guy, who reeked of cat piss and underarm funk, in his little apartment on Avenue C. He was a greasy, older White dude who looked and acted like the character in every gangster movie who snitched and ended up in a dumpster. He looked as if an appropriate name for him would've been Ratso. I gave Scrapper the go-ahead, though, and he took the whole package from Brooklyn to this shady dude.

That was the last I saw of Scrapps for over a month. I knew he was alive because he came to our apartment when I was at work to drop stuff off. One day, I saw a brand-new boom box in his room, and a few days after that, a pair of crisp new Dr. Martens wing tips. There were also some Ben Sherman and Fred Perry shirts hanging in his closet.

One night, with murder on my mind, I went looking for him in his home bar, a bucket of blood on Avenue A called Lucy's. He wasn't there, but every one of the regular rude boys who hung out at that bar had the same glassy eyes and grinding teeth. They all swore they hadn't seen him.

A week later, I was about to crash on my floor mattress when the front door to my "bedroom" opened and there stood Lord Scrapps, looking dapper. The prodigal rude boy had returned. I pulled out the claw hammer I kept next to my bed and set it in my lap. In a calm, even tone, I asked, "Do you have my money?"

Scrapper replied, "Well…"

Christmas Miracle I (The Resurrection)

ON CHRISTMAS EVE, the year David Dinkins was elected the first Black mayor of New York City and a mob of young white men beat Yusuf Hawkins to death in Brooklyn, I was working at a little art supplies store in Park Slope. I didn't even know my mom had my number at that shop, so I was super surprised to get a call from her there that afternoon. She said my brother Dee was being rushed to St. Mary's Hospital in Bed-Stuy. She said it was serious. Mom didn't provide any other details, but she wasn't one for exaggeration. I knew if she said *serious,* it was very bad.

I don't remember how I managed to get from Park Slope to Bed-Stuy so quickly that day, but I do remember arriving at St. Mary's and running through the emergency room doors into a scene that could've come out of a documentary about a third world hospital in wartime. In 1989, the crack epidemic in NYC was at its height. Some neighborhoods were a lot like war zones, and St. Mary's was at the epicenter. There were desperate, dangerous-looking people jammed into this small emergency room, some laid out on the floor. The suffering was palpable. Doctors and nurses running around doing triage. Blood that clearly hadn't been mopped up for hours. There was loud cursing and crying and bodies covered in white sheets lined up along the hall.

I found my mom sitting by herself in a corner. She told me a neighbor had rung her bell to tell her Dee was next door and something was wrong. Dee had been living down the block from Mom at the time, and he often hung out with the people who lived in the building next door to hers. She said, "The apartment was empty when I got there. I found him lying face down. It looked like he'd fallen off the couch. He wasn't moving, and I couldn't tell if he was breathing."

I loved my older brother, but we weren't close by then. He was living his own life, always involved in some kind of hustle, always looking for ways to get over, usually not very successfully. He was clever, but too nice to be a good hustler. Cocaine was everywhere, and I knew he dabbled—almost everyone did.

Earlier that day, Dee had gotten his Christmas bonus from this gig he had as a busboy in a restaurant at the World Trade Center. Apparently, he'd been hanging out with the neighbors, celebrating and snorting coke, and at some point, he started to complain about his heart racing and beating out of his chest. He couldn't catch his breath and he felt weak. He fell off the couch and went into a seizure.

The people he was getting high with took the rest of the drugs, emptied his wallet, and left him there convulsing. It was only by God's grace that the upstairs neighbor felt something was wrong and went to check. She had enough sense to call 911 and contact my mom.

I had only just sat down next to my mom when a nurse came over, asked our names and our relationship to Dee, then told us to follow her. She led us into the emergency room, and as we walked through the doors, we saw a doctor pulling the sheet over my brother. He said they'd done all they could. He said Dee was gone.

My mom wouldn't accept this. She pushed past them and pulled the sheet back down. "No!" my mother screamed. "Try again! No! Do something else!"

The doctor explained my brother had OD'd and gone into cardiac arrest, that they'd tried everything but couldn't get his heart to restart. Mom refused to hear it. She wouldn't let go of my brother's hand, wouldn't let them pull up the sheet.

The doctors had an exasperated attitude of *just another dead nigger drug addict.* The hall was lined with them. They were already disconnecting tubes and writing on their clipboards, but my mother wouldn't budge. "Try again, please, please try again! He's not gone."

I couldn't process what I was seeing. I stood there unable to move. Finally, the medical staff realized my mom wasn't going to let go, so with an attitude that seemed to say *Let's just do this so we can move on,* the doctors placed the paddles against my brother's chest. The first bolt made his body jump up off the gurney. I turned away. It was too much to see. I heard the second bolt, followed by a big gasp and intake of air. Then the faint sound of a beep. Then another beep.

My brother had been officially dead for nearly two minutes, and he would have stayed that way if my mom hadn't insisted. If she hadn't *made* them try again. As my mother literally fought for her son's life, I knew I was witnessing the most powerful example of a mother's love. The doctors seemed embarrassed. They were apologetic as they asked us to wait in the waiting room. They said it was still unlikely he'd make it.

We waited and prayed for hours, during which time I saw the best and worst of humanity. There were the shouts, cries, and moans of the wounded and their loved ones. Arguments and fights broke out, but I also witnessed love in its most real, raw, and powerful manifestation. People comforted one another. People held the hands of strangers and offered countless acts of kindness and generosity.

After some time, a kindly doctor spoke to us. She explained that Dee's vitals had stabilized and his body was strong, but they weren't getting any brain activity. He was in a coma and would likely stay in a comatose, brain-dead state. Dee might live, but he'd probably be a vegetable. None of their words registered with me. They didn't know my brother, how strong he was. And after just witnessing the power of my mother's love, I didn't accept the prognosis.

For the next three weeks, I visited my brother every day after work. There was no change in him. Day after day, he lay there, eyes closed, perfectly still, hooked up to machines. The doctors occasionally stopped by to tell us the prognosis wasn't good, that he'd gone too long without oxygen to the brain. The damage was irreversible. They were implying he'd never come out of the coma and we'd need to make a decision soon.

I was sitting with Dee, watching the rise and fall of his chest in his otherwise motionless body. I thought how boring it must be for him to just lie there with only the beeping of machines to keep him company. When I got home later that evening, I decided to make him a mix cassette tape of all the music we grew up on, all the artists I knew he loved—Stevie Wonder; Earth, Wind & Fire; Sly and the Family Stone; and his all-time favorite: the Persuasions.

The next day, I placed my Walkman headphones on my brother's ears and hit play, then I sat with him as a couple of songs played. Nothing. He didn't so much as twitch, so I went back to sitting in the waiting room.

A few minutes later, a scratchy, moaning sound came from Dee's room. It sounded muffled and weak, but it was distinctly my brother's voice. I ran to his bedside. His eyes were glazed over but open. *He was singing!* He was way out of tune, but he was never that great a singer in the first place. It was the sweetest sound I had ever heard. Within a day or two, Dee was talking and making jokes. He was clearly damaged cognitively. He would need both physical and cognitive therapy, but he was definitely back. The doctors called it literally a miracle.

Months later, Dee told me he remembered wandering in an empty place. Then he heard the music and started walking toward it.

White Devil

COCAINE IS "Sir Nose D'Voidoffunk" by Parliament, "Ziggy Stardust" by David Bowie, and every disco record. Cocaine is diet soda sweetened with cancer. It's cheap caviar and fake jewelry. Cocaine is greasy and slippery. Cocaine is sleazy. It's a liar and a thief. It pretends to be champagne, but it's actually back-alley piss. Cocaine is a bad magician in a filthy polyester tuxedo pulling insidious innuendoes from a hat. It's an egotistical philosopher spouting absurd profundities and gem-encrusted bullshit. It's a facade, a cruel con man, and a phony pimp. It's selfish and slick, vain and violent. Cocaine is delusions of grandeur. It's opulent and depraved. It's starving debauchery and a decadent deceiver. Cocaine is a gaslighting narcissist. It's fake fantasies in stained, skintight spandex. It's a gold-rimmed glory hole in an upscale gas station bathroom. Cocaine is a dry pussy and a limp dick. It's all show and no substance.

Cocaine is a control freak.

I avoided coke, held myself above it for many years, but in the late '70s and through the '80s, it was everywhere. Every generation had its definitive drug. For my generation, it was the powder that became the rock.

I called it "white devil" because from early on, I recognized its power, deception, and evil intent. It had no spiritual application. Wine, weed, and psychedelics will have you talking to God at some point, but cocaine had you doing deals with the devil, right away.

I loved getting and being high, and I was open to experimenting, but I refused to touch blow, even though it was all around me. The homies and the hippies were doing it. Coke was the hip high. It was the in thing, but to me it was a black cloud made of white powder. I watched it change vibes and moods. I might be somewhere chilling and having a cool time, smoking some weed and drinking, enjoying an enlightening or funny conversation, when, inevitably, coke would show up and suck the joy out of the room. It snorted up the positivity and replaced it with a dark energy. Conversation would become sleazy and self-absorbed. The laughter would dry up and people would start acting shady and secretive or aggressive and full of boasts. From my perspective, it simply didn't look fun. Nobody looked happy on coke.

By the time I was fifteen or so, powder was ubiquitous. My uncles had been doing it for years, and like with everything they did, they made it look cool and stylish. Naturally, my older brother, who, like me, idolized them, got into it. He turned on to cocaine about the time an even more potent way to use it came into vogue. Dee got into a thing called "freebasing," which involved cooking cocaine to get it to the pure form of white rocks, then smoking it. Apparently the rocks got you extra high. Overnight, everyone became a chemist and a cook.

The other thing about freebasing was it made the white devil addictive.

I got a sense of the power of this new craze early on when my brother brought a friend over to my basement, specifically to cook up some rocks. His friend was drop-dead gorgeous. She was seventeen and probably the most beautiful and sexiest girl I'd ever shared a space with. She had an eight ball of blow and a box of baking soda. She said she wanted to make freebase, but what she was actually preparing wasn't freebase. It was what would become known as crack.

She went into my tiny kitchen area, where she boiled water and worked out the coke–to–baking soda ratio. She was in such a good mood. She said we could smoke together once it was done. I told her she was welcome to stay with me and smoke but I wasn't interested in partaking. That seemed to make her even happier. I was falling in love with her.

All of a sudden, she began to scream. Scream like she was in deep pain. Scream like she'd just watched someone she loved get murdered, or like she herself was being killed. It was bloodcurdling. Her cries went straight to my spine.

She'd messed up something with the proportions and ended up with coke soup. She'd wasted the cocaine. It was a ruined concoction.

She lay on my bed and bawled. Had a tantrum. She kept saying, "I wasted it, I wasted it!" I asked how I could help. She was inconsolable. She needed the hit. It was all she was interested in. I offered her my weed, my vodka. I offered her me.

She wouldn't stop crying. It was like she'd lost her baby. It broke my heart, but it also scared me.

About a year later, I saw that same beautiful young woman, and I hardly recognized her. She'd gone from a full-bodied girl with a bright white smile, flawless, glowing skin, and a head full of rich, healthy curls to a bone-thin, practically toothless, ashy, gray zombie.

She was a ruined concoction.

A cautionary tale. I vowed never to allow any substance to control and ruin me like that. I vowed never to touch cocaine.

I broke the vow.

I am an addict.

I used coke for the first time with my friend Chris because I trusted him. We'd been getting high together since before we were teenagers, and he was always experimenting with new ways to get high. We went from regular bush weed to sticky sinsemilla and sweet Thai stick. Chris brought us quaaludes and black beauty amphetamine pills to try. He wasn't much of a drinker, but he knew I liked alcohol, so he'd often come over with bottles of fancy whiskey or gin. I considered him a good friend, but in truth, we didn't have much in common beyond our love of getting high.

He'd been secretly snorting blow for years. Chris knew I wouldn't allow cocaine around me, and he kept those things to himself. When he finally came out as gay, he came all the way out. He told me about the coke. As he spoke freely about his gay life, he started snorting in front of me. I tolerated this because he supplied me with alcohol and weed.

One day, I was telling Chris how much I hated coke when, for no apparent reason, I said, "Give me the straw!" Two lines went up my nose before I even had time to consider what I had done. We were both surprised. I think I had the need to show cocaine who was boss. I snorted like a pro. I'd seen people doing it for so long, it came naturally to me. I knew how to hold one nostril down as I vacuumed up the line of powder into the other. I knew how to wipe up the residue with my pinkie and rub it on my gums for a "freeze." I knew how to sit with my head back after the bump and pinch my nostrils. I knew all of that, but I didn't know how it would make me feel.

I felt like a beautiful, brilliant god.

I felt smart, slick, and sexy. My mind raced with fantasies and visions of grandeur. I was a rock star and a porn star, a famous actor, a world-renowned artist, a fashion model, and a great philosopher. I was bad and bold, and nobody could fuck with me because I was so fucking cool.

I liked it.

A lot.

This thing I'd despised and avoided for so long I now wanted all the time, but I told myself I'd do it only with Chris.

I still only hung out with Chris once every few months, and it became all about the cocaine. I think Chris liked the idea of me using it because it allowed him to get flirtier and more suggestive. He knew my attraction to the coke was his allure and power. In the months between our hanging out, I thought about coke constantly, but I resisted finding out where to get it on my own, and I didn't partake when it was offered to me.

Then I moved in with Rico, and things took a turn. Rico was a half-blind Haitian dread who was part of the Flatbush Black punk scene. He was a brilliant poet and artist—abstract, eccentric, and just a little crazy. He lived with his mom in a huge, beautiful old apartment in the last building on a dead-end block called Westbury Court. It was all high ceilings and hardwood floors. The Q train ran right under its windows. The block had been a quiet enclave for years, and most of the buildings on it were owned by a local Haitian church. But when the crack epidemic hit in the mid-'80s, that block became the center of it, and there was a mass exodus by the God-fearing people. Overnight, the buildings emptied of nice Christian Haitian families and became crack houses. In the evenings, the dark dead-end block turned into an open-air crack market. Wild, depraved, and dangerous. It truly became a dead end.

Rico's mom moved back to Haiti and left the lease of the apartment to him. The first thing he did was take a sledgehammer to the bathroom, destroying the tub, sink, and toilet. It was his brilliant idea of how to justify not paying rent, because who would pay to live in a place that didn't have a usable bathroom? The once-beautiful apartment became a crash pad and a squat. Guys with names like Wire, Buzz, Skelly, and Dog started coming through and trashing the spot. These dudes were part of the rock and roll outlaws, a set of mostly Trinidadian bad boys who were into punk rock way before it was considered cool to be Black and punk.

At the time, I was without a place to live, and Rico graciously gave me a room. I spent most of my time in the city and usually got back to the squat after midnight. Turning the corner of that block was always a trip. I never knew what I might see: somebody selling a TV set or a whole stereo system, some crackhead sucking dick between parked cars or in a doorway, some bloodied body lying in the gutter, lighter flashes as stems were lit, or muzzle flashes as guns were fired. Walking that one short block, I'd often be solicited, threatened, propositioned, and offered stolen items, sexual favors, and various drugs. I had to run the gauntlet all the way to the apartment door because even the building lobby was a marketplace.

"Nah...I'm good. No, not tonight, baby," I recited like a mantra once I hit that block. It got to the point where I didn't even register the madness anymore. Insanity and danger became the norm. I was good with my bag of weed and forty-ounce of Colt 45. I steered clear of the crack rock. This went on for months.

I'm not really sure what made me say yes one night. Maybe I had some extra money or the desire to get higher than usual. Boredom is a dangerous thing for an addict. I bought a five-dollar vial of crack in the lobby of my building, then locked myself in my room, crushed the rocks up, mixed it with my weed, and rolled it into a joint. In Brooklyn, we called mixed joints like this "hoolas"; uptown and in the Bronx, they were called "bazookas." Crackheads were universally looked down upon, so nobody bragged about smoking crack, but hoolas were acceptable. A lot of the homeboys and even some Rastas smoked them. You got the mellow weed high with a little cocaine rush. I liked it a lot.

The next night, I bought another vial of crack and did the same thing.

I am an addict.

In short order, I found myself wanting only hoolas. Plain weed just wasn't doing it anymore. I wanted the extra kick that was similar to snorting but not as craven. I don't know how long this practice of smoking crack rock crushed into my weed went on, but one night I got the four little rocks in a five-dollar vial, and I smoked crack by itself for the first time. Rico had this smelly dude named Blew staying with us who was smoking crack in the apartment with impunity, and he left his stems and crack pipes lying around. I found one and took it to my room. The five-dollar vial was gone in minutes, so I went out and down one flight of stairs to the lobby, where a dealer I had passed every night for months was posted up. I spent the rest of the night going up and down those stairs until I was broke.

I am an addict.

The following night, I found some weed, but all I was really thinking about was getting a hit of crack. It doesn't take much to addict an addict. I kept telling myself the "just one vial" lie. On my way to buy it, I was accosted by a skinny, unkempt young brother who asked me for change. He was barely a teenager.

"I'll take anything you got, a quarter, a dime. I can get you a new Walkman for mad cheap. You need anything moved or cleaned up in your house? I'm a good worker."

I brushed him off.

"Nah, I'm good. I can't do nothing for you, man."

He grabbed my arm and said, "I see you around. I know you be smoking, too. Hook me up. I got a stem."

Something about him saying he recognized me as a smoker hit me hard. He recognized me as a fellow crackhead.

Then he said under his breath, "I'll suck your dick."

It broke my heart, and it made me angry in equal measure.

I never bought crack again.

For the Love of Him

CHRIS WAS ONE of the last White boys left in my neighborhood growing up. When we first moved to the block, he lived around the corner, and he was my sworn enemy for about a year. Chris rallied the other kids into hazing us with racist taunts, throwing firecrackers at us, and dumping bags of dog shit on our stoop.

All that stopped when I punched him in the face. I think the punch and the fact that the other White kids moved away humbled his ass.

We were the same age, and around the time we turned twelve, he became friendly. The fact that he always had the best toys, the coolest bikes, all the new gadgets, and a wicked fireworks connection helped me forgive and forget. Chris was a bit socially awkward and we didn't always agree on simple things. He liked sports, I liked music and art. He was sloppy and I was neat. We had different tastes in most things, but in time we became good friends. We hung out pretty regularly, and everything was cool until we turned thirteen or so and things got weird.

By that age I was already in love with weed, but I could rarely get hold of any, partly because I never had any money and partly because I didn't really know where to get it. My older brothers always brought the joints. Somehow, I must have gotten a joint for myself, though, and I decided to turn Chris on to his first smoke. It was love at first puff. What made this good for me was I had unknowingly created a weed monster who had money and a connection. Turns out the people he got his fireworks from also sold weed.

Chris became my pothead partner overnight, which was very fortunate for a "budding" young weed head like myself. We got high every chance we could.

Over summer break, I was pretty much unsupervised and left to fend for myself. Neighborhood kids used to meet up at my house, and we'd play all day in the backyard and basement. Chris was one of the kids who frequently hung out, and he was always welcome because he usually had a joint or two.

My mom used to buy our breakfast and lunch stuff from the no-frills aisle at the supermarket. We got the industrial-sized no-frills oatmeal, no-frills cheese, no-frills margarine, no-frills bread, no-frills jelly, and no-frills peanut butter. We made do with this food throughout the summer.

The peanut butter came in these big plastic gallon tubs. When I first opened the lid, the peanut butter was nice and smooth, but after a few days, a sinkhole developed in the middle of the tub. It was a strange phenomenon. I could never figure out what would make it do that. We'd finish the whole tub, sinkhole and all, and the same thing would happen with the next one.

Chris would hang in our backyard and go in and out of our house to use the bathroom, or sometimes make himself a sandwich if we happened to have bread. All the kids did it. One day we were in the backyard, playing with some of the older kids, when Chris quietly disappeared. It was around lunchtime, and I went inside to make myself a peanut butter and jelly sandwich. I was looking around the kitchen for the tub of peanut butter when I heard sounds from the basement. A kind of moaning. Curious, I quietly followed the sounds downstairs.

There was Chris on the couch with our family dog, Dizzy, between his legs. His pants were down by his ankles, and next to him was the tub of peanut butter. Dizzy was licking peanut butter off his dick.

I grew up with brothers, male cousins, and uncles, and by this point I'd seen and participated in many dick contests and activities, so seeing the dog lick peanut butter off Chris's wasn't even that extraordinary. What made this scene particularly fucked up was I realized I'd just discovered the mystery of the sinkhole in the peanut butter.

It's one thing to slather peanut butter on your dick to get a lick job from your friend's dog. To each his own. But it's another thing to put your whole dick *in* the peanut butter, especially the communal peanut butter. I mean, if you're going to fuck the peanut butter, then get doggie head, at least use your *own damn* peanut butter. I'd been making peanut butter, dick, and jelly sandwiches all summer!

A few awkward moments and a couple of joints later, all was forgiven.

* * *

Chris was an only child with an old dude for a father, so I wasn't overly surprised when he started making dick-curious statements and dropping hints. Chris and I used to smoke in my basement and sit around listening to music and cracking typical pubescent jokes. Every once in a while, I caught him staring at my crotch, which made me uncomfortable, but a couple more puffs of his good weed and it didn't seem to matter.

I spent most of my time in the basement during the summer, and it was where I showered in the morning. Chris started doing this thing where he'd show up in the basement *exactly* as I was stepping out of the shower. It was uncanny. I don't know how many times I stepped out of the shower naked to see Chris sitting on the couch, rolling up a joint and staring at me. He would always laugh at my embarrassment and light a joint as I quickly got dressed.

I remembered something my dad had told me when I was still really little—"All White guys are curious about Black guys' dicks"—and I figured that's what was up with my weed buddy Chris.

He started bringing over *Hustler* magazines. These were like precious currency. I always said, "Hey! Can I borrow this for later? I'll get it back to you tomorrow, I promise!" But Chris always wanted us to look at them together, which to me completely defeated the purpose.

One hot summer evening, Chris came over really late. It was a surprise, because he usually had to be home no later than 8 p.m. All the other kids had long since gone home. He let himself into the basement and was acting strange, like he was super high, in la-la land. I was always down to smoke, so I was willing to put up with a little weirdness. He said he'd taken a quaalude, which was like a horse tranquilizer pill. We smoked and he started acting like he was out his mind, like he didn't know where he was or what he was doing. He'd brought some new *Hustler* magazines with him, and he laid them out on the couch. Then he complained that he was too high and it was too hot and he needed to sleep for a minute before he went home. He lay down on the couch and looked like he was falling asleep. I sat next to him, and I guess half out of the boredom of just sitting there high and with no one to talk to, I started flipping through the magazines. I was deep into the magazines and got a hard-on in my gym shorts. I remember thinking, *I wish this dude would wake up and leave already so I can jerk off in peace.* I even thought of leaving him there and taking the magazines into the bathroom. Right then, Chris rolled over and rested his head in my lap. He was still "sleeping," but now using my lap as a pillow. It was an incredibly awkward position to be in, your friend's head in your lap with your big hard-on just inches from his face.

I don't know exactly what happened next, but somehow I found myself sitting on my couch looking at a porn magazine while my dick was in my friend's mouth. I remember both not understanding what was happening and desperately trying to make believe it wasn't happening.

I was still technically a virgin. I'd only had heavy make-out sessions with my girlfriend, Sharon, in the staircases of the Vanderveer projects. I'd even gotten to third base with her. I'd also been humping and playing with my next-door neighbor Waynetta for a couple of years, but I'd never had anything close to a mouth on my dick.

And what made everything worse was Chris obviously

must have known what he was doing because Lord help me, it felt good.

I came.

It was over, and somehow my dick was resting peacefully back in my gym shorts and Chris was still "sleeping." We never mentioned what occurred in the basement that night. It was like it never happened, and I began to wonder if I had somehow made it up.

A few weeks before I started my freshman year at James Madison High School, Chris totally hooked me up. He got me a weekend job working with him at the Glenwood flea market, but even better, devised a credit card scam where we went shopping at all these different stores, buying fresh new clothes, sneakers, and jewelry. When we maxed his cards out, he called to report that they had been stolen. It was brilliant, something I would have never thought up on my own. It's partly because I was so "dripped" when I started high school that I was able to pull one of the most popular fly girls in school. Linda was my first love. We met in September, and by December, I was so in love I was telling people we were going to get married as soon as we turned eighteen. I was dead serious.

Chris had started dating one of Linda's friends, this fine Trinidadian girl. We double-dated, going to the movies and shopping malls together. We were the cute "it" couples *and* I wasn't a virgin anymore. Far from it. Linda was way more sexually advanced than I, and she showed me all kinds of new things. We were constantly at it.

Right before Christmas, I was hanging out with Chris and bragging to him about the gifts I'd bought Linda and how in love we were. How we were going to get married. Something washed over Chris. He got quiet and distant. Finally, he came out and said, "I can't take it anymore. You deserve to know." He continued, "I've been seeing Linda. We've been fucking for the last month. I bought her all the new jewelry she's been wearing!"

I had noticed her new gold necklaces and tennis bracelets. She'd told me they were gifts from her uncles.

In the course of one minute, I went from sky-high to crashing to the lowest low I'd ever felt. My fifteen-year-old heart completely crushed. With one sentence, I'd lost the love of my life and my best friend.

But then he said something it took me at least a decade to come to grips with: "The only reason I got with her is because I knew I couldn't get with you. She was the closest way I could come to having you. I'd ask her to let me know when you had fucked her and I'd tell her not to bathe until I could get there to eat her pussy." He dropped his head. "I've always wanted you. I'm in love with you."

I wasn't emotionally mature enough to handle his confession. I had no tools to deal with and process the hurt. I was a mess. Completely broken.

I stopped seeing Linda.

I stopped talking to Chris.

Two weeks later, my dad died.

That was when I began to seriously self-medicate, when my drinking and drugging really took off.

A decade later, I was still trying to numb the pain. I went from smoking weed and drinking an occasional beer to drinking as much of any alcohol as I could physically tolerate and taking any drug I could get my hands on. There was rarely a time when I wasn't under the influence of some substance, and consequently, my life began to fall apart. I was desperate. I worked, stole, borrowed, and begged just to stay high.

About that time, Chris reentered my life.

I don't remember how we got back in touch after a decade of absolutely no contact. Right after he told me about Linda and professed his love to me, I completely removed him from my life. All that time passed but somehow there he was. Back in my life.

One day, seemingly out of nowhere, he invited me over to the little apartment by Brooklyn College he was sharing with his dad. The years hadn't been too kind to Chris, either. He'd come out as gay pretty much right after his confession to me, and he, too, had gone right to drugs. Then he'd bounced around from job to job and apartment to apartment, finally ending up renting a room from his old dad, who was rarely home.

We got high together again. Smoked his good weed, snorted his good coke, and I drank his dad's booze. As always, he had the best drugs and plenty of alcohol. We caught up and made up, careful not to mention anything about what had happened between us all those years ago. He spoke freely about his lifestyle and seemed relieved he could now be open with me about being gay. I shared stories about my girlfriends and my sexual conquests, and he told me about his boyfriends, the clubs, the orgies, and all the naughtiness he had been up to. We laughed a lot. We were friends again.

As I was leaving that evening, still reveling in the glow of friendship and good drugs, Chris asked if I could use a couple of bucks. I was down-and-out, and there was no way I could refuse. As soon as he passed me that twenty dollars, our whole dynamic changed.

We hung out maybe six times over the course of the next two years, and during that time, my financial situation got progressively worse. I had become basically homeless, and I never had any money. All I had went to my need to stay high, and Chris took advantage of it. The vibe shifted from two old friends getting high and hanging out to a sleazy kind of game of cat and mouse. I would show up and Chris would have the lights low, porno on the screen, lines of coke laid out, and a bottle of vodka for me. He'd also be dressed in things like short shorts with crop tops, things that made him look feminine. It all made me uncomfortable, but I *needed* to get high, and I *needed* money.

He made not-so-subtle innuendoes and slick suggestions, and he even brought up what had transpired between us in my basement all those years before, teasing, "I know you liked it." I did my best to ignore all of this, pretending to be naive and oblivious. I dressed as baggy and "butch" as possible, thinking it would be a deterrent, only to find out it had the opposite effect. Part of what he wanted was to seduce a straight Black man. For me, the game was to try to do up all his drugs and get him to give me some money and get out of there without anything sexual happening.

The first couple of times, it worked. The third time, he came straight out and said, "If you're going to do up all my drugs and expect to take my money, I want something, and I think you know what it is."

The first time, I got fifty dollars and a small bag of coke. All he wanted was to give me head, so I closed my eyes and tried to make believe it wasn't happening. So much like the basement incident. As soon as it was over, I snatched up the money and drugs and dashed out without looking at him or saying goodbye.

Each time, I demanded more money and drugs. It was always the same act, and I always did my best to check out and make believe I wasn't there, but I never got used to it. I felt horrible afterward, so disgusted and dirty it would take me months before I could even consider picking up his calls. It was a secret that burned a hole in my soul. Addiction and desperation had turned me into a prostitute.

The last time was different.

It was the night before his birthday. He'd told me on the phone he wanted it to be special. I arrived to find Chris completely done up. He had shaved his mustache and body hair. He was wearing little cutoff pum-pum shorts, stockings, garters, panties, the whole nine for my whole nine.

He had three crisp hundred-dollar bills and an eight ball of coke on the table next to the couch.

He said, "I want you to make love to me like you make love to a woman. Like I used to imagine you doing with Linda. I just want you to love me. It's all I've ever wanted."

I was stunned. I stood there, speechless and motionless.

"Look, if you won't do it, then just leave, but I'm not giving you any money." Chris said it in a defiant way, but I could tell he was trying to cover up his feelings.

He lay on the couch and turned on his belly. Buried his head in the pillow, pulled the shorts and panties aside. As desperate for money and drugs as I was, as depraved and hungry as I was, I remember staring down at him and being washed over with a deep feeling of sorrow.

The whole scene just felt desperate and sad.

This was my friend Chris.

And this was me standing there, considering fucking a friend for money and drugs, and him asking me to just love him.

In that moment, I realized it really all came down to my loving him. All we'd been through since we were ten years old was about him wanting me to love him.

And I did love him.

I loved him so much I simply turned around and let myself out of the apartment.

I left the money and drugs.

I left Chris lying there on the couch.

Untouched but deeply loved.

Psychedelic Shaman

PSYCHEDELICS WERE "ATMOSPHERE" by Funkadelic, *The Dark Side of the Moon* by Pink Floyd, and all Indian raga music. Psychedelics were Day-Glo posters, incense, and peppermints. They were the groovy witch doctor. They were staring into a flame and speaking to God in foreign tongues.

The first couple of times I took magic mushrooms, the effect was so mild it was almost unnoticeable. It could've been the quality of the shrooms, or because I was also smoking weed and drinking wine and couldn't distinguish what was getting me high. I certainly didn't get the trippy effects I hoped for. I expected an altered reality, and what I got was a mild euphoria and a mellow distortion. I got pleasant and safe vibrations when I wanted shaman visions and melting clocks. Mushrooms did enhance things a bit. The colors were a little more vivid, sounds a little more intense, but it wasn't the bang for the buck I was looking for. I wanted to lose my mind.

Then, someone gave me blotter acid.

Acid (or LSD) was a throwback to the '60s. The hippies and freaks had done it, then made music, art, and a movement around it and moved on. I remember asking around for it from older heads, who would smile knowingly with a nostalgic gleam in their eyes and an attitude of *Aw, now isn't that sweet?* and offer quaaludes or cocaine instead. But I wouldn't be satisfied until I saw fluorescent paisley floating around me and heard the voices of the angels.

It was a neo-hippie kid from across the tracks who helped me realize my spaced-out aspirations. Bobby lived on the other side of Glenwood Road, literally across abandoned railway tracks. He was one of those third-wave Deadheads, all tie-dye and patchouli, but still a Brooklyn kid with street sensibilities. I'd met him when I worked at the Glenwood flea market, and we became casual friends over time.

One day, I randomly ran into Bobby. He said, "Dude, I got tabs of Mickey Mouse." He was referring to blotter acid that came in tiny squares of paper with an image of Mickey on them. "Ya dig? I got that Disney dizzy that would make Snow turn White, the Seven Dwarfs start a Stones cover band, and get Goofy groovy. Two hits for five dollars. Out of sight, maaaaan!"

I bought six tabs. He cautioned me to take only one and see where it took me. He told me, "This shit is super strong. Acid can be tricky, dude. It reacts differently to different people. You don't want a bad trip your first time, maaaaan."

I took all six at once.

I got the shaman visions and the dripping Salvador Dalí clocks.

I didn't have a bad trip. I had a divine journey that lasted three days. I lost and gained time. I lost and gained my mind. My senses made no sense. I tasted colors, heard smells, saw sound. The angels and fairies, the devils and demons, visited me. I didn't sleep. I was in a dream state in which I experienced different planes of existence. I was in an altered reality. I felt awe but no fear. My skin was super sensitive to the slightest of stimuli. A breeze sent me into ecstasy, a butterfly landing on my arm was bliss. I understood the language of the chirping birds and buzzing bees. The cacophony of city sounds became an exquisite symphony almost too perfect to endure. I felt the universal vibration pulsing around and through me, and I vibrated at the same frequency. I fell into perfect harmony and rhythm with the *All*. I melted and melded into the cosmic *One*. I couldn't tell where I began and where the atmosphere ended. I fully understood for the first time the interconnection and interdependency of *Everything*, and it was all glorious.

During those three days, I could only manage to drink water and eat a little fruit. It took me an hour to eat an orange. Its color, smell, and structure were overwhelmingly beautiful, and its flavor intense. I could taste it in my soul. I could taste *its* soul. I felt the orange sacrifice its being to feed my physical body, and I cried with gratitude. I was absorbed into the whole, yet I was aware of my unique existence. My body lit up from the inside out, and I became a beacon to myself. I spoke to no one. I walked and walked. Over the bridge into Manhattan at night, the city lights and the stars in the sky became one twinkling masterpiece. I ended up sitting alone in a zone on Brighton Beach as the dawn broke and the sun rose on the final day. Mesmerized by the majesty of the ocean and losing myself in the ebb and flow of the waves, I waded into the water and felt anointed and reborn. Baptized. I gently eased back to reality, but I was forever altered.

I dropped acid many more times, but I never got to quite that place again. I thought I had gone as far as I could go with psychedelics.

Then I met Freddy.

He was absolutely one of a kind. A walking contradiction. Freddy may have been the most unpretentious intelligent person I'd ever met, but he did some of the stupidest shit imaginable. He was dark-skinned and handsome with sleepy eyes that made you think he was dull and unaware, but he was the opposite. Freddy was sharp as a razor, and he didn't miss anything. When he seemed to be drifting off on his own cloud, he'd suddenly say something so astute and precise, he'd leave you speechless. He was sophisticated and he was savage. He was a highly disciplined hedonist. He was a shaman and a mystic, and he was a thug and a gangster. He was a hustler, a con man, a thief, and a priest. He could quote chapter and verse from the Bible, Quran, and Bhagavad Gita, and he kept those holy books on top of a stack of German porno magazines. He read Thomas Aquinas and Marcus Aurelius for fun, and he never left the house without a gun.

Freddy was a trickster. He was Loki and Pan. He was a mischievous spirit made flesh. He was Baron Samedi.

When I met Freddy, he'd already risen to the level of a hood god. A local legend. He'd robbed a bank around the corner from his house and gotten into a shoot-out with a squad of police. He emptied his gun at the cops and somehow managed to escape over backyard fences to his basement apartment. He stashed the stolen money, reloaded his gun, changed his clothes, and went back around the corner to mingle with the crowd of onlookers. He even had the nerve to ask a cop what happened. Freddy didn't give a fuck.

Freddy was initiated in the Ife Yoruba faith. He was a Babalawo, a high priest in that order. He made connections in West Africa and started importing ancient African masks, sculptures, and statues. Not pretty tourist items but sacred ceremonial fetishes used in rituals. His basement apartment was jammed with powerful and frightening pieces. There was never anyplace to sit. Many of those pieces were still caked with the blood of sacrifice.

Freddy was also openly into BDSM, so in his apartment things like handcuffs, a whip, and a leather bondage mask sat next to some magical African mask. A full latex catsuit draped over an ancient sacred sculpture. The juxtaposition was always disturbing.

Freddy sold the African sculptures and things that fell off the back of a truck.

Freddy sold drugs.

Specifically, mescaline.

Well, it wasn't actually mescaline. I'd read about mescaline in books by Carlos Castaneda that told the story of a Native American shaman who used it, along with peyote, to give himself otherworldly experiences and allow himself to commune with the spirits. It was a purple cactus one ingested in dried "buttons." It was psychedelic and holy and to be used in ceremonies and rituals. It was what I wanted, but what Freddy actually sold were manufactured little purple pellets that masqueraded as mescaline. Microdot was called Purple Haze, which was most likely LSD mixed with amphetamine. The effect was trippy and speedy at once, a party drug that preceded Ecstasy and Molly. Freddy sold some of it at underground clubs like the Paradise Garage and the Tunnel, but I think he sold the majority of it at the gay and swinger clubs he frequented. Purple Haze made me feel spiritual and sexy at the same time. It made me want to talk about God while I fucked.

It cost three dollars per microdot, and you needed about three hits to get a really good trip that would last eight to twelve hours. I was buying hits daily. After a while, Freddy dropped the price to a dollar apiece for me, and eventually he just started giving me the microdots by the handful. He was getting them from some Mob dudes he worked with for cheap and could afford to give them away. Plus, he was really making his money from heists and moving cocaine in quantity. The Purple Haze was just a plaything for him.

For me, those tiny dots were definitely not a plaything. They were salvation. The summer of my twenty-first year, I tripped every single day. I started each morning with three hits and a spliff. It got so everything I looked at had a purple aura. Literally everything glowed fluorescent, like I was viewing the world through a black light. I saw all motion in trails; movement was broken down into still sequences, like an old film rolling slowly through a projector. I would drop another three or more hits in the evening. I stayed under the influence and in a constant state of illusion. If you had licked my sweat that summer, you would've tripped. I slept and ate very little as a result of the amphetamine. I fucked a lot, and I spaced out. I lost whole days at a time. The missing days turned into weeks and months. Big gaps where I lost all conception of who, when, where, or what I was. I stayed in this state for the better part of a year. Nothing seemed important or real. I was floating in a purple haze.

I met LeTrisha over the Christmas holiday that year. She

was down from Stony Brook University on break. My friend Ish introduced us. I liked her, but I wasn't interested in a real relationship. I wasn't in a state to be serious about anything, let alone a relationship. Over the course of the week she was in town, we made love a few times. I was tripping on each occasion.

Two months later, I received the news I was to be a father.

I reacted to that news by taking a handful of microdots. I went far, far away.

I am an addict.

Express

I GOT A job as a bike messenger for a company called Express. Their office / bike garage was down near Chinatown, but messengers were sent all over the city. Every morning, I rode my own bike from Flatbush into the city and spent the day going back and forth to the base to get more pickups and deliveries. Messengers were paid a flat rate of three dollars an hour, but we made fifty cents in commission with every run. The more you rode, the more you made.

Long before emails and sending attached documents, New York was full of bike messengers zipping in and out of traffic, uptown, across town, through Central Park, down to the Village and Wall Street. We saw one another everywhere, and we were like a band of brothers. We were bike warriors. Messengers shared unspoken respect, conveyed with a nod or an "I see you!" shouted as we rode by each other. It didn't matter what messenger service you worked for, didn't matter if your bike was a Cannondale ten-speed or if you were on a homemade fixed gear you cobbled together yourself (usually the case) — if you carried a messenger bag filled with big manila envelopes and mailing tubes, you were a brother.

It was the closest I'd ever felt to being in the military. We were at war. It was us against the whole city: the taxis, trucks, pedestrians, cops, and, worst of all, the recreational bike riders. The taxis treated us like a regrettable nuisance, the trucks didn't even register us, pedestrians didn't seem to understand the sidewalk was theirs but the streets belonged to us, the cops were indifferent, and as far as recreational bike riders, I speak for all messengers when I say, wholeheartedly, "Fuck 'em!"

It was hard, exhausting, and dangerous work, but there was an exhilarating freedom to it, too. With everything we were up against, our biggest enemy was probably the weather. I started working toward the end of the summer, and I caught some of the hottest days of the year, the type of days when I saw heat genies dancing up from the sidewalk, when touching the hood of a car could burn my hands and my bike tires got soft. I was literally burning rubber as I rode. No amount of water could keep me hydrated on those days, and the black smoke and grit from riding in traffic didn't wipe off. It was incredibly unhealthy and hard on my lungs. Like a lot of messengers, I wore a bandana wrapped around my face, but I still developed a black cough by the end of the season.

The fall was actually quite pleasant to ride in. Crisp and brisk. Not so cold you had to bundle up and not so hot you lost twenty pounds every shift. Then came winter, and winter was painful. Sometimes on a long run, my hands would freeze and I couldn't even hold the pen to sign myself in to a building. But it was an added burden to layer up against the cold because it restricted mobility. Bulky clothes not only added weight, they made the aerodynamics brutal, made it difficult to turn on a dime, and dragged us down. We felt (and sometimes looked) like circus bears on those tiny bikes. The best thing I could do was dress lightly, keep my extremities covered, and keep moving to try to generate as much internal heat as possible. When the temperature dipped below freezing and there was freezing rain, it was pure torture to ride. The cold damp seeped into my clothes, layer by layer, until I could feel it in my bones.

In a typical day of riding, I crisscrossed the city many times. All the way west to the Hudson River, across to the East River, up past Central Park, and down to Battery Park. It was a great way to learn the city.

Bike messengers didn't often stop for red lights, but when we did, we talked about the weather, gossiped, and gave each other directions and shortcuts. A conversation at a stoplight might go like "I see you! Hotter than a mafukka today, yo! Who you with?" To which you might reply, "Express. Yo! I gotta go down to Wall Street. What's good?" The reply might go something like "Bro, from here your best bet is Broadway down to Church and swing east. Yo! Tell Esau that Fat Jose from Quick Drops said what's up! One!" And off you went.

One bitterly cold winter day, I was going back to the office in Chinatown from a drop I'd made up by Central Park. The streets had frozen up, and it had started raining the kind of rain that makes you rethink your career choices. It was gray and foggy, and the road got super slippery as freezing rain covered the ice. It was miserable and scary.

A brother messenger pulled up to me at a light. We were wedged between a big delivery truck and parked cars. We greeted each other, and he asked for directions. I recognized him. We had passed each other on the streets a few times. I told him the route I'd take for where he was going.

As the light changed and we began to pull off, he said, "Yo! Be careful out here today, bro, it's—"

I never heard the end of his sentence. What I heard was the grinding of truck brakes and the crunching of metal. Just that quick, his bike had slid out from under him. His lower half was crushed under the wheels of the delivery truck.

I got off my bike and walked it all the way downtown to the office. I left it there and never went back.

Christmas Miracle II (The Nativity Scene)

I WAS LIVING on Fourth Avenue in South Park Slope with my beautiful girlfriend, Glenda, and a cat named Dog. Glenda and I had been together for a few years, and we'd just moved in together to this new apartment. Between my working part-time for minimum wage in an art supplies shop and trying to make it as a gigging musician with a drug and alcohol problem, and Glenda hustling to get decent-paying modeling jobs, we often struggled to make ends meet.

LeTrisha, my son Omari's mother, and I had landed on an arrangement where I had him on most weekends, some holidays, and all of Christmas Day. I picked him up from his grandmother's house in Bed-Stuy on this freezing Christmas morning and looked forward to spending the day with him. We always had great times together. He was going to spend the night for the first time in our new apartment.

Omari was now four years old. He was sickly with severe asthma at that age, and because of it he was a little timid and fearful because he always worried he'd have an attack that would leave him struggling to breathe. Despite this, he was usually in good spirits. We hung out all Christmas Day and played with the toys I'd gotten him, the Stretch Armstrong doll he'd wanted and some other action figures. By 9 p.m. it was past his bedtime, and he was yawning, could barely keep his eyes open. He was also having a little trouble breathing, but that wasn't unusual.

I put him to bed on a little cot I'd made up for him in my bedroom, then I stayed up drinking and smoking weed in the living room until about 1 a.m. When I finally lay down, I noticed his breathing had become very heavy and erratic. Earlier, he'd said he was having a hard time breathing, but I thought it was because he was overstimulated.

Into the night, I listened with concern to his broken breathing, and I became really worried at around 3 a.m., when it seemed his episodes of not breathing were becoming more frequent. I wondered what I should do. At about 4 a.m., I realized he'd basically stopped breathing and wasn't responding when I tried to rouse him awake. In a panic, I bundled him up and headed out into the freezing night, carrying my limp son in my arms.

I lived about a mile from Methodist Hospital, and I thought I could catch a cab on busy Fourth Avenue and be there in minutes. It was the coldest night of the year, the coldest Christmas I ever remembered. Everything was covered in ice, and I stood on the corner in my light jacket with only a T-shirt underneath, Converse sneakers with no socks, no hat or gloves, and my son cradled to my chest. I tried everything to hail a cab, even standing in the middle of oncoming traffic. Plenty of cabs passed, but the drivers only slowed down, looked at us, and kept going. Omari seemed to have stopped breathing and was beginning to turn blue. I was desperately clutching him to my chest, hopping up and down and calling his name, trying to get him to respond. "C'mon, buddy! Wake up for your dad! Take a nice deep breath for me! We're gonna get you some help! Please, just start breathing, Omari!"

Finally, a cab stopped. The driver looked at us, rolled down his window, and asked where we were going. I told him, "My son is sick! He's not breathing! I need to get him to the hospital!" The cabbie didn't even say anything. He just pulled off.

I began to run to the hospital. All uphill blocks on icy streets. I fell a couple of times, making sure to protect Omari by cradling him like a running back and rolling so as to keep him from hitting the ground. I ran without thinking of the cold or distance. I ran and prayed and hugged my dying son to my chest. I ran through the snow and ice for a mile. I felt no cold or pain.

As soon as I stepped into the emergency room, a nurse saw the state I was in, took one look at my son, and without a word, took him from me. Immediately an intern ran up, checked Omari's vital signs, and they rushed him away beyond the doors.

I sat in the waiting room in shock and watched the minutes tick by on the lobby clock. A nurse finally came over to me. She brought a cup of warm water and a cloth. She said, "They're doing all they can."

It was only then that the pain hit me. I looked down and saw that my hands and knees were shredded and covered in blood. I could feel that my toes, nose, ears, and fingers were nearly frostbitten.

I alternated from sitting and waiting to standing at the nurses' desk to ask what Omari's condition was. No one would tell me anything. They only asked questions like "How long had he stopped breathing?" and "Was he on any medications?" while not looking me in the eye.

I prayed with every bit of my soul to a God I didn't know.

Eventually, a nurse I hadn't seen before came over and said in a low, conciliatory voice, "You can go back and see him now." I was sure her tone was telling me I was about to see my four-year-old son lying dead on a hospital gurney.

I walked behind that door to a world of masked faces and beeping machines. There were rows of people, mostly older folks lying under white sheets and connected to all types of wires and tubes.

And at the very back of the room, there he was, my son, sitting up straight on a plastic chair, feet swinging, and a big smile on his face. I grabbed him and pulled him into a tight hug. I kissed his cheeks, his hands, and the top of his peasy head. I held my boy and rocked him from side to side and thought, *I will never, ever let him go.*

When I settled him back onto the chair, I saw he was chewing gum. A lot of gum. It made his cheeks puff out. I thought it would be strange for doctors to give bubble gum to a child who had just been brought in blue from lack of oxygen.

I asked, "Omari, did the nice doctors give you that gum?"
He shook his head no.
"Did the nice nurses give you the gum?"
Again, no.

"Where did you get it from?"

He shyly pointed down to the chair he was sitting on.

I thought, *Oh! God, no!*

I leaned forward and looked underneath the chair. There must have been twenty dried wads of previously chewed gum stuck there. Old hospital sick-people gum.

The Strand

IN 1987, I got a job at the famous Strand bookstore in Union Square. My ska band, the Boilers, rehearsed down the block at a place called Giant Studios, and I stopped in the Strand one day with every intention to steal a book but instead decided to ask if any positions were open.

Every NYU student, downtown artist, and aspiring writer wanted to work at the Strand. It was a status job. It was hip to be seen wearing the iconic red Strand bookstore T-shirt only employees got.

A young woman who was as dark as the night and as beautiful as a sunrise handed me an application. I filled it out and was lucky enough to be sent directly to meet Fred, the store's owner, in a cramped little space he called his office. The interview lasted less than a minute. Fred looked me up and down and asked, "What's the last book you read?"

"I don't remember the title," I said, "but it was something by Vonnegut."

Fred told me to come back the next day. I was assigned to the store warehouse, and when I stepped inside it, I realized why Fred wanted to be in charge of who was hired. I was fairly sure he was conducting a social experiment.

We had two floor managers. John and Paul, like the Beatles and the popes. John was an old throwback to a Haight-Ashbury hippie. All long hair, tie-dyed shirts, and bell-bottom jeans. He was always noticeably stoned. He moved and spoke slowly, started and ended every sentence with "Maaaaan," and took frequent naps at his desk. He was basically Chong from the Cheech & Chong movies. Paul was completely different. He was in his early thirties and super energetic, like methamphetamine-energetic. A total leather queen, complete with the thick mustache and the supertight black leather outfits. He buzzed around the warehouse giving out orders and shade. If he could have gotten away with it, I guessed he would have literally "cracked the whip." The secret joke we warehouse workers shared about Paul was that one of the guys had found a picture in a Robert Mapplethorpe photography book of a skinny White dude with a thick mustache wearing leather chaps. He had the handle of a big black leather whip shoved way up his ass. It was Paul.

There were about ten of us who worked the warehouse floor, including the managers. Our job was to keep the store stocked, fill mail orders, and receive shipments of books. It was a lot of time on our feet, walking up and down aisles, climbing pallets of books, and lugging heavy boxes. Our crew was as motley and unlikely as could be imagined.

We had Chelsea, who looked like the love child of Howard Stern and Joey Ramone. Years later, when I saw

Marilyn Manson for the first time, I swore it was Chelsea. I'm still not convinced it wasn't. Every day, Chelsea came to work in that dusty, dirty warehouse dressed in a pink or yellow ballerina's tutu and combat boots. Long before people were talking about gender nonconformity or gender fluidity, there was Chelsea. This tall, gaunt, pale, skinny being was in a serious romantic relationship with a stud lesbian called Bobbi, who also worked in the store. Bobbi was short, round, and fat, and all trucker hats and flannel shirts. The two of them making out in the stairway was indeed a sight to behold.

We had two other Black guys on the crew. One was Nathaniel, who suffered from the worst case of eczema I'd ever seen. Every visible inch of Nathaniel looked like alligator skin. It flaked, peeled, and cracked, and he was constantly scratching. When he sat down at our break table to eat lunch, he left flakes of himself all over the chair and the table. You knew when he'd used the toilet because his dried, flaked skin sat in a ring around the seat.

Eugene was a bit older, but he always looked as if his mommy had dressed him. Creased, high-water corduroy pants and too-tight sweater vests and off-brand sneakers. He had the most unkempt afro I'd seen since middle school. I had to fight the urge to tell him to pick his shit out. Eugene wore thick glasses and had a gentle, scholarly air about him. He was soft-spoken and well-read and always eager to discuss philosophy or the Bible. Eugene was a devout, churchgoing, born-again Christian with a secret.

Sometimes, when I was filling an order in the quiet warehouse, I'd suddenly hear a loud "Suck my motherfucking dick, you faggot bitch!" or "Lick my shitty asshole!"

Eugene had Tourette's. He had a verbal tic he couldn't control. Once I got used to it, I teased him about it. One day, after a particularly vile outburst, he said, "They really love me in church. They think I've been possessed by a demon."

Boo-Boo Fuff was the dirtiest kid I'd ever met. He was poor White trash from the Rockaways and looked like a mix between a young Bob Dylan and Shaggy from *Scooby-Doo*. He was a really sweet kid. Our hippie manager, John, actually gave him the nickname. Joey (soon to be christened Boo-Boo Fuff) messed up an order badly one day. He got really upset and started to tear up. John put a consoling arm around his shoulders and said, "Maaaaan, you've gotta toughen up, dude! You can't go through life being Boo-Boo Fuff, maaaaan!"

Fuff used to bathe in the warehouse bathroom. I saw him scrub his face with soap and water, and still it looked like he'd just pulled it out of a bus exhaust pipe. He was genetically dirty. Dirt was in his DNA.

Lastly, there was Natz. Natz was my boy. We hit it off right away. I didn't know it at first, but he was somewhat of a local legend in the Lower East Side and East Village punk scene. He was a bass player who played with everyone but was best known for his time with two iconic bands on that scene, the Undead and Cop Shoot Cop.

Cop Shoot Cop was at the height of its popularity as a noise industrial post-punk band. When Natz first told me about the band, I thought the title was literal; as in cops shooting other cops. He explained it actually meant the cycle of a junkie's life, as in "*cop* dope, *shoot* dope, *cop* dope" and repeat.

Natz and I had a catchphrase: "You think it's easy?" It's how we greeted and said goodbye to each other. I hung out with him after work in Tompkins Square Park and around Alphabet City, where he was hailed as a minor celebrity by the local punks and junkies. He was pretty recognizable: six foot three and bone-skinny with crazy, unkempt hair and a habit of wearing long black trench coats and heavy engineer boots—even in the dead of summer. I went to a couple of his shows, and I was the only Black guy for miles. But Natz always made me feel welcome. At one matinee show, a bunch of Nazi punks showed up and started harassing the band. Natz calmly unstrapped his bass and smacked one of those Nazis across the face with it, and just as calmly picked up playing where he'd left off. Punk rock!

Natz lived in a big apartment off of Avenue C with his girlfriend, who was also somewhat famous in the dark, post-punk-art Lydia Lunch world. We had hung out in Tompkins Square all night, and I had to be back at work in a few hours, so he invited me to crash at their spot. I slept on the floor in the smelly, nasty, roach- and rat-infested space. They had cats but no cat box. They had a refrigerator but no electricity. Everything was rotten and foul. The toilet didn't flush. Things crawled on me and things nibbled at me. Natz and his girl thought it was cool to live like that. They actually bragged about it.

A couple times a week, Fred came up to the warehouse to check on his social experiment. I think he really got a kick out of playing God as he chose one of us to work the store floor for a few hours. It was a reprieve to be out of the dusty warehouse and among the public, and some of the cashiers were kind of cute. One day, Fred selected me to work the floor, and I struck up a conversation with one of the cute cashiers. She was a punk chick, new to the city. She was a big fan of Cop Shoot Cop, and she knew Natz and I were friends. She suggested we hang out after work.

We ended up getting drunk together till pretty late, and

found ourselves on a secluded bench in Tompkins Square. We made out a bit. She unzipped my pants.

I was living in a squat that had no bath or shower. The best I could do was take a cowboy bath in the kitchen sink, and I hadn't even done that in a week. I was cheesy and nasty. I grabbed her hand and said, "Baby, you don't want to do that. I stink like a homeless bum. Let's wait till I can get washed up." She was persistent but eventually stopped trying. She'll never know the favor I did her that day.

I quit the Strand by simply not showing up anymore. One day, I was on my way in and a voice came to me as if God herself whispered it in my ear. "It's done," the voice said.

Homeless Stew

AFTER I LEFT the Strand, I spent more and more time in the East Village. I roamed Alphabet City, looking for the next high, be it a drink, a drug, a fight, or a woman. Tompkins Square Park became like a second home. Literally.

Tompkins Square was *the* place for artists, musicians, punk rockers, B-boys, addicts, and the homeless, and I was pretty much all of the above. There was always something jumping off. I saw people get stabbed there and heard guns popping off. I saw people shooting up and smoking crack, people fucking and fighting. There were parties and music and the occasional celebrity. One afternoon, I fell asleep high and drunk on a bench and woke up to find myself sitting next to H.R., the lead singer of Bad Brains, a hardcore legend and a hero of mine. We sat on that bench and reasoned for hours about our lives, injustice, and Jah.

Another time, I shared a bench with a timid, nerdy White guy. Eventually, we struck up a conversation, making pleasant small talk. He kind of reminded me of an owl. I told him so, and he thought it was not only funny but accurate. He introduced himself as David. He seemed to be getting a lot of attention for such a nondescript guy, and it was only after we parted ways that I realized he was another one of my heroes. He was in a band called the Talking Heads.

At that time, the park was a melting pot of grit and glam, poverty and fame. But despite Tompkins Square Park being one pot, like so much of New York City, it was naturally segregated. The Puerto Ricans and B-boys tended to stay on the Avenue B side, while the punks and artist types congregated near Avenue A. The homeless had no boundaries. There was a little homeless shanty town erected in the middle of the park, a homeless homeland. It was made up of people from every ethnic group and demographic. It was a homeless United Nations.

I was still living in Brooklyn, bumming on couches and trying to get in where I fit in, but I often ended up crashing on a bench in the park. I roamed freely throughout Tompkins, day and night, to the north and south. I was making almost no money selling poor-quality weed, and I had a few regular customers from both sides of the park. I mingled with the punks and chilled with the B-boys, but I was most fascinated and entertained by the homeless. There were some outstanding characters among them.

There were the three Petes: Sneaky, Sticky, and Stinky, or the Re-Petes, as some of my friends and I called them. Sneaky Pete was an older, skinny White dude who skulked around the park, always looking like he'd just stolen something or was about to. No one trusted him. Then there was Sticky

Pete, a young Black guy who was simple and sweet but really needy. If you gave him a dollar or started any kind of conversation with him, he'd stick to you all day like flypaper. Lastly, there was Stinky Pete, who was stinky to an extraordinary degree, even among the homeless.

Calamity Jane was one of my favorites. I never spoke to her, but I liked watching her. I didn't know her real name, but I secretly thought of her as Calamity Jane because no matter the weather, she always wore a little red cowboy hat with matching red cowboy boots. This was an easily two-hundred-pound Black woman, and sometimes the hat and those boots were *all* she wore.

There was Transgenda Linda, a Puerto Rican character whose appearance was so confusing, we could never figure out if "she" started out as a "he" or vice versa. There was Cuckoo for Cocoa Puffs, a chubby White kid who was always in deep conversation with himself and seemed to eat only boxed cereal. Stone Mug Doug always looked like he was deep in thought and never cracked a smile. I asked him once what he was thinking about, and he said, "I'm trying to solve the problems of the world."

I enjoyed them all, but my all-time favorite was Big Black, a teeny White dwarf. He looked like an old leprechaun, but for some reason, when he spoke, you could swear you were hearing an old Black Mississippi Delta bluesman. He sounded like a mix of James Earl Jones and Howlin' Wolf, and he was always dropping folksy pearls of wisdom. In his deep, growling voice, Big Black once told me, "The best way to chill out your woman in the midst of an argument is to say nothing, do nothing. Now repeat it like a mantra, son, and you just might be all right."

Like my homeless companions, I was almost always

hungry. Any little money I made selling weed, doing odd jobs, and hustling in general went to my head. Drink and drugs were the priority, and food was an afterthought. I'd get a free meal a couple of times a week from the Hare Krishnas who set up at Union Square, or from the Christian Ministries that occasionally came through to feed the homeless. I also did my fair share of dumpster diving. It was surprising how much good food restaurants threw away every night. Sometimes I'd score a whole untouched meal, with dessert included.

I had a friend named Manager, whom I'd known for years from back in my rock and roll outlaw days in Flatbush, when there were precious few Black punks to be found. His real name was Pete, too, but he got the nickname Manager from the Trinidadian punks in Flatbush because, somehow, at eighteen years old, looking totally crazy and unkempt, he "managed" to get a job as the night manager of the iconic McDonald's on Flatbush and Parkside Avenue, right across from Prospect Park. He didn't keep that job long, though. Once upper management found out he was feeding every Black punk in Brooklyn for free, he was fired. I ate a lot of McDonald's for a minute there.

Manager and I had a lot in common. We were the same age, both biracial from dysfunctional alcoholic families, and alcoholics ourselves. We were street-smart social chameleons.

For a few months, Manager and I set up a sidewalk flea market next to Trash and Vaudeville on St. Mark's Place, where we sold vintage clothes, hip old vinyl LPs, and used books. We bought the stuff from the Salvation Army on Flatbush Avenue, and it was all mad profits. We'd buy records for fifty cents each and sell them for five dollars. An old pair of funky army boots might cost us a dollar, and we'd sell them for twenty to some poseur punk from New Jersey. It was all gravy until the cops started harassing us, asking for permits and threatening to fine us.

On a fall evening, I was chilling on a bench in Tompkins Square with my boy Manager, sharing a joint and a forty of Budweiser. Neither of us had eaten yet, and we were complaining about our growling stomachs when this White dude with long, greasy hair showed up carrying a big, steaming pot, then walked right by us, set the pot down, pulled some paper bowls and plastic spoons out of a bag, and proclaimed, "Anybody hungry?"

I recognized this cat. I'd seen him around. He really didn't look any different from half the people in the park, and I don't think he would have registered at all with me if it wasn't for two things. One, he also sold weed in the park, so he was kind of low-key competition, and two, he used to walk around with a live rooster on his shoulder.

He didn't have the rooster with him that day.

A couple of the homeless people came over to accept his offer. He dished out the soup to them. I remember wondering if he'd made rooster stew.

Manager looked at me and said, "Fuck it! We were just talking about being hungry."

I walked with him to the soup guy. Manager accepted a bowl of soup. It didn't smell too bad. It looked okay, a clear, light-brown broth with bits of nondescript meat floating in it. I was hungry. It was free. Fuck it. I took a bowl, too.

We went back to our bench, and Manager started slurping away at the soup. He seemed to like it well enough. My stomach growled, and I was just about to lift the bowl to my lips when some kind of instinct kicked in, something inside me that warned, *If you eat this, you'll get sick.*

I set the bowl down and lit a cigarette. Manager finished his soup and, without asking, picked up mine and finished it off.

I forgot about that day until around a year later, when I read a newspaper article that sent a jolt to my heart and a cold shiver down my back.

The article was about a man named Daniel Rakowitz, a self-proclaimed satanic priest and marijuana dealer who lived across the street from Tompkins Square Park and was known to walk around with a live rooster on his shoulder. He was charged with murdering his roommate in his apartment, dismembering her body, and making soup from her head.

In the early fall of 1989, he served the soup to the homeless people of Tompkins Square Park.

Hand of Death

IN 1992, I was dating a dancer who lived on the Lower East Side. I had cleaned up my act a bit and was living with a roommate in a nice two-bedroom brownstone in South Park Slope. I managed an art-framing store that served a well-to-do clientele, and was making good money on the books while lightening the register every chance I got to feed my addictions. The dancer and I partied a lot together, and we often hung out with her friends, who were all dancers, models, and actresses. Never have I hung out with people who drank and drugged like they did. I thought people whose profession it was to look good took better care of their bodies, but nope, some of these well-known folks made me look like an amateur when it came to alcohol and drug consumption. The only time I ever saw someone fill a bong with super-expensive vodka, pack the bowl with high-grade weed, dump half a gram of coke on top of that, light it, smoke it, and then drink the bong vodka was when my girlfriend's best friend, a famous model, did it with the ease of someone slurping a wholesome bowl of bran flakes. It blew my mind. Even I wasn't that hardcore.

One summer night, we hung out until nearly dawn, bouncing from party to party. I ended up at the dancer's place, making love and "putting a little tickle on the Jones's head," which meant more drinks and more blow. It was all great, except I eventually realized I had to be at work in a few hours. I had ridden my bike over the bridge to her place, and at 5:30 a.m., I decided to ride back home. I was ripped out of my skull, and all I wanted to do was try to get an hour or two of sleep before clocking in.

The fog was dense and damp, but luckily it was early enough that the city was asleep and the streets were mostly bare. Once I got over the bridge, I'd be home free. It was a struggle; I felt like I had twenty-five-pound weights tied to each leg.

Just as I made it to the Brooklyn side of the bridge, a drizzle began to fall. I welcomed it. It was refreshing and sobered me up a bit.

Fourth Avenue was a Brooklyn speedway, a four-lane thruway that was a favorite truck route. I was only a few blocks from home when, up ahead of me through the rain and fog, I saw flashing lights on the otherwise empty avenue. I could make out cop cars, EMT vans, and a big tractor trailer jack-knifed in the middle of the avenue.

As I rode closer, I saw cops waving in my direction, motioning for me to go around. I thought, *I'm only on a bike—they must be waving at oncoming cars.* I continued ahead past cops and yellow police tape. Obviously there had been a bad accident, but that was nothing new for the avenue. I simply rode through, minding my business.

I passed the tail end of the truck. Cops yelled at me, and my bike almost slipped out from under me. I had ridden through a deep puddle, and the road was slick and wet. I kept riding.

Finally back home, I locked my bike up in front of my building and made it up to my third-floor apartment. I fell into bed. No brushing teeth, no getting out of my soaked clothes.

Maybe three hours later, I woke to the sound of my annoying-ass roommate, Orville, knocking on my door, asking me if I saw the terrible accident that happened right around the corner from us. "Did you hear? It's a mess! I think some poor fool got run over by a giant truck!" He ran back into the living room to watch the news.

I lay there, trying to reconcile with reality. Looking down, I noticed my sheets were splashed with red. Had I spilled something? Then I noticed my still-wet clothes were also splashed with red, particularly my lower half. I was bleeding! I jumped up and checked myself all over. Nothing hurt except my hungover head.

Ever so slowly, it began to dawn on me what the red might be. Still in the blood-soaked clothes and looking like a madman who had just committed multiple axe murders, I stumbled out to where my bike was locked up. It, too, was splashed with rusty red and, most peculiarly, had fatty white flesh-looking bits stuck in the chain and spokes.

I went back upstairs, where Orville was waiting by the door. He was so wound up, he didn't seem to notice the state I was in. He blurted, "The news said around 5:30 a.m., some drunk dude wandered into the middle of Fourth Avenue. A speeding tractor trailer hit him and rolled over his head!"

I went into the bathroom to strip off my clothes and shower. It was then that I really looked at my hands for the first time. They were literally covered in dried blood. I had death on my hands. I retched, and for the thousandth time, I vowed to myself to get and stay sober.

I bought a pint of vodka on my way to work. Just to calm my nerves.

Smooth Operator

I WAS STILL playing music when I worked at the frame shop. I was doing gigs, playing drums for my friend Gary Dourdan's band. Gary, despite having a blooming career as an actor and model, was, like me, trying to make it as a musician. I met Gary through a mutual friend years before his acting career began to take off. He had a regular spot playing at Nell's, a super-hip venue on Fourteenth Street. Nell's was the club where actors, musicians, models, and the hip Black bohemian crowd went to see and be seen.

One night after our set, I was packing up my drums when a dude came alongside the stage and shouted, "So, how does it feel to play for Prince?"

I said, "I'm sure it would feel great, but I don't know what you're talking about."

He pointed to the left of the stage. I followed his finger,

and sure enough, there was Prince himself sitting front row at the side of the stage. Apparently, he'd come in during our set. I was glad I didn't know he was there until afterward. Trying to drum knowing Prince was listening only a few feet away probably would have made me lose my shit.

The club emptied out after our show, but Prince stayed, and when our van pulled up and we began loading in our gear, Prince came along. He didn't speak to us, nor we to him, but he was *with* us. It was weird. If you didn't know any better and just looked at the scene, you would have probably assumed we were Prince's band and he was waiting for us to load up for our next gig. Being that close to him, I distinctly felt his magical, otherworldly presence. Prince was a physically tiny man with a huge, palpable aura. I could literally feel his vibration. He lingered with the band until we were all packed up, and then he went back inside the club. It was surreal. If the bass player hadn't mentioned it at the next rehearsal, I would have thought it had all been a lucid dream.

About two weeks later at Nell's, we had finished playing a show when a skinny White guy with a British accent hopped onstage and asked, "Have you ever heard of a singer called Sade?" It was such an odd and silly question. Sade was one of the biggest stars in music. She was also, hands down, my greatest celebrity crush. The guy introduced himself as Stuart and asked if I'd be interested in filling in for Sade's drummer, who was having some visa trouble and was stuck in England. He said the gig was just to play along to one song for a live BBC broadcast being shot in a sound studio in Queens in two days' time.

"Umm, I guess I could move a couple of things around," I said.

The day of the gig, a limo pulled up to my door and I was whisked off to the soundstage in Queens. I met Sade's band. Super warm and funny guys. The camaraderie was instant. They had the dry British wit I so appreciated, and I fell right in with them.

I was dressed in the Afro-bohemian style Gary and I rocked at the time: dashiki, faded flared jeans, and big ol' work boots, accessorized with African necklaces and rings. I reeked of patchouli and Egyptian musk. Sade's band had a sophisticated, coordinated look my style didn't quite fit, so the keyboard player, who was about my size, let me wear his spare suit. I was led to a makeup chair and fawned over. "So, you're the new drummer, huh? Definitely an upgrade."

Stuart turned out to be the cat who not only played guitar and saxophone in the band but also wrote and produced most of the music. He came into the makeup room, looked me over, and said, "Right. You'll do nicely. Glad you could make it."

I followed him onto the freezing soundstage, where the band and I ran through the song "No Ordinary Love" a few times while the cameramen worked out angles. I didn't really need to rehearse. The song was a big hit and one of my favorites. I knew it like it was etched on my soul.

When everything was in order and they were ready to start the broadcast, Sade walked in.

Shoeless, unpretentious, humble. Beautiful. She greeted everyone, stopped in front of my drum kit, and smiled. "Don't be nervous. This is going to be fun!"

We performed "No Ordinary Love" for the British show *Top of the Pops,* and the performance went beautifully. During the song's guitar solo, Sade faced the drums and smiled and winked at me. It took every bit of concentration and discipline for me not to leap from behind the drums and snatch her up.

I was escorted to the dressing room after the performance. As I was changing back into my Afrocentric hippie uniform, there was a soft knock on the door. I opened it to find the love of my dreams standing in front of me.

Sade smiled. "I just wanted to thank you for coming on such short notice and for doing such a great job. Did you have fun?"

I stammered out that I had and that it was my honor. I was taken by how physically small she was. There was a slightly awkward moment when she looked me up and down, smiled, and in a kind of shy but knowing way, leaned in. Sade kissed me gently on the lips. Then her assistant appeared and moved her along.

I closed the door and I stood there, feeling the tingle of her kiss on my lips. When I finally went to move, I nearly tripped. It was only then I looked down and realized that when I'd opened the door to Sade, I'd been in the process of putting my jeans on. I guess I'd dropped them when I saw her in front of me. I was literally standing there in my underwear with my jeans around my ankles. And that's where they were for our entire brief but unforgettable encounter.

Smooth operator.

About three days after the gig, Stuart called me. He said, "You did great, mate! Sade and the band love you!"

I stammered my thanks.

He continued, "Listen, our regular drummer is still stuck in England with passport issues, so we were wondering if you'd be interested in filling in for the rest of the US tour." I knew this was a dream offer. It meant more money, by far, than I'd ever made before. It meant exposure and a chance to woo the love of my life. It was a no-brainer. An opportunity of a lifetime.

Stuart said, "I know it's short notice and an inconvenience, but we'll need your answer by tomorrow morning, at the latest. You can call me at this number. We all hope you can do it, mate!"

I went out and got a pint of vodka, a bag of weed, and a twenty-dollar bag of blow. I stayed up all night celebrating the gift I was being handed.

In the morning, hungover, I began to feel trepidation. What if I can't get high on the road? What if they need me to stay sober? What if I can't score any weed and coke?

Noon rolled around. I never called.

Gangsters II

BACK WHEN I was in high school, I briefly befriended an Italian kid named John Chevalino. John looked, spoke, and dressed like a character straight out of *Saturday Night Fever,* but despite that, he was anything but stereotypical. He was, in fact, really progressive, liberal, and intelligent but in an unpretentious way. What I most appreciated about him was that he was always authentic and honest.

We cut classes together often to get high and talk shit. At the end of the school year, John invited me to spend the night at his house. He admitted his neighborhood wouldn't be very welcoming to me, but he assured me I'd be okay. He implied his father "knew people" and the neighborhood knew better than to mess with him or his friends, "even niggers, as long as they ain't walking with an Italian girl." He was one of the few White dudes I allowed to say that word to me. Somehow, when he said *nigger*, which was rarely, it didn't feel racist.

That summer, I hung out with John a few times in his neighborhood and spent the night at his house. His family was warm and welcoming.

His dad wasn't usually home when I was there, but there were pictures of him all over the house. Mr. Chevalino with Frank Sinatra, Mr. Chevalino with soon-to-be Mayor Giuliani, lots of pictures of Mr. Chevalino with guys who looked like they ate children for breakfast, and a few of him with a dapper gentleman named John, who everybody was quick to tell me my friend was named after. That John's last name was Gotti.

One night, John and I snuck out late to get high. We crept back in at around 2 a.m. and raided the fridge. We were sitting at the table eating ice cream when Mr. Chevalino came in. He didn't seem to mind that we were up and obviously high. Mr. Chevalino was obviously high, too. He didn't even try to hide it, and whatever he was on put him in a talkative mood. He kept us up until dawn, telling us a lot of pretty thinly veiled and risqué stories about the guys he grew up with. As naive as I was, even I could tell he was talking about Mafia dudes.

As the sun began to rise, he yawned and said, "Listen, Imma hit the sack, but before I hit the sack, lemme give youse some advice that'll keep youse alive. There are certain people that'll want to offer youse things for free or volunteer to do you favors. *Never, ever* take them up on it. Youse politely and respectfully decline, and when those same certain people tell you a joke, you laugh your fuckin' ass off, even if it ain't funny."

Years later, the advice would pay off.

* * *

When I was in my early thirties, I found myself in need of a job. I wasn't picky, and I wasn't making career moves. I just needed some steady employment. A friend who worked doing the lighting for the famous NYC strip club Scores was about to quit and suggested I take over his position. When I readily accepted, he said, "And don't worry about that thing people say about strip clubs being owned by the Mafia. It's not true. It's a totally legit business like any other. I got you a meeting with Frankie, the manager, next Friday."

That Friday, I showed up to Scores clean and on time. Before this, I'd never been to a strip club of any kind. I expected it to be dark and sleazy, smelling like the peep show booths on Forty-Second Street, and full of perverts in trench coats. It wasn't any of that.

I arrived about an hour before the doors opened. The lights were up, and the place was immaculately clean and tastefully decorated. It felt like the lobby of an upscale hotel.

I met Frankie. He immediately reminded me of Vinnie Cuccia from middle school, all grown up. He had on a gray silk suit and a diamond pinkie ring. His hair was slicked back, and in his mouth, he held a toothpick that bobbed up and down when he spoke. Frankie had a *giant* guy named Bobby who followed him around like a puppy. To me, Bobby was Big Tony from middle school all grown up.

Frankie said, "So you're da new guy I'm hearing about, eh? You come recommended. Youse gonna give me any trouble?"

I said, "No, sir! No trouble from me!"

"Good!"

He came over to me from behind the bar, where he'd

been counting money for the register, and looked me in the eyes, sizing me up. Satisfied, he gave me a friendly, not-so-soft smack across the cheek. "What kind of cigarettes you smoke? Bobby, give him a carton of whatever he wants."

That was the job interview.

I worked at Scores for three years. I ran the lights for the girls doing their pole dances, and I learned how to do the best lighting for the ones who tipped me out best. I made sure none of their flaws showed. For the girls who were lousy tippers, I hit the bright yellow lights, which made even the youngest, cutest ones look old and haggard. I became an artist with the smoke machine and strobe light, creating spectacles of choreographed lights coordinated perfectly with the music. The girls tipped me, the DJ tipped me. Sometimes even the customers tipped me. I made a ton of easy money.

There were Russian hard guys who did security there, and they scared me worse than any other people I'd ever encountered in my life. The Russians had dead eyes and hands like iron. They were really nice guys, which somehow made them even scarier. I saw them remove rowdy drunks and break up fights nightly. They never lost their calm, never broke a sweat.

I witnessed some crazy shit, and heard even crazier shit, but I kept my head down and minded my business.

While I worked there, I was readily offered "favors," all of which I politely declined. And whenever I was told a joke, I laughed my ass off. Even if it wasn't funny.

Over the Hump

I WAS STILL spiraling downward on alcohol and drugs when I got the gig at Scores. I worked part-time, Friday through Sunday, and got off at 2 a.m., then didn't get back to Brooklyn until after 3 a.m. By the time I left the club, I'd be half drunk and full horny. Six hours of tits, ass, and Jägermeister shots always left me pretty sloppy and randy.

It was about a ten-block walk down Nostrand Avenue from the train to where I was living, and the avenue was quiet and empty by the time I got off the train, especially on Sunday nights, so I was surprised one sweltering summer night when I was about halfway home and looked up to see a young woman sitting by herself on the steps of an apartment building.

As I walked past, I tried to take her in without seeming lecherous. She looked up at me. Our eyes met for a split second, and I thought I saw just the sliver of a smile cross her lips.

She was young, maybe in her early twenties, and looked South Asian, Indian or Pakistani. She was tall and slim, and she wore only a thin white wifebeater and very short denim cutoffs. In that quick glance, I noticed she was braless and the nipples of her small breasts were erect. Her brown legs were long, smooth, and shapely. Her hair was straight and long. She was really beautiful.

I kept walking, but I thought about her all week. On my way home the following Sunday after finishing my shift, I hoped I'd see her but accepted there was very little chance the beautiful young woman would be sitting out by herself again at 3 a.m. But there she was. As I passed her, my heart sped up in my chest, and my mouth suddenly got dry, but I flashed her a full smile and said a polite "Good night!"

She smiled and gave me a knowing nod. As I walked away, I could swear I felt her eyes on my back.

For the next week, I played the encounter over and over in my mind. Had she been waiting for me? Was her smile an invitation to stop and speak? Had I blown it?

By midweek I concluded I'd blown it, and I very much doubted I'd get another chance to speak with her. The next Sunday morning at 3 a.m., I exited the train station and walked out into the summer rain. I thought, no way would she be sitting out in this weather. But when I passed her steps, I saw she was standing in the doorway. I was so surprised, I stumbled to say something, anything. She spoke first. "It's raining. Would you like to come up?"

My heart jumped to my throat. I would've been happy just to exchange a "good night," but here she was, inviting me up to her apartment. "Y-yes! D-definitely!" I stammered.

I followed behind her up the stairs, which gave me a chance to really check her out from behind. She was about my height with long, athletic legs and graceful arms. Her hair was thick and fell down her back, ending right above her tight denim shorts, which accentuated her ass, a perfect peach.

I was busy checking her out, so it took me a second to register where she was leading me. The one flight of stairs to her apartment was dark and tight, and I couldn't see much, but I did smell the distinctive stench of an old tenement building. Ancient cooking smells, body odor, and a faint but definitely discernible stink of old piss. It smelled like poverty.

She let me into her apartment and another smell hit me. One I'd encountered too many times in my life. The smell of infestation. When roaches and rodents take over a space, they leave a very distinctive smell, and this was it. It was funky. A sickly-sweet funk like perfume over unwashed ass.

The front door opened into the kitchen, and that's where she directed me to take a seat. She sat across from me, and for the first time in the dim light, I could really make out her face. She was beautiful in an exotic way, but everything about her face seemed somehow just a little too extra. Her cheekbones were almost too high and sharp. Her eyes were captivating but maybe just a bit too large. Her full lips just a tad too full. She had a look that would be great for a runway model, but up close it was overpowering.

We started to make the smallest of small talk. Her name was Cynthia, and wasn't the rain a surprise? Hadn't it been a really hot summer? I detected a slight accent and asked where she was from originally. She said she was from Guyana and had been in the States for only a year. I was having a hard time paying attention because everything in the kitchen was moving. There were conga lines of roaches marching across the walls, ceiling, floor, and table in crisscrossing patterns. There were mice popping in and out of the overflowing garbage can in the corner and running freely over the stove and under our feet. Not just a few mice. A colony of mice. It was stifling hot in the kitchen, the kind of sticky, humid heat that made you feel greasy. It didn't help that above us, circling like a merry-go-round, was a swarm of fat flies.

The juxtaposition of this beautiful, healthy-looking young woman sitting in this menagerie of insects and vermin was off-putting, to say the least. I kept trying to stay focused on our small talk while keeping an eye on the roaches and mice. I didn't want anything crawling on me, and I didn't want anything to come home with me. As discreetly as possible, I lifted my feet off the floor and placed my knapsack on my lap.

Cynthia seemed completely oblivious to everything going on around us. She even began to get a little flirty. Complimenting my physique and strong hands, she said she'd been lonely since coming to the States and didn't have any friends or a boyfriend.

We were both sweating. Her wifebeater was starting to stick to her chest, making her nipples stand out even more. She started to rub them, and at one point even let out a little moan between words.

I could see where this was heading, but as hot as she was and as drunk and horny as I was, I just couldn't concentrate. There was too much creature activity going on. When a mouse boldly jumped on the table and strolled between my hands, that was it. I stood up. I was about to excuse myself with a *Well, okay, it's getting late,* but Cynthia stood up, too, grabbed my hand, and without a word led me to the room adjacent to the kitchen, a room empty except for a naked mattress on the floor. She sat down and pulled me down next to her. Still without speaking, she undid her shorts and pulled them down halfway, revealing red see-through panties. She spread out on her stomach on this dank mattress and said, quietly, "Rub it on me."

At first, I didn't really get what she meant, but then she started wiggling and gyrating her ass, and again, she said, "Rub it on me."

I got what she meant.

I rubbed it on her.

In fact, I dry-humped her like I was in Digital Underground riding a camel on a Wednesday. Humpty Hump riding humps on hump day. I humped like I hadn't humped since I was thirteen and my next-door neighbor Waynetta let me rub it on her till we were both raw and sore. I humped Cynthia with lustful abandon. We were both still fully dressed. We rubbed through our clothes. We hadn't even kissed. When I tried to slip my hand down her shorts she kept pulling away, and try as I might, I couldn't get her to turn over.

I guess none of it mattered, because I finished on her back. Then came the awkward moment of trying to find something to clean up with. Cynthia reached to the side of the mattress to retrieve a cloth, and for a quick second, she rolled over. Just long enough for me to see her manhood.

Whitey and Speedy

WHILE I WAS working at the strip club, I was still managing the frame shop part-time. There was an old salt who hung around the avenue, a neighborhood character named Whitey, who made the rounds sweeping up in front of the mom-and-pop shops and running errands for change. It was a subtle kind of extortion.

Whitey had grown up in the neighborhood, and he knew everybody. The newer shopkeepers paid him mostly out of wanting to be accepted on the block by an old-timer. He had the old-school Brooklyn way of speaking that was dying out with his generation — he said "youse" and pronounced the number three like "tree." Whitey sounded like a mix of Popeye, Bugs Bunny, and the Bowery Boys.

Whitey often hung out at the shop with me, telling me

stories of the old Brooklyn street gangs, the Bishops and the Chaplains, and their rumbles over turf. He told me about playing stickball and other street games. He bragged about sneaking into Ebbets Field to see the Dodgers play when he was a kid. Whitey was usually pleasant and in an upbeat mood, but I started to notice that at around 5 p.m., he would begin to get moody and antsy. I'd see him make a sudden dash out to a white Chevy that had just rolled up. He would get in the car, and they'd pull off. In a few minutes, they'd be back and Whitey would be in a better mood.

One day I asked what was up with that, and he said, with a wink, "Oh! That's just my friend Speedy."

I wasn't completely naive. I figured out what was happening, and after about a year of knowing Whitey, I asked, "So, your friend, you think he might know where I can get some blow?"

He said, "I'm sure we can work something out." For the next two years, Whitey and Speedy became my whole world.

It started with a twenty-dollar bag of blow on Sundays. Then it was a twenty-dollar bag on Saturdays and Sundays. Then one bag each Friday, Saturday, and Sunday. Then two bags on those days.

I lived for those weekends. Planned and plotted and counted days all week. I got my bags of blow at 5 p.m., when Speedy pulled up, then I counted the minutes till 6 p.m., when I'd be able to lock up the store and start snorting it.

This habit took a toll on every aspect of my life. I went MIA from socializing, my health suffered to the point that it was really difficult to do simple things like climb a flight of stairs or ride my bike. I was dating a beautiful woman named Tamela, whom I loved, avoided, and lied to. I was trapped and stuck. My whole life centered on coke and the decadent isolation of the weekend.

One Friday, I got my two twenty-dollar bags, as usual, and headed home to get them in my system as soon as possible. Oddly, one of the bags wasn't full of the regular white powder. Instead it was full of a golden-brown powder. I thought maybe it was a different strain of blow. I snorted and smoked the first bag of the white coke and immediately started in on the second bag. I took an initial snort and immediately realized it wasn't coke. The word *dope* floated across my mind. Then I thought, *Fuck it, one little bag of heroin ain't gonna make me a junkie, right?* I snorted it. I smoked it.

I got sick. I threw up. I got a very slight sense of euphoria toward the end of the bag, but mostly it made me feel miserable. It was horrible. Lesson learned. Heroin wasn't for me.

Whitey was all apologies the next day. Somehow, he had mixed up the bags. The dope was meant for him. All was forgiven.

I continued my weekly coke binges. About two months had passed since the "dope mix-up," and I handed Whitey two twenty-dollar bills and waited for him to return with my powder. He didn't come back for a long time. I started panicking when 6 p.m. rolled around and there was still no Whitey. I didn't know what to do. I couldn't imagine getting through the night without something to snort.

Just as I was pulling down the store gates, Whitey rolled up. "Listen, kid. There's no blow to be found. That's what took me so long. Things have dried up. Me and Speedy were driving around trying to make a connect. No luck." He reached out to hand me back my money.

"Can I get some dope, then?"

Whitey took a step back like I'd punched him in the chest. "C'mon, kid. You don't want to go down that road."

I had to convince him it wasn't a problem. I practically begged him to score me a bag of dope. Eventually, when I promised on my living mother's grave this would be the last time, he gave in. An addict conning an addict with words we both knew weren't true.

I snorted and smoked the heroin, then sat on my bed. I don't remember much of the evening except I had a brain orgasm that lasted for hours.

I wanted more.

I am an addict.

I didn't see Whitey the following weekend or for the next couple of weekends.

I was a mess. I was in crisis. My body craved powder, white or brown. It was all I could think about.

I searched all over for Whitey, but he was nowhere. I asked around. No one had seen him. I began to suspect he'd died. Then, after about a month, I saw Whitey. He was sweeping up in front of a store a couple of blocks down the avenue. I asked where he'd been.

He said, "I been around, kid."

I asked if we could get with Speedy later. I said I wanted to get a bag of blow and a bag of dope and that I'd even buy him a bag.

Whitey looked at me for a long time. I could tell he was struggling with what to say. His eyes welled up, then he shook his head and said, "No more, kid. I don't want this for you." He turned his back on me and kept sweeping.

That weekend, I had an anxiety attack. I was closing the shop on Sunday evening, and it occurred to me it was over. I probably could have found another coke and dope connection, but somehow I knew this was it. This chapter of my life was over. The look in the old junkie's eyes said it all.

My heart started pounding, and I couldn't catch my breath. I began to walk the two miles toward home rather than take the train, because I thought if I stopped moving even for a second, I might die. I managed to get to a liquor store, where I downed a half-pint of vodka in two gulps. Then I walked to Methodist Hospital's emergency room and told the nurse at the front desk I thought I was having a heart attack. I'm sure she smelled the alcohol on my breath and saw the sorry state I was in. I looked like what I was, an addict. She asked if anyone in my family had ever had a heart attack. I said yes. She asked if I'd been drinking. I said no. She asked if I used drugs. I said no.

They admitted me. I was told I wasn't having a heart attack but a common anxiety attack. Still, they said they wanted to keep me for a couple of weeks. I was in bad shape. I needed to detox.

For two weeks, I rested and ate and vowed never to allow myself to become addicted to anything ever again. It was the first time in over twenty years I'd gone more than a day without a cigarette, a drink, or a drug. Oddly, I felt no urge or compulsion to smoke or drink. I had no cravings or longings. It was like I'd been miraculously cured of my alcoholism and addiction.

I was done.

It was over.

I was free.

At the end of those two weeks, I was stronger, clearer, and more hopeful than I'd been since I was a preteen. I felt like I had a new lease on life and that this time, things were going to be different.

I was discharged early on a weekday morning. It was a glorious morning. The air was fresh and crisp, the sun was shining, and the birds were chirping. I stood appreciating the beauty. I thanked God for my freedom.

Then I walked to the bodega across the street. I bought a pack of cigarettes and a forty-ounce of Colt 45, and I went looking for Whitey.

I am an addict.

Hard Break

I FIRST SAW her when I was in my late teens. She lived with her family just three blocks from where I grew up in East Flatbush, and when I walked to school I passed her house, hoping to catch a glimpse of her from across the street. Many times, she was out there, sitting on her stoop. She was an angel. My dream girl. Golden brown with long, soft, curly hair and big, beautiful, intelligent eyes. Her family was Panamanian-Jamaican, and she was exotic and mysterious. I thought about her constantly over the years.

About ten years later, my friend Ish invited me to a Christmas party at his cousin's house, which he said happened to be three blocks away. I walked into the party and there she was, the exotic girl of my teenage dreams. Ish introduced her as Tamela, and she was even more beautiful than I remembered. She'd married a naval officer and seemed happy. She had two babies, a one-year-old girl and a newborn boy. I held them. On that day, I fell in love with all three of them.

Two years later, I was playing a gig at Nell's. Ish said he wanted to hear the band. I put him on the guest list, and when he asked for a plus-one to be added to his name, I expected to see him show up with a date, but I looked out at the audience from the stage and saw him sitting front row center, next to Tamela.

After the show, Tamela and I spoke briefly. She was shy. So was I. She said, "So, I was wondering if you might like to meet up at the park tomorrow afternoon?"

"I'm sure we can make that happen," I replied coolly, with my heart thumping out of my chest.

It was a gorgeous spring day, and Prospect Park was blooming and blossoming with rebirth. Tamela was perfect. I was hungover. We made awkward small talk at first, but quickly the conversation turned tender and vulnerable. She said she was divorcing the naval officer. "It never really felt right," she said. "And after I saw you at that Christmas party, I *knew* it wasn't right." She said she'd thought about me constantly since that day. She said she'd fallen in love with me as I held her children.

Within months, we were living together. I was thirty-six years old and somehow living with a beautiful woman and her beautiful children.

Tamela came into my life when I was losing the battle with my addictions. In some ways, I hoped she would be my salvation. I thought our love could save me from myself, would somehow exorcise my demons. I was spiraling toward my bottom, and I held on to her and her children as if they were my lifeline. It was foolish and unfair.

We moved into a big three-bedroom apartment on Nostrand Avenue, above a famous Caribbean bakery. All day long, our apartment smelled of fresh-baked bread and addiction. I tried my best to be a good partner and a loving stepfather to Brittany and Steve. I picked them up from school every day and helped them with their homework. I cooked for them when their mom was too tired and made sure they took their baths. I consoled them when they cried, and I romped and played with them like a clown. I showered them with cheap gifts and priceless attention. I loved them as my own, but I was in the grips of a power greater than myself. As much as I loved and cherished them, they simply were not my priority. Getting and staying high was, and even the greatest loves of my life to that point weren't going to stand in the way of it.

For a few years we were relatively happy. The kids called me Patty, a name they came up with on their own. I was too oblivious at the time to recognize their Patty, which they said like *Paddy,* was their way of calling me daddy. They loved Omari and he loved them. When he came on weekends, it felt like we were a healthy, beautiful family. We were the Huxtables.

Tamela had it together. She was responsible and organized. She was a great mom and a loving partner. She handled all the affairs of the house, paid the rent and bills, cooked and cleaned, and cared for her children.

I was becoming uglier inside and out. I was falling apart,

yet I felt that as long as I could show the world this beautiful woman by my side, I was all right. Here I was approaching forty, and I'd never had a checking account or credit card, never had a driver's license, and never been on an airplane. Stunted and stuck. Sick and suffering.

I began to lock myself in a tiny room in the back of the apartment, a room no bigger than a closet. I called it my "studio." It was there I ran to every day with my bottle, locking myself in and drinking until the bottle was done and I was knocked out.

I told myself, *I'm not abusing anyone. I'm simply neglecting them, and that causes no harm.* My own childhood had told me that was a lie, but during those years with Tamela and the kids, I convinced myself I wasn't hurting anyone.

I'd gotten to the point where the last thing I did before crawling into bed at night and the first thing I did in the morning was take a drink. On weekday mornings, I pretended I was asleep as my beautiful family readied themselves for work and school. I couldn't wait for them all to leave. When they finally went down the stairs at around seven thirty, I was right behind them. We lived across the street from a bodega, but I didn't go to that one in the morning, because that was where I bought my respectable beer in the evenings. Instead, I went to the all-night, crackhead bodega three blocks away by the train station, the bodega that sold only beer, tobacco, and lottery tickets. The bodega where I could buy two forty-ounces of Colt 45 at seven thirty in the morning and not feel judged.

I was always anxious to get the beer and get back to the apartment as quickly as possible. Although it was so close to the apartment, I rode my bike. I reasoned that walking took too long, plus, my head and feet hurt. This morning routine of sad depravity went on for nearly two years.

One morning like any other, I was riding back from the bodega against rush hour traffic. On Nostrand Avenue, this wasn't a wise thing to do, particularly if you were unstable and holding two forty-ounce bottles of beer in a plastic bag. I was pedaling faster than usual and steering with my left hand while struggling to hold the bag of beer in my right. The next thing I knew, I was flipped head over heels. I literally saw my feet against the sky. I managed to tuck my head, which kept me from breaking my neck or bashing my skull into the road, but I landed hard on my left arm. The sound of breaking bone was loud and clear.

The bag of beer had swung into the front wheel of the bike, which abruptly stopped the bike, and my momentum caused both the bike and me to flip into the air and into the oncoming traffic. I heard the screeching and saw the truck tire that came to a squealing halt less than a foot from my head. The bike wasn't that lucky. It was run over and mangled. The broken beer bottles surrounded me in a puddle of foam and glass.

In perfect Brooklyn style, a dude (there's *always* this dude) came over to me as I lay there and, in a voice loud enough for everyone to hear, said, "Yo! I seent the whole thing. You fucked up, homie. Trying to ride with that beer. You lucky you ain't break your neck or get your head runt over. Yo! Your arm is definitely broke, though, bro. I heard that shit snap! Yo! This nigga fucked up."

I didn't need the commentary. I knew my arm was broken. I knew I'd fucked up, but as I started to get up from the street, the only thing on my mind was the five dollars in my pocket, which meant I could get two more forties to replace the broken ones. I left the bike and broken bottles right there in the middle of Nostrand Avenue and ignored all the drivers who were cursing me out and all the people staring at me, some shaking their heads and some pointing their fingers and laughing. I limped back to the bodega.

The Messiah

TAMELA, HER KIDS, and I lived four long blocks from Prospect Park in Brooklyn, and I often took drunken walks to the park to commune with nature. Omari spent most weekends with us, and sometimes I'd take him with me on these drunken walks. I called them our "adventure walks." There was one entrance to the park near Flatbush and Ocean Avenues, just up from the zoo, where a lot of homeless folks gathered. It was the nearest entrance to my apartment and the one I most often used. I began to recognize some of the regulars who camped out near the entrance.

Most of those folks were clearly drunks, drug addicts, mentally ill, or a combination of all three, and they acted accordingly—erratic, sometimes loud and violent, sometimes quietly desperate, but there was one character above all who intrigued me.

The Messiah.

Omari was about thirteen years old at the time and beginning to find his own independent voice. He gave the homeless man the name when we saw two beautiful red cardinals alight upon his shoulders and rest there one day. But there was also an inexplicable light about the man. He somehow glowed through his filthy rags. He seemed to emanate peaceful vibrations. We both found him magical, mysterious, and mystical.

The Messiah always sat in the same spot on the same bench right outside the park. He was a big man made bigger by the layers and layers of coats and pants he wore. Winter, spring, summer, and fall, he never deviated from those layers and that spot. I saw him there in freezing winter blizzards and in blazing summer sun. Rain and snow fell on him, orange and yellow leaves stuck to him.

The Messiah didn't speak, and he kept his face covered from the nose down with a thick mask that looked to be made of newspaper, tape, and cloth. Not once did I ever see him without the mask. The only visible parts of him were his eyes and his hands. He was a dark-skinned man, and as time went on, it seemed like his clothes and skin took on a kind of shiny black patina. It was like those layers of clothes and dirt became a stiff outer casing, an armor that had melded to his flesh, and I couldn't tell where he began and his layers ended.

Omari and I made up stories about him. We imagined he was a magical knight of an ancient order condemned to an eternity of silence for his misdeeds in a mythical realm. He was a fallen angel sent from heaven to observe mankind. He had been a powerful man who had spoken words that caused the deaths of hundreds, including his family, and he now lived out his days in self-imposed silence as a penance. He was a big black Buddha who took a vow of silence and poverty but who held the wisdom that could save the world.

He was the Homeless Messiah.

At first, I observed him only from a distance. He scared me. I also assumed he smelled terrible. But as time passed and when I was alone, I began to get closer to him, and as I did, I noticed some surprising things. First, when I was near him, instead of fear or apprehension, I felt only a swelling of inner peace. It was like he exuded serenity and love. Second, and much to my relief, he didn't stink at all. He actually smelled earthy, like wet grass and a breeze across fresh flowers.

The Messiah showed up in my life around the time I was feeling most hopeless and helpless. I was lonely and depressed. I'd regularly buy a forty-ounce of malt liquor and walk to the park and sit on a bench a short way from the Messiah and drink it, imagining what it would be like to be him. Homeless and holy.

One evening I walked to the park and sat right on his bench, only a few feet from him. In all the time I'd observed him, I'd never seen anyone share his bench. All the time I sat there, he didn't stir, but somehow I could tell he was aware I was there. I smelled his flowers, and I felt peaceful.

Over the course of the summer, I must have shared his bench a dozen times. He never outwardly acknowledged me, but I was drunk most of the time when I visited him. One night, after I'd had a bad fight with Tamela, I went to his bench to sit with him. I needed his peace, but he wasn't there, and I had the oddest sinking feeling in my chest. I sat on his bench, but it felt meaningless without him.

I told Omari the Messiah hadn't been at his bench. The fact that he had gone missing somehow added to his legend.

We speculated about what may have happened to him. We said maybe his mission here was completed, and he'd moved on to another bench in another part of the world. We said maybe his brother and sister angels had finally found him and released him from his silent bondage. Maybe heaven had called him back. All of these sounded better than what I knew had probably happened to the Messiah. Either the city had scooped him up and put him in a shelter or he had died.

By winter, I had a weekend job in Park Slope, and one morning, Tamela was giving me a lift in. We drove along the side of the park, up the hill on Flatbush Avenue, and as we passed the Messiah's bench, I casually looked that way.

He was there.

That evening after work, I got a forty-ounce and went to see if he was still there. He was. It was too cold to be drinking beer, but that didn't deter me. I sat on the Messiah's bench a couple of feet away from him and felt his radiating peace.

I quietly finished the beer and thought I should go get another bottle while also wishing I could stop. As I got up to leave, I spoke directly to him. "I missed you."

I heard a sound come from him. It was rough and deep, muffled through his thick newspaper mask. "Yes."

I didn't go to look for him for at least a month after that. I think I told myself I was too busy, but the truth was, when he uttered that single word to me, he touched something deep in me. Something that wasn't ready to be touched. I felt fear, but not the spooky kind of fear for my safety. I felt the kind of fear one might feel in God's presence.

When I finally got up the courage to walk to the park, I was relieved to see the Messiah on his bench. I sat next to him, but I immediately felt something was different. The flower smell wasn't there, and I didn't feel the radiating peace. I felt nothing. He was too still. His hands were on either side of him on the bench, as if he was holding himself up or perhaps preparing to lift himself.

I stared at his shiny black hands for a long time. They didn't move. There was no life in them. I sat there with him for a long time, even though I knew he was no longer here.

When I finally got up, I bowed deeply to the layers of empty black rags that were his shell.

I said, "Thank you."

Yesterday I Died

I AM AN alcoholic. I am a drug addict.

I drank and drugged daily for twenty-three straight years, from the time I was sixteen years old to the time I was thirty-nine. I had a perfect record. No days off. From adolescence to young adulthood and mature adulthood, and practically up to middle age, I was constantly under the influence of alcohol and substances. I lived those crucial developmental years in one of three states of being: on my way to being drunk and high, totally drunk and high, or coming down from being drunk and high.

I knew I had a problem from early on. By the time I was seventeen, I could see how my life was being controlled by a force greater than myself—a destructive force. I knew I didn't have an "off" switch. Once I started, I couldn't stop.

Getting and staying high was my primary purpose, and I

would work, beg, borrow, steal, lie, cheat, and prostitute myself to get what I needed. I hung out in places with people who repulsed me. I did things that made me ashamed and embarrassed. I lost my moral compass. It's said that the alcoholic stops maturing emotionally when he starts drinking. That means I lived most of my adult life with the emotional maturity and coping skills of a sixteen-year-old. Arrested development. All my major life decisions were tainted and dictated by my addictions. Addictions told me where to live, whom to date or befriend, what jobs to take or decline. They shaped my attitude and controlled my moods.

Alcohol was the greatest thief and liar I ever encountered. It slowly and systematically stole from me everything that was good and positive—my health, my relationships, my financial stability, and nearly my sanity. And the whole time it lied to me, telling me I didn't really need those things.

It spoke to me in my own voice. *So what if she leaves you? She was getting in the way of our drinking anyway.*

So what if another tooth falls out? You don't need teeth to drink.

So what if you get kicked out and have to live on the streets? You won't have to pay rent—that means more money for drinks.

Alcoholism is a progressive and patient disease. It's cruel, like a cat that plays with its prey before breaking its neck. Its goal is to break you, to get you alone and wretched, to disconnect you from God, to make you a pariah to your family and friends, to make you unemployable, to break down your body so you're weak and sick, useless, a burden to yourself and society, and then, if you're lucky, it will relieve you of your misery and kill you.

And that's basically where it brought me.

By the time I was thirty-eight, my body was destroyed. I couldn't walk up a flight of steps without stopping to catch my breath. A pack of Marlboros a day for twenty years will do that. I always felt I was on the verge of a heart attack. Snorting cheap cocaine for decades will do that. Someone told me if I took aspirin it would help prevent a heart attack, so, like a good addict, I took them by the handful. I started my day with a handful of aspirin from the ninety-nine-cent store, then washed it down with a forty-ounce of Colt 45. It ripped up the lining of my stomach. For the last two years of my drinking, the toilet was deep red with blood every time I moved my bowels. A booze-and-aspirin breakfast will do that.

I was sick and suffering physically, but the real suffering was at the emotional and spiritual level. Yes, I was dying. My body was giving me all the signs, but it's amazing how another drink or another hit will make you forget your physical anguish. Yet no amount of drink or drug could numb the pain in my soul. My heart had become cold and my eyes empty. I had become joyless and spiritually barren. I hated myself. I'd look in the mirror and spit at my own reflection.

I lived with the torture of seeing my life fall apart and yet felt completely powerless to stop the wreckage. I was in the worst kind of bondage, and I couldn't figure out how to get free.

Every night for at least ten years, I said to myself, *Tomorrow is going to be different*, but tomorrow never was. It was like running headfirst into a brick wall every day. I knew the wall was there. I knew it was going to hurt. I didn't enjoy anything about hitting the wall, yet I couldn't find the willpower to stop myself. For a decade, over and over again, I said, *Tomorrow I'm going to figure out how to get through the wall.*

I was committing a slow, miserable suicide. I was a bloody,

broken mess, yet I kept picking myself up and kept running into the wall. Being caught in this cycle was the worst kind of torture imaginable.

I also had this totally insane idea, an idea only an addict can delude himself into believing: I thought all I needed was one perfect night of getting high, then I could quit. For years, I believed all I needed was the perfect amount of good weed and coke, just the right amount of beer and vodka, and a place where I could be undisturbed. Just one perfect high, then the next day I'd start a new, clean, sober life. All I needed was to get it all out of my system by first putting it all in my system. I really believed this. I would mark a weekend on my calendar months ahead, then think, *I'll have the apartment to myself. I'll have just gotten a big paycheck. I know the dealers with the best stuff. This is it! On New Year's Eve, I'll have the perfect night of decadence and debauchery. Then I'll wake up and start a new life.*

Of course it could never work. An addict can never get enough of what they don't want. If by some impossible miracle, everything had lined up perfectly and I'd had the night I imagined, there was no way I would have quit the next day. Addiction is a disease of more. It's like the hungry ghost that gorges itself on all the foods of its desire and never satisfies its hunger. My greedy ass would have wanted to do it again, and again. Ad infinitum.

Tamela suffered from my suffering. This beautiful, loving woman whom I'd often stare at with hate in my eyes, thinking, *How can this women love me? I am a waste and a piece of shit.* I hated myself and I hated her for loving me. Eventually, Tamela had enough. She realized she had a problem and did something about it. She kicked me out.

I became homeless.

I packed a knapsack and headed to Prospect Park, where I slept on a bench on Ocean Avenue outside the park, not far from where I used to visit the Messiah. It was a warm spring that year. "My" bench had a lovely willow tree above it and was only steps away from a liquor store and a twenty-four-hour bodega.

I had three hundred dollars in savings, the most money I'd saved in my thirty-nine years. In my voice, alcoholism said, *You're doing okay. And this is what you deserve.*

On some strange impulse, I had packed in my knapsack a book I'd had for twenty years and never cracked open once. *Alcoholism: The Family Disease* was basically a medical journal describing alcoholism and its links to heredity. My aunt Chris had given it to me on my eighteenth birthday because she'd recognized I had a problem. I'd carried the book with me to the many places I lived. When I got my first apartment with Scrapper, I used that book to prop open the kitchen window. In Rico's squalid crack-house squat where I crashed, I kept that book under my filthy mattress, but I never read a single word.

On that warm spring day, sitting on my park bench, sipping vodka, I read the book cover to cover. I was going to cure myself with knowledge. The book broke down different theories about the causes of and cures for alcoholism. I had to read sections over and over because I'd get drunk and forget what I'd read. But I always remembered the last chapter was about recovery, and it said that in the opinion of all these learned doctors with all their years of extensive research, the greatest chance for recovery for the alcoholic was a twelve-step program.

I didn't want to hear that shit. All I needed was another

forty-ounce and to be left alone. I didn't need or want help. I'd figure it out on my own.

My friend Ishmael got word I'd been kicked out. He had a recording studio in Greenpoint, Brooklyn, where he produced and engineered for mostly up-and-coming rap acts, and he offered to let me stay at the studio, sleeping on the floor. It was a better situation than my bench. I took him up on his kind offer.

I moved in with plans to get myself together and find a place within a month. I stayed for three months, probably the most important three months of my life. I knew I was in trouble, and I knew it was alcohol and drugs that had brought me so low. And I knew I was powerless over my addictions.

I had my last puff of weed at Ish's studio.

Ishmael had a rap duo scheduled for a session. They rolled in with a big crew, and the crew blazed the whole time they were in the studio. After they left, I searched through the space and found two half-smoked blunts in an ashtray.

I sat on the studio couch and lit up. I thought I would hit it only a couple of times and savor the high. I glanced up at the clock on the studio wall. It was 5 p.m. The next thing I knew, it was almost 8:30 p.m. I hadn't fallen asleep. I was sitting upright with the blunt butt still between my fingers, but somehow, I'd lost three and a half hours. I'd gone blank. I couldn't remember what had happened or what I was thinking during that lost time. I was stuck in place like a fly in amber. And I couldn't move my limbs. I began to wonder if I'd had a stroke. I couldn't detect my heart. I felt no beat. I wondered, *Is this what death feels like?*

I looked around the room and down at my body. Can a

dead person look around? My chest wasn't moving. *I am not breathing!*

I hadn't been breathing since I "came to," and at least an hour had passed. I looked at the clock again: 8:35 p.m.

Wait, I hadn't drawn a breath in five full minutes!

How does one breathe?

I was suffocating with paranoia.

I was overwhelmed with fear and anxiety. I was overcome with confusion.

I was disoriented and completely unable to move.

It was no fun. It was torture. I stayed in this state of misery for nearly another three hours before I started to come down enough to gain some semblance of control. As the clock inched to midnight, I was finally able to move my body enough to put the blunt butt down.

I made it through.

As the clock moved ever so slowly past midnight, I thought, *Yesterday I died.*

For years, Ishmael had a tradition of throwing big blowout Fourth of July parties at his studio. Maybe a hundred people would swing through for music and dancing and drumming and fireworks and a lot of drinking. People brought cases of beer and bottles of all kinds of liquor. It was a blast.

I tried for the first half of the party to act like I wasn't drinking. I wanted word to get back to the beautiful woman who had kicked me out that "Patrick is doing great. He stopped drinking." I was telling anyone who would listen, "Yeah, I stopped drinking! I'm clean and sober now. I feel great!" I made a big show of "not drinking."

What I was actually doing was excusing myself every half hour to run to the bodega two blocks away to buy tall boys of

Budweiser and down them in two gulps before popping some breath mints and hustling back to the party. I must've excused myself a dozen times. I was coming back from one of my covert trips when Ishmael stopped me in the hallway, handed me a beer, and said, "Here, man, you can stop now. You ain't fooling anybody."

Now I could drink with impunity and abandon, so that's exactly what I did.

The party went on until the afternoon of the fifth. There were cases of beer and many bottles of booze left over. I don't remember much of the following three days, but I know I drank. I know I didn't eat or bathe. I know that when I woke up on the morning of July 8, all the cases of beer and the bottles of booze were gone.

I know now I'd been trying to drink myself to death.

When I realized there was no alcohol left, I panicked. I had no money, and the haze was lifting. Everything hurt. In desperation, I went through drawers and looked between couch cushions. I came up with enough change for a forty-ounce of malt liquor, then stumbled to the corner store only steps away. It was about 8 a.m. on a sweltering weekday morning. People were getting their morning coffees, heading to work. I was wearing the same clothes from the party, clothes I'd pissed in and vomited on and slept in. I got a forty-ounce, and I couldn't even wait to get it back to the studio. I drank it right outside of the bodega.

Nothing happened. I felt absolutely nothing.

Then an anxiety welled up in me that choked my breath. This thing that had for over twenty years worked to get me out of myself, to numb me to reality, suddenly stopped working. I made it back to the studio in a panicked state. With shaking hands, I scrounged around, looking under furniture and going through the closets. I came up with just enough dimes, nickels, and pennies to buy another forty-ounce. Maybe twenty minutes had passed since I'd been in this bodega. I poured my change on the counter and took another forty from the fridge.

Then grace happened. It happened in the form of a look from a stranger.

The Arab bodega owner behind the counter gave me a look I'm sure I'd received before but never noticed. He looked at me with a mixture of pity and repulsion. He looked at me like one might look at a mangy, dying dog. A look that said, *I'm really sorry for you, but please get the fuck out.*

It hit me like a punch in the stomach.

I crawled back to the studio with the forty-ounce. I sat on the roof and drank it. The sun was merciless. I sat there for I don't know how long. A puddle of sweat and tears gathered at my feet. I contemplated suicide. I knew there was no more gray area. It was all black-and-white now. Drink and die or stop and live. I'd reached the end.

Something stirred in me, and I began speaking to it. To *something* that might save me. I cried out to that *something*. I pleaded with it, I begged it, "Please help me. I can't do this anymore."

I must have said it a hundred times.

I surrendered.

I fell asleep.

That forty-ounce was the last drink I ever had.

Ninety days after that moment of grace and surrender, I was coming home from my job at the strip club. It was 3 a.m., and I sat on the empty 4 train, thinking about my journey. I thought of my dad. It occurred to me he was thirty-nine years old when he got sober, same as me. It occurred to me he'd had to hit a bottom of pain, desperation, and misery before he, too, surrendered. It occurred to me I'd never cried when my father died.

Three in the morning, alone on a Brooklyn-bound 4 train, the tears came. They came and they didn't stop. Twenty-three years' worth of tears.

I was finally free.

Second Chance

BACK WHEN I lived with Tamela and her beautiful children in Flatbush, where I'd created a self-made jail cell I locked myself into so I could get high, I'd sit by the room's little window that looked out onto the avenue and blow smoke from my cocaine-laced joints as I watched all the life passing me by.

Across the street was an old majestic Catholic church. I noticed that on most evenings, a motley group of people would emerge from the side of the church and congregate. They were of mixed race, age, and gender, and looked like they didn't belong in the same company, yet they would gather there smoking cigarettes, laughing, and hugging. I became obsessed with them. I couldn't figure out who these people were or what had brought such a diverse group together. They looked happy and healthy. I hated them.

Later, when I moved into Ishmael's studio in Greenpoint and was still buying forties from the bodega, I used to pass a church where I often saw a diverse group of people hanging out front. These people looked different from the group hanging out in front of the Catholic church in Flatbush, a little younger and hipper-looking, and yet, oddly, they seemed like the same crowd. They laughed and hugged, too. Sometimes I'd cross the street and watch them for a while. I hated them, too.

One evening as I stood watching, a guy broke off from the group and walked across to me. He held out a card. "Hey, I just wanted to pass this on to you in case you ever feel like you might need it." The card read *Alcoholics Anonymous Intergroup*. It had a number and address. I thanked him and stuffed the card in my pocket. I hated him. After that evening, I took a different route to and from the bodega.

On the morning of July 8, 2001, I pulled the worn, torn card out of my wallet and called the number on it. I was miserable and wretched. I was in pain. I had hit the bottom. I was dying.

I held the phone in shaking hands, desperately hoping that somehow, this call would save my life, and at the same time hoping it wouldn't.

A voice answered on the third ring. "Hello. How can I help you?" The voice was warm and raspy, like coffee and cigarette smoke. It was familiar. I wanted to answer. I wanted to say, "Please help me. Please save me." But I couldn't speak.

The voice continued. "It's okay. I'm glad you called. I made a call like this over twenty-five years ago, and I couldn't speak, either. I was dying. That call saved my life. That's what you're doing right now, saving your life."

I began to cry. He asked my name. I mumbled it out.

He said in a cheery, faux-Irish brogue, "Ah! Patrick! Well, that be a fine name for an alcoholic!"

I don't remember most of what was said during that five-minute call, but I will never forget three things he said: "It's going to be all right" and "You deserve a second chance at life." Then he said, "I'm proud of you, kid." He was kind and funny. He had a gruff, old-school Brooklyn Irish accent. He was an angel. He sounded exactly like my dad. He asked for my address. He said he would mail me an AA meeting book to find meetings in my area. I fell asleep. When I awoke two hours later, there was a meeting book waiting at the door.

I found a meeting for the following evening, just blocks away from Ish's studio. By 5 p.m. on July 9, I was a wreck. I hadn't had a drink in over twenty-four hours, the longest I'd gone without alcohol in my system for many, many years. It had been a hot day, and the evening air was still sweltering. I was melting, detoxing, and sweating buckets. By the time I showed up in front of the church, my clothes were soaked through. My sweat was sour and rank. I felt weak and frail. I was terrified. I wanted desperately to be embraced and surrounded by people willing to help me, and at the same time, I felt if anyone so much as said hello to me, I would leave and never come back.

The church gates were locked. I double-checked the address, the day, the time. It was right there in the meeting book. I thought, *Well, I tried. I might as well just go get a drink.* As I turned to walk away, a car horn beeped. The driver waved me over. He rolled down his window.

"Hey, I was just driving down the block and saw you

rattling the gate. That meeting closed down recently, but there's another one around the corner that's not in the book. If you hurry, you can make it. They should be just starting." He wrote down the address and room number. He said, "Good luck!" He was an angel.

I found the place. It was in the basement of an old dilapidated community center. I walked down the dark, dank, musty corridor looking for the room. There were puddles and trash on the floor. A fat rat scurried in front of me. I'd been in basement corridors like this many times, the familiarity put me somewhat at ease.

Then I opened the door to my first AA meeting. There were about ten unkempt men scattered about the small fluorescent-lit room. It smelled of urine, sweat, and stale cigarette smoke. I was home. I sat in the back as close to the door as possible. No one paid any attention to me. In fact, the men all seemed to be in worlds of their own. Some looked half asleep, some rocked back and forth in their chairs, others sat drooling into their laps. I felt comfortable there, funky and sweating in this stuffy little room. I fit right in.

At the front of the room were roll-down shades with writing on them, twelve steps on one, twelve traditions on the other. I couldn't understand a single word of it. My mind was *scattered* and racing. Between the shades stood a man who was speaking to the group. He looked clean and healthy. I don't remember what he said, but I remember feeling safe. I felt like I belonged. I felt anonymous.

I didn't drink that day. It was the first full day in over twenty years I hadn't used some substance to self-medicate. The day started my sober journey. I got a second chance at life.

I went to that AA meeting every evening for about two weeks. The fog slowly began to lift, and my thinking began to clear. At some point, I remember looking at the drooling, rocking, mumbling men around me and thinking, *Wait a goddamn minute! These motherfuckers are crazy!* And, in fact, they were. I found out later why the meeting wasn't in the AA book. It was because it wasn't technically an AA meeting. It was specifically for MICA (mentally ill chemically addicted) patients. No one questioned my being there. I fit the profile. It was exactly where I needed to be for those first couple of weeks. In those first days, if I'd walked into a nice clean church room filled with nice clean recovering alcoholics, I would have turned right around and left. I would have felt judged and unworthy. Wretched and unwelcome.

During my first weeks of being clean and sober, I felt as vulnerable and delicate as a newborn baby. I felt hypersensitive and raw. Every bit of me was tender. It was as if a layer of skin had been stripped from me and every nerve exposed. For over twenty years, I'd been using alcohol and drugs daily to numb myself and shut out the world, but now I was feeling *all* my feelings without any anesthesia. It was frightening and exciting. I began to see colors again. I was able to taste, smell, and hear again. I marveled at a blooming flower, birds chirping, fresh-cut grass, and the sounds of children laughing. Apparently, all this beauty had been around me for years, but I'd been too high to notice. I cried, totally overwhelmed by how exquisite these things I had missed for so many years were.

I was determined to stay sober, but I'd be lying if I said the beginning was easy and without temptation. I have the disease of alcoholism, a disease that's cunning, baffling, and powerful. A disease that speaks to me in my own voice. A chronic disease that wants me to drink and, ultimately, wants me dead.

By the time planes were crashed into the World Trade Center, I had two months and two days of sobriety. I was living in Downtown Brooklyn, and on the sunny morning of September 11, I saw the sky darken, and I smelled the smoke from the burning buildings. I looked out my window and saw people covered in soot and ash walking like zombies down my block.

My disease spoke to me loudly and clearly that day. It knew how vulnerable an event like that could make me, so it swooped in and tried to pull me back. It whispered, *Man, you can drink today. You haven't been sober that long. You can't get through a tragedy like this without something to take the edge off. No one would blame you.*

I was listening. I headed out to the liquor store, feeling the fear, panic, and confusion in the streets. The first liquor store I went to was closed, so I headed to another. There was a line out the door, so I headed to another. I told myself, *Let me walk just a little farther, and I'll stop at the next liquor store.* I kept walking and telling myself, *I'll stop at the* next *liquor store.* Then I found myself in front of an AA meeting.

I sat in the meeting between two people who had just come from the city. They were covered in ash. People spoke about the gratitude they had for another sober day. They spoke prayers for the sick and suffering. They offered each other support. There were hugs and tears. It was a typical AA meeting.

I had just gotten a sponsor to help me through the twelve steps. He met me at the meeting, then we walked to his house. We sat on his roof and spoke about sobriety. We prayed as we watched the towers burn.

During those early days of sobriety, I was desperately in need of work. I had to deal with the financial wreckage of my past, and I owed a lot of money. I was working two six-hour shifts a week as the lighting guy at Scores, and though it was a shitty place to try to stay sober, I couldn't afford to quit.

I counted days in AA. I went to multiple meetings daily, did the steps, and sent out résumés. I must have sent out one hundred résumés in the first months of sobriety. I applied for everything from art-teaching gigs to construction work. I didn't care what kind of job I got. I heard nothing and I got no callbacks. I was broke. I had no real money coming in and yet, somehow, I always had just enough to pay my meager rent to Mr. Kim, pay other bills, feed myself, and put a dollar in the basket at the meetings. I was being taken care of by a power greater than myself.

It's recommended in AA that newcomers attend ninety meetings in ninety days to get a real foundation in sobriety. I must have made 270 in that time. I basically had nothing else to do except make meetings and look for work. I was learning how to "live life on life's terms" without a drink or drug. I began to learn how to maneuver and show up as a sober man. I became steadfast and honest. Reliable and accountable. I learned many lessons and equally unlearned behaviors that no longer served me.

On my ninetieth day of sobriety, I began to get callbacks and responses to my résumés. They came flooding in. There's a saying that coincidence is God's way of staying anonymous.

I don't believe for one minute that the tsunami of callbacks was a coincidence. A power greater than me knew I needed a solid foundation in sobriety before I went back into the workforce.

I went on several interviews. Three places offered to hire me. I took all three jobs. Technically, I wasn't qualified for any of these positions, but somehow, I'd talked and charmed my way into getting hired. God never left my side. During the week, I worked two part-time jobs, starting the first at 8 a.m. and leaving at noon to get to the other by 1 p.m., where I worked until 7 p.m. I needed the money, and I needed to stay busy. On the weekends, I went back to managing the art store/frame shop. All this while making at least one AA meeting a day.

I worked seven days a week without breaks or vacations for the first six years of my sobriety. It took that long to pay back all my debt.

After three years of sobriety, I managed to cofound a men's AA group in Clinton Hill. It was in that meeting I really learned how to be a sober man, a solid man. I was thirty-nine years old when I surrendered to my disease and admitted I was powerless over alcohol and drugs, but at the time, I had the emotional intelligence and coping skills of a sixteen-year-old and was still working from the playbook and teachings I'd gotten from men who were as damaged and misguided as I was. The men's meeting brought a cross section of sober men together and gave them a safe place to share and be supported. We had badass, tough street hustlers and dudes straight out of the penitentiary share that they'd been scared their whole lives. In that meeting, those hard guys and alpha males felt comfortable crying in front of other men. Things like that would be considered absolutely taboo in their world of hypermasculinity.

That group offered me my first experience with safe touch from other men. We hugged and held hands as we prayed and cried together. We also laughed a lot, the kind of laughter I hadn't experienced since before I'd started drinking. Pure, joyful, uninhibited laughter. In that meeting, I learned that real sober men could express their feelings and admit when they were wrong or made mistakes, that a real sober man could ask for help and admit when he didn't know the answers. That a real sober man's word is bond and that his honesty and integrity are his currency and worth. I learned that I can humbly admit when I am afraid, and I can express love freely without worry of being perceived as weak or soft.

I learned more and gained more spiritual wisdom from a group of ex-hustlers, -thieves, -pimps, -drunks, -dope fiends, and -crackheads than any self-help guru or program could have ever taught me.

I am a miracle. I mean that literally. A miracle is defined as *an action or occurrence that goes contrary to natural progression.* I am an alcoholic. I say this without doubt, apology, or reservation. As an alcoholic, I'm genetically programmed to drink, and the natural progression for me is institutions, hospitals, jails, and a lonely and wretched death. I've seen this progression play out in my own family, and yet, by some impossible miracle that I attribute to the grace of God, I do not drink, a day at a time.

In sobriety, I lost my beloved uncles Billy and Danny and my older brother Michael to the disease of alcoholism/addiction. But I did not drink. I gained and lost jobs. But I did not drink. I felt the exhilaration of new love and devastating heartbreak. But I did not drink. Through the mundane and extraordinary, the triumphs and failures, the accolades and disappointments, and all the polarities of life, I did not drink. Through all of life's adventures and surprises, both good and bad, and the hundreds of times I could have found an excuse to, I did not pick up a drink. And yet I am not cured. I am a work in progress.

Sober Feet

TO EXPLAIN HIS bad feet and bad temper, my dad told me his father had bad feet and a bad temper. "I'm just like my father," he said, "and you'll be just like me." Prophecy.

I remember seeing my dad from a distance as he shuffle-walked the one block home from the bus stop after work. He was usually already half drunk, but that didn't really explain his awkward gait. Dad always walked gingerly, as if his feet were made of thin glass and if he stepped too hard, they might shatter. He was only in his early thirties then, but he moved like an old man.

Dad was the foreman in a paper warehouse, and the job required him to be on his feet all day. The first thing he did when he got home was take off his brogans and put his sour-smelling feet up on the La-Z-Boy in front of the TV. On the little table next to him sat his ubiquitous pack of Pall Mall cigarettes, ashtray, shot glass, and pint of Gordon's gin. My job was to shuttle back and forth to the refrigerator, delivering fresh cans of Rheingold beer and taking away the empties. He didn't move from his chair once he got home. "Dame una cerveza, por favor" was the first full sentence of Spanish I ever learned.

I was an active little kid. I played sports pretty well, so I never got picked last. I ran around all day and walked for fun, but by the time I turned seventeen or so, my feet started to hurt, too. It happened gradually. I assumed it was the family affliction catching up with me.

By the time I was twenty, I'd accepted that life meant waking to sore, tender feet, staying in bed, and holding on as long as possible to avoid the painful first steps to the toilet for the morning release. I knew it would feel like I was walking with hot gravel in my shoes. I called it "the agony of de feet." Most days, the only way I could function was by downing aspirins by the mouthful.

Unbeknownst to me, by the time I was twenty, I had acquired a nickname among my closest friends. The Grouch, or, sometimes, Grumps. They were appropriate nicknames. It's difficult to be happy and upbeat when your feet feel like they're constantly being skewered with hot pokers. My boys would want to hang out, go out clubbing and dancing, play touch football or pickup games of basketball, all things normal, healthy young guys do. But not me. No way. Those activities sounded like medieval torture. I may as well have been asked to walk ten blocks on hot burning coals.

This malady also put quite a cramp in my dating life. I was definitely *not* the dude who was taking long romantic walks along the beach and in the park. I was great on a couch or stoop, though. I mastered stationary charm.

By seventeen years old, I'd stopped growing vertically, and I was wearing a size eight and a half shoe. When I went shoe shopping, it meant I somehow had money to spare, which meant I also had enough money to get high. I never went shopping sober, and I'd be half drunk and high by the time I made it to the store. I was the dude who stank of rank alcohol, old weed, and stale cigarettes and stood there unsteady, talking way too loudly while holding a tall boy in a brown paper bag and drinking it with a straw.

My feet smelled like things that were dead and rotting, and I knew taking off my shoes in a public place could be considered an environmental hazard and a crime against humanity. The salespeople were always patronizing and impatient with me, which was why I never tried on shoes in stores. They were happy when I announced with a slur, "Gimme the Adidas shells in an eight and a half. Nah! I don't need to try them on! Just ring them shits up!"

My story had become a drunken, addicted life of stinking, painful feet. In my mid-twenties, I found myself "walking in my father's shoes" when I got a job in the warehouse of the Strand bookstore. A job that kept me on my feet all day. I walked up and down long aisles, filling book orders while wearing Dr. Martens boots. These boots were my prize possession, a status symbol. They were rare in the States then and only came in European sizing, and I messed up and got the conversion wrong. I bought a pair a size too small. They were ridiculously expensive (a hundred dollars!), and I couldn't afford to return them. I wore them daily, which required downing a handful of aspirin every morning and holding my breath as I squeezed my poor feet into these stylish instruments of torture. I was akin to the Chinese women who had bound their feet and lived in miserable pain in order to be aesthetically pleasing.

I was living in the Ditmas Park section of Brooklyn and sharing an old house with two musician friends. I had my own room, and, much like my father before me, all I wanted to do when I got home was pull my contorted, rotten-smelling feet out of my boots, sit unmoving in one spot, and get high until I felt no pain and crashed out. Our old house was a straight five-block line from the train station, and on the five-block strip, I could have all my addictive needs met. It was the perfect setup for a drunk with bad foots.

I planned my life around taking as few steps as possible. A block from the train station was Bumper's Variety Store. This was basically an empty storefront with some sun-faded boxes of Pampers in the window and a sad rack with bags of dusty old potato chips on the inside. It was always dark in there, which didn't stop Bumper from wearing sunglasses. It smelled of incense and dank underarm funk. Bumper and his partner sold weed and loose cigarettes from under the counter. I'd known Bumper for years, before he even opened this spot. We had mutual friends in the reggae music scene. He was a Jamaican rude-boy dread with a thick accent and a stutter. "Ah wwwha de bbbloodclaat ah gggwaan?!" was his usual greeting. I would stop there first to buy a bag of weed and make some small talk.

Next stop was the liquor store on the next block, where I would pick up my half-pint of Georgi vodka. I never knew the name of the Korean man behind the thick bulletproof glass, but it didn't matter. He knew me and he would have the half-pint in a bag and rung up without a word passing between us.

Next was the twenty-four-hour bodega another block

down. Merengue music, the cat you had to move out the way to get to the beer, and Primo, who stayed on the phone and basically ignored you. Perfect. "Two forty-ounces of Colt 45 and a pack of Marlboro, por favor, papi." Usually standing on the corner was Flaco, who greeted me with an elaborate handshake to disguise the pass-off of the twenty-dollar bag of blow. It was a meaningless gesture, as everyone knew what was up. I think Flaco just liked the theatrics of it.

Within four blocks of getting off the train, I had everything I needed for a night of oblivion where I could numb out and forget the pain in my feet until the next morning.

I had this daily routine going for over a year. Again, what made it so perfect was *no wasted steps,* because by the time I got home from being on my killing feet all day in the warehouse, I was trying to take not even *one* extra step.

This one fateful day, no different from any other, I got off the train in my too-small Dr. Martens boots, walking glass-footed like my dad. I mindlessly began the routine I'd done a hundred times before. I was about to make the first stop at Bumper's when, for no logical reason whatsoever, *something* said, *You should go get your gin and beer first, then double back to get the weed.* This made no sense for someone with regular healthy feet, let alone someone in my condition. Why would I take *all* those extra steps? It defied logic, yet for some reason, that's exactly what I did. I looked in Bumper's and saw it was dark, as usual. I made out the silhouettes of a couple of guys standing at the counter. All pretty standard; there were usually customers coming in and out at that time. I decided to pass it by and come back, questioning myself the whole time and cursing my feet and my fucked-up genetics.

It couldn't have taken me more than five minutes to stop in the liquor store and bodega and hobble back. I had the ten dollars for the dime bag ready in my hand when I walked into Bumper's. I stopped just inside the door. I immediately knew something was wrong. It was darker than usual, and I smelled the distinctive stink of gunpowder. The smell was strong. So strong it overpowered the incense and funk. I took another step into the darkness and slipped a bit. I was standing in a puddle. I heard a low groan to my left and could just make out what looked like Bumper's partner lying on his back. My eyes adjusted enough to the darkness to make out three more bodies. All lying in puddles of blood. I saw my friend Bumper among them. His sunglasses had been blown off, blood drained from the side of his head, and his eyes stared up, unblinking, at the ceiling.

I immediately read the scene.

When I'd looked in earlier, what I was witnessing was a robbery about to happen. Bumper and his partner were known to carry guns, which is why they didn't bother to have a bulletproof partition in their spot. A shoot-out had ensued, and everyone in the store was shot and in different stages of dying when I walked in. Somehow, from only a block away, I hadn't heard the shots.

In that crucial moment, as I stood there in that scene of carnage, I was not struck with any grace, generosity, or gratitude.

I did not think, *Thank* God *I decided to pass by and wasn't here when the shooting started!* Nor did I think, *That's my friend Bumper lying there! I need to call for help!*

I'm ashamed to admit my *first and only* thought was *Fuck! Now I'm going to have to* walk *all the way to the projects to get my weed.*

Many years later, free of alcohol and drugs, I found myself in need of a new pair of sneakers. My first pair of "sober shoes." I showed up at the shoe store clean and clear-eyed, and I was surprised at how genuinely welcoming and helpful the salespeople were. I saw a pair of sneakers I liked and asked for them in a size eight and a half, as I had done since I was seventeen years old.

I was prepared to take them without trying them on, as I had always done as well, when the salesperson said, "Are you sure you're an eight and a half? Why don't you take your shoes off and let me measure your foot." My hygiene had improved, so I wasn't embarrassed to take off my shoes and step on the Brannock shoe-sizing device.

A device that clearly showed I wore a size ten.

From Haiti with Love

ONE OF THE most important people in my adult life was Constant Bernard. He and his brother, Lionel, were in two popular ska bands, and it was through them that I was introduced to that scene and began to play with a popular NYC ska band myself.

When I was nineteen years old, I lived in the same neighborhood as the Bernard brothers, and whenever I got the chance, I dropped by the little apartment off Flatbush Avenue where they lived with their mom. I'd make up any excuse I could think of to swing through. I loved hanging out with Constant and Lionel, but my main goal was to get some food. I knew the brothers would feed me, and I knew the food was going to be delicious and plentiful.

One Thanksgiving, the Brothers Bernard invited me to have dinner with them and their mom. Mrs. Bernard was genuinely one of the most loving, kind, and joyful people I'd ever met. She made me feel welcome in their warm, cramped apartment full of tantalizing smells and kompa music. The Bernards were Haitian and served the most delicious traditional Haitian foods. The griot, tassot, and soup joumou were like manna from heaven, but it was the djon-djon rice I most looked forward to. They also served traditional American Thanksgiving staples, including the best turkey and mac and cheese I ever had. Everything on the menu was culinary bliss.

Besides the amazing food that came plate after plate, and the beer and Barbancourt rum that flowed freely, it was the love and laughter that fed my soul. Mrs. Bernard took such joy in watching people eat. She would sit with a big smile on her beautiful face, and literally as soon as anyone finished one thing on their plate, she'd be up dishing out more. I had never before and have never since eaten food as good as hers. I think besides the fact that she was a truly gifted and experienced chef, what made her food delicious and satisfying was the love she poured into every dish she touched. It was such a blessing to be part of this feast, and I was grateful to be invited back every year for close to a decade.

Mrs. Bernard practically adopted me. I was treated like the third Bernard son. I was struggling with active alcoholism and addiction during those years, and every Thanksgiving I was more lost than the year before, but Mrs. Bernard always treated me with warmth, love, and generosity, even as I was sinking deeper and deeper into the depraved darkness of addiction.

On Thanksgiving in the year 2000, I was in a completely wretched state. Dinner was supposed to be at 3 p.m., and I knew Mrs. Bernard wouldn't let anyone sit down to eat until I got there, but I was on an alcohol and cocaine binge. I was already drunk by noon and trying to score drugs. I wasn't able to get what I needed until 7 p.m., and when I did, I immediately snorted half a bag. I got to Mrs. Bernard's four hours late, drunk, high, and empty-handed.

She made me a plate, but I refused to eat. Instead, I sat at the side table drinking her rum and beer, running to the bathroom every fifteen minutes to snort a line, and stepping outside several times to smoke a cigarette or a joint. I was miserable, mean, rude, and inappropriate. I'm surprised the brothers didn't kick me out and kick my ass, but, like their mother, they were creatures of love and forgiveness.

As I was leaving their home that Thanksgiving, Mrs. Bernard gave me a big heavy bag of plates and Tupperware full of food. She said, "You didn't eat, baby. Maybe you'll be hungry later." I half thanked her and asked for the rest of the rum, which she gave me without hesitation.

I got home and drank, snorted, and smoked till 6 a.m. When the drugs and alcohol ran out, I was hit with hunger. My body cried for food after having gone forty-eight hours without eating. I ate all the delicious food that had been made with love, but I tasted nothing. I shoved it in my mouth and swallowed without chewing. I finished everything in less than fifteen minutes and immediately threw it up. It was too much too quick. My body couldn't handle it. I was miserable and in pain. I needed someone to blame, so at 6 a.m., I called Mrs. Bernard, that beautiful, loving woman, woke her up, and said her food had made me sick. I blamed her for my throwing up. I scolded her. Mrs. Bernard cried and apologized over and over. I wanted her to feel as miserable as I did.

Calling that wonderful, kind woman that morning and

making her cry was the beginning of the end for me. A part of me died. I knew I had hit bottom.

By God's grace, I got clean and sober in July of the following year. I was invited again to Thanksgiving, despite my despicable behavior the year before. I arrived at Mrs. Bernard's early, with gifts in hand. I purposely got there before anyone else arrived, and I asked if I could speak with Manman Bernard privately. She and I sat down, and I began apologizing. I tried to make amends for my past behavior. She wouldn't let me finish. She hushed me and said, in her lovely Haitian accent, "Baby, I knew you were sick. I am thanking God you are better. This is my thanksgiving today." I had a wonderful Thanksgiving that year with her and the family.

It was our last.

Mrs. Bernard also knew by then that she had terminal cancer and less than three months to live, but she'd told no one. She laughed and danced and heaped food on plates and sent people home with to-go containers full of her delicious food. She hugged me like I'd never been hugged before and like I will never be hugged again.

I met pure love once, and she cooked like an angel.

Christmas Miracle III (The Dove)

ONE OF THE many jobs I applied for when I was newly sober was the position of art therapist for an organization called B-PAN, which had offices at Kings County Hospital. The position required a degree in art therapy and work experience in the field. I had neither. But somehow, I got the job.

B-PAN stood for Brooklyn Pediatric AIDS Network. My job was to work with children who were HIV positive or had AIDS, children who had been born with the virus. I was given a tiny room next to the doctors' offices where the children came for checkups twice a month. There were some basic art supplies in the room, some toys, and some board games. My job was to entertain and calm the children as they waited to see the doctor. Although it didn't list it in the job description, my job was to love the children.

I saw a cohort of about thirty young souls on a revolving

basis, from toddlers to twelve-year-olds. Sick children, the most beautiful beings I'd ever been blessed to encounter. In my brief time in the role, I had the profound honor of meeting the brightest, most courageous, and strongest human beings. They had the pure, infectious joyfulness of children and the sage wisdom of people far beyond their years. They were bright lights in the process of dimming. They were angels in transition.

I'd been working with the kids for a few months and had established a steady routine. I had gotten to know and love all the children on my roster, and I'd thought my heart was as full as it could be. Then Elijah showed up. And my heart simply melted.

I was reading a story to a small group of children when Elijah and his dad came into the art playroom. I paused the story to introduce myself and to welcome them. Elijah's father shook my hand, then excused himself and went to sit in the room next door, where the other parents waited. He left a strong smell of alcohol behind.

The first thing that impressed me about Elijah was his actual physical presence. He was seven years old, but he was tiny, the size of a healthy four-year-old. Despite his diminutive size, he filled the room with his bright smile. He stood erect and walked with an air of royalty. He walked around the small table and shook the hands of the other children, introducing himself: "Hi! I'm Elijah. What's your name?" When they replied, he'd find something complimentary to say about them. "Nice to meet you, LaKenya! I really like your braids!" "Hi, Jose! I bet you're really good at sports!" There was something noble about him. When he made the rounds and got to me, he actually bowed.

The other outstanding thing about Elijah was he

dressed like a scholar. Always in a tie, his little sweater, and khaki or corduroy pants. I complimented his father on Elijah's outfits, and he said, "I wish I could take credit. He's been picking out his own clothes and dressing himself since he was four years old."

While the other children came twice a month, Elijah started coming once a week, then two or three times a week. He was very sick, but he never showed it in any way. I used to love to watch him play and interact with the other children. He was always warm, patient, and loving with them. So kind. He made us laugh when he did silly dances. He put on impromptu puppet shows to entertain us. He played dolls with the girls and roughhoused with the boys. He took the younger kids by the hand and read to them. When they cried, as they often did, he spoke softly to them and rubbed their backs. He was compassionate and empathetic.

As soon as the last child left the room, Elijah's demeanor would change. He'd still be sweet, but a seriousness would come over him. A heavy sadness. With just him and me in the playroom, Elijah talked about his life, about his mother's death and how much it had destroyed his father. He told me about his father's drinking and said he was worried about his dad's future. He wanted his dad to be happy more than anything else.

He told me about the severe and persistent pain he was in. He told me how scared he was.

Whenever we had these talks I mostly just listened, holding his hand. He spoke with a child's vocabulary but with a profound awareness. While most of the other children, even the older ones, didn't know exactly why they had to see the doctor so often, this angel knew exactly why he was there. He knew he was dying.

I worked the morning shift with the children, 8 a.m. to 12 p.m., and then went to my other job as a youth counselor and teaching artist at an organization called the Center for Family Life in the Sunset Park area of Brooklyn. It's where I was when I got the call that Elijah had been rushed to the hospital and wanted to see me. I was helping to create props for a play the kids were putting on that afternoon, but I dropped everything and rushed to see Elijah.

At the hospital, Elijah's father sat in the lobby with his head in his hands. He didn't look up when I passed him.

I entered Elijah's room, and there he lay, the most beautiful human being I'd ever known, with tubes coming out of him everywhere and an oxygen mask covering his face. When I got to his bedside, he sat up. He hadn't even seen me; he just *knew* I was there. He pulled his mask down and smiled his angelic smile. Then he lay back down. The effort to simply sit up took all his energy.

In the days since I'd last seen him, Elijah had shrunk. He'd become frail and weak. I sat with him, holding his hand as he lay still and quiet. He squeezed my hand with a strength that surprised me. Then suddenly he sat up and screamed, a scream that came from his soul and rattled his body. A long, loud, gut-wrenching scream. It was the scream of someone in deep pain. A scream of intense suffering. But there was something else happening. He was trying to let go. It looked to me like he was trying to expel his spirit, his life force.

The doctors and nurses rushed in and asked me to leave. Elijah gripped my hand, and a nurse had to gently pull his fingers back to release his hold. He turned his head to me and looked into my heart. I heard "I love you" as clearly as if he'd said the words.

For the next two weeks, I couldn't get word of Elijah's

condition. He'd been moved from Kings County Hospital to Methodist in Park Slope. His father didn't respond to my calls. I prayed for that little boy around the clock, and every time the door to my playroom opened, I held my breath, hoping it would be Elijah.

Then, early one morning, Elijah walked through the door. He was alone. His dad was waiting for him in the hallway. He was dressed in his tie and sweater, as always, but they were baggy. He was still standing erect and dignified, but his walk was slow and measured. I'd been sitting on one of the little kiddie chairs, writing in the daily journal, when he walked in. The other children who were scheduled to visit hadn't arrived yet. Elijah bowed as he had the first day, then crawled up in my lap. He put his head against my chest.

"It hurts so much," he said.

"I know, baby."

"I'm so tired."

"I know, baby, I know." I hugged him to my chest.

A tear rolled down his cheek. "I'm scared."

He fell asleep in my arms. I rocked him. I cried.

About a week later, on Christmas Eve, there was a major storm. Snow fell all night. I was living in Downtown Brooklyn in an apartment with a window that looked out onto the roof. The next morning, all I could see was a blanket of perfect white snow. Then I registered a movement. On my windowsill, looking directly at me, was a dove, a dove so pure and white it was hard to make it out against the backdrop of the snow.

It was an odd sight. I'd never seen a white dove like that in Brooklyn, and I had certainly never seen one up close. It was beautiful. It sat perched on my windowsill, looking in, and it didn't move, even when I got right up to it. We stared at each other through the glass, and after a minute, it turned its back to me and settled in.

I left for work and didn't get home again until early evening. I'd forgotten all about the dove, which was why I was surprised to see it was still on the windowsill. As I walked toward it, the dove turned to look at me through the glass. Again, I was taken by how incredibly pure and beautiful it was and how it didn't move, even as I got right up to it. I was still staring at the dove when I got a call from Elijah's father. He said, "I just wanted to let you know that Elijah left us this morning. He asked me to tell you that he wasn't scared anymore."

I turned back to the window just in time to see the white dove fly away.

Stardust and Rainbows

SHANTI WAS MY first sober relationship. We met when she came to B-PAN to lead yoga sessions with the children. My newly opened heart fell for her immediately, but the relationship was pretty contentious from the start. We dated for about a year. I really loved her, and we really tried, but it simply wasn't a good fit.

I watched her walking away that autumn morning and I knew it was really over. We'd been slowly breaking up for months. She'd walked away before, but this time was different. I knew she wasn't coming back. My tender heart broke.

It was a cold, dark, and gray day, and my mood matched the weather. I sat there staring at the sky long after she was gone. I had turned forty just a few days before, and this was the saddest birthday present.

My phone rang. I didn't want to speak to anyone. I wanted

to wallow in my misery. I let the call go to voicemail. A minute later, the phone rang again. I let it go to voicemail. When the phone rang the third time, I thought I should at least see who was calling.

Richard worked across the hall from me at Kings County Hospital. I'd known him only a couple of months, but he'd already become dear to me. It was impossible not to like him. His positivity and bubbly personality were infectious. His whole affect was like that of a fairy godmother.

Richard was slight of build and about my age. Sometimes he'd be the only White face on the entire floor, but I don't think he was even aware of it. Like a pixie, he floated around dispensing love and good cheer. There was something about him that made me feel that no matter what he was wearing, what I saw was him in a frilly pink tutu, waving a wand that sprinkled stardust and rainbows.

Richard was gay. Gay to the highest degree of gaydom. Gay ad infinitum, gay squared, the gayest a gay person could possibly be with additional gay added. If Liberace and Richard Simmons had had a son, it would have been Richard. He was a living, breathing show tune. He floated when he walked and sang when he spoke.

He had a secret, though. Whenever there was an attractive woman around, Richard would go into super-turbo gay mode. He would disarm these women by being "just one of the girls," and because of that, he got away with murder. I watched him basically maul women under the guise of being friendly. We worked with a nutritionist, a super-attractive young Asian woman with curves galore. Richard would get really "friendly" with her. One day she was in my room, reviewing some case notes, when Richard slid in behind her, grabbed her generous breasts, and started massaging them while simultaneously humping her round bottom. If I'd done that, I would've been fired immediately for sexual harassment and assault, and rightly so, but Richard got away with it. "Oh! Richard, you're so naughty!" She laughed. But I saw Richard's face. Richard wasn't being "one of the girls." Richard was getting off. When she left, he said to me, in a low, lecherous voice, "Mmmm, titties! I like titties."

I finally checked his message, thinking it may have been an emergency. We worked with some of the same kids. A couple of them had full-blown AIDS and weren't doing well. I prayed it wasn't bad news.

"Hiiiiiii. It's Richaaard! Call me baaaack!"

"Hey, Richard, it's Patrick. What's up?" I said flatly.

"Oh! You are what's up, honey! I was sitting here, and your face came up before me. You were sad. Something told me I needed to call yooou!"

I told him I was indeed feeling sad. He knew I loved Shanti, and he knew it wasn't working out.

"Oh, I felt your pain, darling. Don't be a Gloomy Gus. Richaaard is here!"

As heavy as I felt, I had to admit Richard made me smile a little.

"Listen! I've got two tickets to a show that I know will cheer you up! You are going with me, and I *will not* accept no for an answer, so get your fanny up and out and meet me at this address!"

The show was at a little theater in Chelsea. I wasn't too familiar with that part of town, and I got turned around a few times, but I made it just in time for the curtain. Richard had saved the seat next to him, and I squeezed in between him and a tall Black man. The lights went down and the show started, and Richard had been right—within minutes, I was laughing. It was an over-the-top campy drama. It was ridiculously funny. The man sitting on the other side of me found it hilarious. He howled and nudged me, making little comments and slapping my thigh like we were there together.

At intermission the lights went up, and I looked around. The first thing I realized was that the whole audience was male. Not a woman in sight. Then I realized the whole audience was White. I thought that might explain why so many people were turning around to look in my direction. The tall Black man and I were the only two Black people in the crowd. We seemed to be getting a lot of attention. I looked at the playbill to distract myself from all the surveying. The playbill let me know that the "women" in the show, some of them quite attractive, were in fact men. There literally wasn't a woman in the entire theater.

Just before the end of intermission, the tall man turned to me, again placing a hand on my thigh, and said, "I can't wait for the second half! The first part was soooo funny!" I had the first real look at my seat neighbor. He had a smooth face, shaved head, caramel-brown skin, and freckles. He had an extraordinary kind of glow about him. We made polite small talk as the lights went down for the second half of the show.

When I'd accepted Richard's invitation, I told him I'd have to leave the show about ten minutes before it ended. I was still in early recovery and needed to make a meeting because alcoholism loves a broken heart. I had looked up meetings in the area and saw one just a couple blocks away. Richard said he understood. I got up as quietly as I could to excuse myself. Richard gave me a kiss on the cheek, and as I passed the tall man, he whispered, "Oh, no! You're leaving? So nice to have met you." He shook my hand for a little longer than I thought necessary.

* * *

The AA meeting had just started. In the book, it had been listed as a "men's meeting." I welcomed this because I thought I might get the chance to share honestly about my breakup. I thought it might be good to get a sober male's perspective. The speaker started telling his story. He spoke about his experience with coming out in high school and how the ridicule and isolation he felt led him to the bottle, which led him to harder drugs and, ultimately, to a methamphetamine addiction. He spoke of contracting AIDS and nearly dying. He spoke of his moment of grace and finding his way to recovery. It was very moving, and as often happens in these meetings, there were many nodding heads and sighs of identification as he told his story. It was powerful.

When he finished, I stood up to get a cup of coffee and looked around the room for the first time. It was a small room, cramped with about thirty men. Again, I found myself the only person of color and, as I took in the whole scene, it occurred to me, probably the only heterosexual. The room looked like a casting call for the Village People. There was practically every gay archetype present. There were leather guys, twinks and twunks, big burly bears, super-effeminate guys, and overly macho guys. When I sat back down and looked at the meeting list again, I saw I'd missed the fine print. It read *Men's Meeting **Gay/GBTQ*.

It was a good meeting. Some of the shares nearly brought me to tears with their brutal and fearless honesty. Some shares, with their campy bitchiness, made me laugh so hard my sides hurt.

When we got to the secretary's report portion of the meeting, the acting secretary asked, as is tradition, "Is there anyone counting days or celebrating an anniversary of a year or more this month?" A few hands went up, and we applauded the miracle and gift of sobriety. Then they did something a bit unusual. The secretary asked if there were any birthdays this month. I timidly raised my hand. The room exploded in hand claps and whistles. Then a group of men stood up, formed a line, locked arms, and sang "Happy Birthday." They did it like a show tune with the cancan high kicks and all. It was excellent. Clearly some of these guys were professional dancers and in the theater. I was overwhelmed.

After the meeting, I walked through Chelsea on my way to the A train. The streets were alive and vibrant with "gaytivity": guys strolling hand in hand, guys making out, bars spilling out onto the street with gay revelry, colors, and sounds. It was a gay wonderland.

I realized that in my brokenhearted grief, I'd neglected to eat all day. The all-night diner at Fourteenth and Eighth seemed perfect, so I dropped in and ordered a grilled cheese sandwich. I sat alone, looking out the window at the passing people. I was startled by a gentle tap on my shoulder. "Oh, how I just hate to see a handsome young man eat all by himself. Do you mind if I join you?" Standing over me was a White man about seventy years old, balding, with thick glasses and a goatee. He seemed harmless. In fact, he seemed vaguely familiar, although I couldn't place him.

"Sure," I said, and he slid in across from me.

He ordered a coffee and looked me over for a minute. There was a wise kindness in his eyes. "Okay, honey, tell me all about it."

I guess he intuited that I was in my feelings. Maybe it was obvious. I immediately felt comfortable with the stranger. He didn't say much. He asked a few questions, but mostly he listened. He called me honey. It sounded like the caring coo of an adult speaking to a beloved child. I opened up to him. Told him about my broken relationship. Told him how much I hurt.

He said, "You'll be okay, honey. Just keep being kind and openhearted, and true love will come to you." He called me a beautiful man. "I'm proud of you, kid," he said.

The man was an angel. He paid my bill. Gave me a kiss on both cheeks. Something about that gesture and the feel of his bristled goatee against my skin gave me a chill.

Kid was what my dad had called me when he was being affectionate. As I stood on the train platform, tears came to my eyes. The man in the diner reminded me of my father. Had he lived, he would've been about that age, and the physical resemblance was strong. His balding head, glasses, and goatee were like my dad's, but it was the twinkle in his eye that really did it. When he kissed me on both cheeks, I got a sensation that brought me back to being ten years old. It was exactly how my dad would say good night to me. No one had ever done that since.

When I finally got home, I saw Richard had been blowing up my phone. He had left five messages. I checked the first one: "It's Richaard! Call meee!"

"What's up, Richard?" I said sleepily.

"Oh my God! *You* are what's up! How does it feel?"

"How does what feel?" I asked.

"To have sat next to a celebrity, of course! *And* I've got news for yoooou!" he sang.

"Richard, what the hell are you talking about?"

Richard could hardly contain himself. "Oh my God, silly man! Didn't you know you were sitting next to RuPaul?"

I had no idea.

"But that's not even the news! When the show was over

people flocked to him for autographs, but before he even signed the first one, he grabbed me and asked, 'Who was your friend?' He wanted to know if you were available!"

I was speechless.

"Ah, hello! Never mind that nasty little Shanti, honey. *The RuPaul wants you!*"

It certainly had been an extraordinary evening. It was entertaining and healing, and for a few days I felt much better about my breakup with Shanti. But as time passed, I found myself sinking again into depression and heartbreak. I spoke with my dear friend Deepa about it. Deepa was a doula and midwife, and a born nurturer and healer. She said, "You should go hug a tree." She said it would help to heal my heart.

To my Brooklyn-born ears, her suggestion sounded like *You should go fuck yourself.*

To me, trees were things usually surrounded by dog shit, wino piss, and broken glass. Not welcoming, and certainly not something to hug. But Deepa swore by the tree-hugging thing and promised me if I did it with an open heart, I would feel better. The tree would help take away my pain. Despite my trepidation, I trusted her.

About a month after that conversation, I got a chance to go to upstate New York to be part of a "rites of passage" weekend with a group of formerly incarcerated young men. Omari, who was in his late teens now, had become part of the group as a youth facilitator. He invited me to be part of the weekend as a coach. It was an intense, powerful three days of activities and rituals specifically designed to break down our walls of ego and fear. It was all about opening our hearts. By Sunday morning, we were all in a beautiful place of vulnerability. The final activity would be each of us going off alone into the woods for a couple of hours to simply be still and commune with nature.

It was a late-autumn / early-winter morning, and I wandered in the cold woods alone. I meditated and prayed and sat still, looking at all the majestic trees and other vegetation. There was a particular tree that kept coming into focus. It seemed to be calling me. There wasn't anything outwardly special about this tree. It looked pretty much like any of the other hundred trees that surrounded me, but there was *something*. At first, I felt silly for even considering hugging the tree, but as I sat there, I realized the silly feeling was just the ego and fear we'd spent the weekend dismantling. I said yes to the call.

I approached the tree, and without knowing what to expect, I hugged it. My arms fit perfectly around it, and I pressed my face into its rough bark like I would a lover I missed. I hugged hard and pushed my heart into its trunk. I felt heat emanating from the tree, I felt it accepting me. I surrendered, and before I knew it, I was crying. Bawling. Releasing pent-up emotions. I felt the tree was receiving my pain, pulling me into itself, holding me and soothing me. I was deeply moved.

I don't know how long I held on to the tree, but when I finally let go, I felt purged and cleansed. I felt renewed.

I also felt forgiven.

It was one of the most profound, incredible, and powerful experiences of my life.

A few months later, back in Brooklyn, I kept having the nagging feeling I needed to hug a tree again. My poor heart hadn't completely mended, and I longed for the connection, the grounding, the healing. I decided to go to Prospect Park to hug a tree.

Prospect Park is Brooklyn's largest park. It's huge. In it are rolling fields, lakes and ponds, dense woods, and even a zoo. The park was like a second home to me. I knew it well, having spent many of my high school days playing hooky there, where I explored and wandered. It was a safe place for me. I thought, if I was going to do the tree-hugging thing again, I wanted to be in a part of the park where no one could see me. It was one thing to hug a tree in the deep woods of upstate New York, but now I was back in *Brooklyn*. Shit, people *knew* me here.

I wandered the park, looking for a completely secluded spot. I went off-trail, and then I went off-off-trail and ended up deep in a quiet wooded area, a part of the park I'd never been in. I was climbing up a steep hill, reciting a silent prayer, when a tree ahead of me caught my attention. Like the tree I'd hugged upstate, there was nothing special about this tree. It looked like any of the other trees I'd seen in the park, but something about this tree beckoned me. It was an old tree, all rough bark and gnarled roots. Not particularly pretty, but undeniably powerful. I thought, *Well, this must be* my *tree*.

I made sure to look all around and listen for voices. I didn't see or hear anyone; in fact, I hadn't seen anyone for some time. *Fuck it,* I thought, *I'm gonna hug the shit out of this here tree.*

I wrapped my arms around it and squeezed it against my heart. The first thing I felt was its warmth. It welcomed me. I lost myself. Pressed my cheek against the bark and hugged with abandon. Again, I had the sensation of the tree receiving me. I felt it connecting to my soul, and I felt its love. It was like this tree was taking my pain and absorbing my fears. I couldn't help it; I started crying again. Crying in relief. Crying with an overwhelming feeling of gratitude, love, and peace. It felt pure and right. It felt like a sacred encounter.

I have no idea how long I hugged the tree, but at some point, I felt renewed and ready to let go. I stepped back and rested a hand against its trunk. I looked up at it and gave my thanks in deep reverence. In this holy and serene moment, I bid my tree goodbye. Then I turned to leave, and as I did, I heard loud and clear...

"You bettah hug that tree, girl!," followed by three resounding snaps. There, standing before me, was a large, middle-aged man with his hands on his hips. In a high, campy voice, he said, *"Yes, girl! You was loving on that tree!"* But then he dropped his volume and pitch and said, in a deep, sincere voice that could have come from Morgan Freeman, "No, but seriously, that was really beautiful. Thank you."

Without asking my permission, he stepped up and wrapped me in his arms. His embrace felt like a blessing.

Then I heard clapping and looked beyond him up the hill. Three robust men stood applauding. I looked down and saw used condoms and wrappers on the ground. That's when I realized I'd wandered into what must be the gay hookup area of the park. Something I always thought was an urban legend.

It was with a full heart that I stepped away from hugging a tree in the secluded woods of Prospect Park to be hugged by a man in a glittery jacket and tight lime-green pants.

Both of those hugs healed my heart.

Godbody III

HINDUISM FIRST CAME to me in the form of a book: *Autobiography of a Yogi* by Paramahansa Yogananda. I devoured the book. It was fascinating and magical to me. In it, I was first introduced to the importance of meditation and the possibility of mystical and miraculous experiences on earth. Soon after that, I began hanging out on the Lower East Side and in Tompkins Square Park with the Hare Krishnas. Theirs was the music and style that most attracted me to the Hindu culture. A lot of their young devotees had been hardcore punk kids; some I even recognized from the scene, but now, instead of getting smashed up in mosh pits and rocking Bad Brains and Minor Threat T-shirts, they were getting blissed out playing Indian drums, chanting "Hare Krishna," and sporting orange robes and shaved heads (well, they already had the shaved heads). I thought the whole Krishna scene was really cool; for a while, I toyed with the idea of becoming a devotee.

I even went through a bit of a Hindu-yogi-monk poseur phase during which I would smoke a bunch of weed and drop whatever psychedelics I could get my hands on, then put on a faux Indian-looking outfit, throw some beads around my neck, and find some visible spot in a public place like Union Square or Washington Square Park to meditate. I'd light incense and stick it around me and sit in a stiff, awkward half lotus posture with my eyes closed, for as long as I could, which was usually no more than five minutes. Then I'd light a cigarette, look around, and hope some spiritual Erykah Badu–type honey saw me "meditating."

When I moved to Downtown Brooklyn, I started frequenting the Hare Krishna temple nearby and often went to their basement cafeteria, Govinda's, for lunch. I liked the atmosphere and the fact that the food was prasada, meaning it had been offered to the deities, thereby consecrated. It didn't always taste that great, but it was imbued with high vibrations, and I always felt uplifted after eating the blessed rice and vegetables.

I got friendly with a Krishna devotee. He was a Southern Black man, about sixty-five years old, who didn't fit the young, orange-robe-wearing, mid-American White convert Hare Krishna template. He was gruff and thick with old, hard muscles. He'd been a marine who had seen combat in Vietnam and was a kung fu master. He told me he'd been quite the ladies' man before taking his vows of celibacy. In fact, he often alluded to having been a pimp before converting, but I think he had too much discretion and decorum to come right out and say it. He'd sit with me and tell stories from his interesting, unconventional life, interspersed with spiritual wisdom and philosophy. I never got to know his name, nor he mine. It didn't seem important. I simply thought of him as the Devotee. I liked his plain talk and his voice. He sounded a little like Billy Bob Thornton in *Sling Blade*.

"How's that there cauliflower curry, young'un? I told them to make it extra spicy today, uh-huh."

After about two years of having these lunch conversations with the Devotee, I heard he'd died suddenly of a heart attack. It left a void in my life because I'd grown to love him like an uncle. The last conversation we'd had was truly a blessing. He'd explained the concept of God, existence, and our place in the universe.

As he and I sat and ate together, he'd delivered the profound esoteric lesson in his own raw and perfect way. "Look here. You, me, Queen Elizabeth, that roach, the tree outside, and the dog that pissed on the tree are all GOD. You unnerstan? God has had a good ol' time being me! All the times I thought I was suffering, or when I was scared to death in some rice paddy in Vietnam, or when I thought I was the hottest ticket going with a girl on each arm and five hundred dollars' worth of cocaine up my nose, all of that was God experiencing God through me. When I forget I'm God and that roach is also God is the only time I really suffer. When I take this thing too damn serious and forget that it's *all* God, well, sir, that's the only time I got a real problem. You dig what I'm putting down?" He helped himself to some of the corn on my plate and continued. "People be coming in here now, talking 'bout 'namaste this' and 'namaste that,' and they don't really know what it means." He laughed. "They think it means 'The God in me honors the God in you,' and that's true, but it ain't the whole meaning, you dig? They ain't really figured out it means not only you and me, but that everything is God and should be honored. See, the problem arises when we start pickin' this thing apart and judging what's good and what's bad." He paused and a mischievous smile crossed his face as he held up a spoonful of corn. "It's like this, man—you know what those yellow bits in your shit are called?" I was about to say *corn*, but before I could, he said, "It's called shit! Everything *in* shit *is* shit and everything *in* God's creation *is* God! Lessons and blessings."

Around the same time I was getting these down-to-earth teachings from the Devotee, I stumbled upon a little halal buffet restaurant when I was coming home from work exhausted and hungry one evening. It was a narrow storefront in a spot I remembered being a pizza joint just weeks earlier. Now it was a self-serve buffet with a couple of clean but well-worn tables. I dished myself out a plate of greens and beans to go and went to the counter to pay. Behind the register was a tall, imposing gentleman dressed in traditional Muslim garb—long white kurta with a matching white kufi on his head. The juxtaposition of the stark white against his dark skin was striking. He looked hard, like he was carved out of rock. He also had a thick scar running down one cheek. "That's all, my brother? No meat?"

I explained that I rarely ate meat anymore.

He seemed to contemplate this for a minute. "I respect that. Brother, it's almost closing, and I'll probably end up having to toss most of the rest of the beans and salad. Please go ahead and take more. Make yourself another plate."

I was in no position to turn down free food, and it seemed to bring him genuine joy when I made another plate.

I began to go to that halal buffet a few nights a week after work. I'd usually get out of the train just minutes before closing, and often, Mr. Mohammad would be alone, cleaning up and putting away the food. We had easy conversations about trivial things, but as we got to know each other more, he began to share his life story. He was twelve years older than I, the age my oldest uncle, Charlie, would have been had he not died. Mr. Mohammad had many of the same mannerisms and speech patterns as my uncle, like the way he rubbed his chin when he was making a point and how he tipped his head back when he laughed. At times, if I closed my eyes, I could swear it was Uncle Charlie talking. Same vocal cadence, same deep, resonant voice. Mr. Mohammad had mentioned early on that he'd grown up in Brownsville, and when I said I had uncles from Brownsville, he asked their names. I told him they were known as the Spellers. His face turned serious. "I didn't know your uncles personally, but I knew of them. Everybody did. Trust me, they knew who I was, too."

Mr. Mohammad had been a notorious Brooklyn gangster, a drug dealer, a pimp, and a murderer. When he told me his street name, it took me a minute to accept I was actually speaking with him. He was a street legend when I was growing up, and his name inspired fear and awe.

Mr. Mohammad had the hip rap of a righteous, street-sharpened Black man from the late '60s and '70s. To me, his words were poetry. Smooth and hard. He spoke like Malcolm X, Gil Scott-Heron, and Iceberg Slim with Arabic interspersed. He knew I knew who he was, and he knew I was familiar with his legend, which I think is why he spoke very little of that time in his life. Or maybe it was because he wasn't proud of the reputation. Instead, he spoke most of his recovery and redemption.

His lifestyle had caught up to him by the early '80s, when he was arrested and sentenced to twenty-five years for armed robbery. He said he entered the penitentiary a full-blown junkie with the same hustler street mentality that got him jailed. He was sent to Attica, and he ran things from his first day. He had whatever he wanted on the inside: drugs, alcohol, other men — but he was dying in there.

After closing out the register, Mr. Mohammad continued, tearing up as he told me how he received grace in the form of a prison shower. "I'd been inside for ten years. I was probably gonna die in prison, and I knew it. I'd made too many enemies and not enough friends. I was still strung out. Shit, I was ready to die; I was already dead on the inside. Then, one day like any other, I went to take a shower and *something* happened. I couldn't move from under the water. I turned the hot water up to the point that it was scalding and told the guards to leave me there. They were scared of me. I stayed under the water for the whole day, crying and asking God to forgive me. I stayed under that scalding water until it felt like I was burning in hellfire. Brother, *something* happened! Alhamdulillah! When I stepped out of the shower, I was reborn. I was washed clean to my soul and had been given redemption. Alhamdulillah!"

I felt myself tearing up as well. Mr. Mohammad went on to tell me he never touched drugs again after that day, and that he devoted his life to Allah and Islam.

Over the course of stopping by to get food and wisdom, I began to notice Mr. Mohammad always found a kind word for whoever entered his shop, and that he often gave out free plates of food to people who seemed down-and-out. He never seemed phony, pious, or condescending. He did it humbly and without asking for recognition or thanks. That's why I was surprised by his behavior when, one evening as he and I sat in his empty shop near closing time, one of the neighborhood junkies came in smelling of piss and sweat. "Mr. Mohammad," the junkie said, "I ain't ate all day. Let me get a plate, brother?"

Mr. Mohammad, the man I'd come to know as being so generous, gentle, and calm, blew up. He seemed to revert back to his old street gangster self. "Oh, you want something to eat now, huh, you nasty motherfucker? You bring your stinking ass in here bumming for a meal for free when I been watching you collecting money up and down the street all day. And now, *now* that you done got high, you want me to feed your raggedy, funky ass. Get the fuck outta my store, nigger, 'fore I break my foot off in your junkie ass!"

The junkie turned around and dashed out of the shop. I think he was as surprised as I was by the outburst. The whole time Mr. Mohammad was cursing the junkie out, he was also making a plate. He was piling on chicken and rice, mac and cheese, and red beans. He said half to me and half to himself, "See, a nigga will spend for what they want and beg for what they need." He filled the container to overflowing, then stopped for a moment and bowed his head and recited some words in Arabic. He lifted his head and spoke calmly to me. "Watch the shop. I'll be back." He was gone for a long time.

When he came back, he blessed me with a supreme teaching. "Thank you for watching my store, brother. Bismillah. I couldn't let the brother go out hungry, no matter how angry I am at him, no matter how wretched he is. I have been him. I *am* him. I was given grace that he hasn't yet received. Inshallah, one day he will receive Allah's grace, too. His book is still open. Truly understanding Allah is like being the wave that understands it is the ocean. I see Allah in myself, and I see Allah in everyone. Believers and nonbelievers, so-called saints and so-called sinners. There is only Allah."

That evening, I reflected on the Devotee and Mr. Mohammad and how much they reminded me of my uncles, the men I considered my first heroes, the men I had lost to addiction. I realized that I had found them again, and I gave thanks.

Christmas Miracle IV (The Something)

FRIENDS HAD INVITED me to an after-hours underground poetry slam in the city that started at midnight. It was the day after Christmas, and people were still in festive moods despite the freezing weather. There was a feeling of holiday glow in the room, and I was really enjoying the show. We were about an hour into the performance when my pocket vibrated. I peeked at my phone and saw the call was from my mother. Usually, I would have let it go to voicemail and called her back later, but my brother had told me earlier, "Mom doesn't seem to be doing too well." He hadn't elaborated.

I excused myself, stepped into the lobby, and answered the call. "Hello?"

My mother's voice was faint, and I had to strain to hear her. "Pat, I'm in an ambulance, being taken to Interfaith hospital. I can't seem to catch my breath, and my pressure is way up—" Then the call disconnected.

I tried calling back, but I kept getting her voicemail. Every three minutes, I called again and left a message. "Mom, please call me back! I'm concerned." When she didn't call back after my fourth try, I left the show and headed back to Brooklyn.

It was about 2 a.m. when I got home. I tried Mom and got her voicemail again, then I called a local cab company, but they had no cars available. It was a frigid Sunday night; the city was pretty much shut down. I called for an Uber, but the closest car was half an hour away. I was now in full-blown fear mode. It had been over an hour since I got Mom's cryptic call. A year before, Mom had suffered a severe heart attack, her second, and had been hospitalized for a couple of weeks. She'd been in fragile health ever since. She'd taken to using a walker to get around, sometimes only taking a few steps before having to stop and rest. My mother was seventy-five years old and hadn't been taking the best care of herself. Worst-case scenarios played through my head.

Cold as it was, I decided to ride my bike. I knew it would offer the fastest way to get to the hospital. Interfaith Medical Center was only about a twenty-minute ride from where I was living in Downtown Brooklyn, and I knew the route well because I'd been volunteering at the detox ward there for the past couple months. In a panic, I bundled up, then grabbed the first shoulder bag handy to store my bike locks as I rode. I slung my still-packed gym bag over my shoulder. Just as I unlocked my bike from the front of the building, snow began to fall. Not a friendly, fluffy, night-after-Christmas-all-is-right-with-the-world snow, but a frozen, windy, stay-your-ass-home snow.

I hopped on the bike and started pedaling. I was about three-quarters of the way there when *something* told me to turn down a block that was off-route. It didn't make much sense, but I listened to *something* and turned the corner onto a quiet, empty street. I saw a pair of Converse sneakers sitting on top of a mailbox illuminated by a streetlight. It was such an out-of-place sight that I didn't give the shoes much thought, but even as I quickly rode by, I could see they were brand-new, and it looked as if someone had carefully placed them there. I took note of it as I kept pedaling as hard as I could. By this time, my hands, ears, and nose were feeling the beginnings of frostbite.

Something spoke up again. It clearly said, *Go back and get those sneakers.*

I argued with the *something.* "I don't need no Cons! I already got two pairs I hardly ever wear, plus those looked way too small for me, anyway. I ain't got no time to be going back. My mama could be dying!"

Something wasn't hearing it. *Go back and get them sneakers,* it said.

After about three more blocks, I gave in. Cursing the cold and the *something.* When I got back to the sneakers, I was surprised to find that despite the hard-falling wet snow, they were perfectly dry. A phenomenon I didn't have the time to contemplate. I could see the sneakers were way too small for me. But, almost begrudgingly and feeling pretty stupid, I put them in my gym bag anyway and rode the remaining half mile to the hospital.

It was about 3 a.m. when I arrived at the emergency room, which was surprisingly full and busy, but I was quickly allowed into the ICU without much hassle. A Black son showing up for his sick mother gets a certain priority with the Black nurses, who make up the majority of the emergency room staff. I'd also learned the three Cs—clear, calm, and compassionate—go a long way in dealing with overworked and underappreciated hospital workers.

The ICU was cold and crowded, and it appeared every bed was taken. Most were curtained off. I could hear the moans of suffering and the beeping of monitors as I walked the hall looking for my mom. I asked several attendants for help, but no one knew which bed she was in. Then, at the far end of the room, sticking out from the curtains, I saw a pair of shriveled feet. I recognized those feet.

I sat at my mom's bedside. Her eyes were closed, and she was hooked up to beeping machines. "I'm here, Mommy," I said, holding her hand.

Her eyes opened. She'd been given something to stabilize her heart rate, and her pressure was going down. I asked her how she felt. She said, "I feel fine now, but I'm so cold." They had given her only the thinnest of blankets, and it barely covered her ankles. I asked a passing attendant if we could get another blanket. I asked my mother where her shoes and socks were.

My mother said, "When I felt the heart attack coming on, I called EMT, and before I could get even halfway dressed or get my shoes and socks on, they were there. Next thing I know, I'm strapped up in the ambulance on my way here." She managed a little laugh. "Baby, I may need you to go back to the house to get me some shoes and socks. I can't be leaving here shoeless."

Without saying a word, I reached into my gym bag and pulled out a fresh pair of socks. I always kept an extra pair in my bag. I gently put them on her feet, feet that felt like icicles. Then I dug in the bag and pulled out the *something* sneakers.

I put them on my mother's feet. They fit perfectly.

She wears them to this day.

Gentrification

WHEN I FIRST got sober, my situation was bleak. I had to get out of Ish's recording studio, where he'd so graciously allowed me to crash out for three months. I had no bank account, no credit, and no references from prior landlords. And I had only a little money saved. I knew the chances of landing any kind of apartment on my own in this city were next to nil. I asked almost everyone I encountered, even strangers, if they knew of any cheap rentals or possible roommate situations, but it wasn't looking good for me. Who wants a thirty-nine-year-old recovering alcoholic-addict with bad teeth and no money as a tenant or a roommate? I resigned myself to the likelihood that I'd either end up back on the park bench or have to go into the shelter system, which would spell death to my spirit.

Oddly enough, it was my bad teeth that ended up being my salvation.

Years of smoking, drinking, and poor dental hygiene had left my mouth a wreck. I still had all my teeth, but they were loose and discolored, and my gums bled constantly. Upon getting sober, I made an appointment with a dentist.

It was late August, and I was in Downtown Brooklyn, leaving a dental appointment. I was kind of wandering around, postponing going back to Ish's for as long as possible, knowing my days were numbered there and trying to be as minimal a presence as I could until I found housing. I started praying and asking for guidance, and while walking, I passed a crowded parking lot around the corner from the Albee Square Mall. At the back of the mall, I saw an Asian man emerge from what looked like a concrete box with windows. It could have been a small storage space, or perhaps a place for the parking lot attendants to use the bathroom. It certainly didn't look like a living space, but something told me to ask the Asian man if the place was available to rent.

Mr. Kim, the owner, explained the space was actually the back of a storefront and didn't even have a proper address. It was built to be a storage unit, but he'd had a bathroom and kitchenette installed just a year before.

The area was designated as a commercial and industrial district and wasn't zoned for residential units. Mr. Kim said in a covert way that it was an illegal apartment but was vacant and could only be rented off the books. He was in a hurry, so I agreed to meet him there the next day to see the place.

Mr. Kim said in his thick Korean accent, "And you bring last bank statement and pay stub when you come."

I had neither, but I had faith.

I met Mr. Kim the next day, a Tuesday morning. We had to weave our way through a sea of parked cars to get to the entrance. The little storage box apartment was on the second floor above the back of a Korean nail salon Mr. Kim also owned. From the salon wafted the smell of toxic chemicals. That chemical smell mixed with the hot stench of the lot next to the entrance of the apartment. In piles as tall as a man, the lot was heaped with rotten debris, old tires and furniture, abandoned car parts, and bags of trash. What bothered me most were the small, tied-off plastic bags. Hundreds of them. Mr. Kim noticed me scanning all the little plastic bags and said, "There's no bathroom for the attendants, not even a porta-potty."

I realized the parking attendants had been shitting in those bags and leaving them around the parking lot.

The "apartment" consisted of two small square rooms that opened onto a roof. It was like a backyard patio except it was enveloped in a cloud of car exhaust. The place was covered in smelly, stained, wall-to-wall carpet. I found out later that local crackheads had found a way in and had been using the place to crash and turn tricks for some time.

Mr. Kim knew I was seeing and smelling the same things he was, so he dove into a sales pitch. "Very quiet at night and plenty light!" That was true. "And very close to all trains!" Also true. I could catch almost any MTA train within a two-block walk from the apartment, but goddamn, it was foul up in there! It was undeniably nasty and toxic, yet something kept telling me, This is your home.

The rent was five hundred dollars per month. I wasn't going to find anywhere else in the city charging 1985 rent rates in 2001, especially since Brooklyn was becoming the *in* destination for young White folks willing to pay big rents to live in the hood. It was like hip-hop had made Brooklyn fashionable and cool, and Mayor Giuliani, with his stop-and-frisk and other harsh policing policies, had made Brooklyn "safe." I knew some hipster would gladly pay three times that for the street cred they could get by renting the nasty apartment. I had to take it.

Mr. Kim didn't like that I had no credit, no bank account, and no pay stubs. He said, "The only way I rent to you, you pay me ten months up front. Cash. By Friday."

I had about two thousand dollars saved up, so that left me three days to come up with three thousand dollars. Somehow, I did it. With no shame in my game, I borrowed from my mom, from my friends, even from distant relatives and acquaintances. I called in debts, made promises, and wrote IOUs. I agreed to pay interest. Whatever it took.

On Friday, I rode the 7 train to Flushing, where Mr. Kim had an office, and I paid him five thousand dollars cash. He handed me the key. After my childhood home, this cement box in a cloud of stench was the second most important place I would ever live. My first solo apartment. My first sober apartment.

I immediately went to work to make it mine. I ripped up the carpet, which I guessed meant I'd just gotten rid of the body juices and DNA of every crackhead from the Whitman projects a couple blocks away. Then I started working on the disgusting empty lot next to the apartment. Across from the parking lot was a loading dock with huge dumpsters on it. I began hauling the mountain of old tires, car parts, and whatever furniture I could lift to the dumpster. Next came the pile of garbage bags. It was like a toxic archaeological dig, and the deeper into the pile I got, the older and grosser the garbage. Years of decomposition made much of what I removed from the lot unidentifiable and absolutely disgusting.

I worked hard as the parking lot attendants looked on from just yards away, saying nothing. By the end of the week, I'd cleared most of the space, and now the time had come to start getting rid of the hundreds of bags of parking attendant shit. I wore a mask, thick gloves, and two layers of everything. My homemade hazmat suit. Some of those bags were old and burst when I picked them up. I gagged, I retched, and I worked.

When I'd been living there for over a week, the parking lot attendants still hadn't acknowledged me. They watched me and talked about me, loud enough for me to hear. I figured they were embarrassed that I was literally cleaning up their shit.

I had just gotten back from dropping bags into the dumpster across the street when I caught one of the attendants about to throw a small plastic bag in the area I had just cleared. A shit bag! "Yo!" I called. "Please excuse my manners. I've been living here for over a week, and I haven't introduced myself. I'm Patrick. I live here now."

The guy reluctantly took my hand and muttered, "Gordo." He was short and chubby but hard.

"Mira, Gordo," I said. "My door is always open if any of y'all need to use the bathroom. Just knock anytime, but this tossing bags next to where I sleep got to stop. Tu entiendes, papi?" He nodded and walked away.

I went upstairs to wash up. Suddenly, I heard, "Yo! Come down here *now*, motherfucker!" I looked out the window. Five parking lot attendants were standing there looking up at me.

I calmly said, "I'll be right down." I felt no fear. I knew this confrontation was going to set the tone for my new living arrangements and could be dangerous. Like the families of cats that lived in the parking lot, these dudes were wild and feral. When I went down, they circled me. I stayed calm. I looked directly into Gordo's eyes and when he spoke, I didn't flinch.

Gordo said, "Yo! Who the fuck you think you are, giving fucking orders? You just got here. We *been* here. If we want to throw garbage and shit in the lot, we gonna do it. Do *you* understand?"

I didn't say anything for a long moment. I stared in his eyes until I saw him shift a little. He was unsure, and I knew I had him. I turned and looked at everyone around me. I smiled at them. "My name is Patrick. I live upstairs now." I opened my arms wide and made a circle. "I been here my whole life." I turned to look Gordo in the face again. "I don't mean no disrespect, but I meant what I said. Y'all are welcome to use my bathroom anytime, but there ain't gonna be no more throwing bags next to where I live. That's my word." I didn't raise my voice and my voice didn't quiver.

Gordo turned to one of the other guys and said something in Spanish and slapped his shoulder. "See! I told you he was an OG!" He smiled and gave me his hand. I shook it.

"Listen, papi, we just needed to see who you was. Nobody gonna throw bags here no more. Trust me!"

I said thank you and nodded to the rest of them. I turned to go back upstairs. Gordo said, "If you need *anything*, papi, I got you. Just ask and it's yours."

I knew better than to ask.

The attendants were a motley crew. Pretty Tony was a big Black dude who believed himself to be a pimp. Johnny was a tough-as-nails White dude who grew up in the projects and was Blacker than I was. Sugar was a skinny, toothless Black dude who was once probably stunningly handsome but had been ruined by drugs. Those three were older heads and had been working in the parking lot for years. Flaco and Gordo, the two young Puerto Rican ex-cons, had been there for only a year or so.

The air quality got considerably better around my new apartment, but I noticed something else disturbing. The space had its own ecosystem and cycle of life. When I moved in at the end of August, the place was infested with ants, an army of ants marching around the apartment with impunity. I didn't mind the little guys that much. They had their own mission and mostly stayed clear of me.

After a month or so, I noticed the ants started to disappear. In their place I began to see roaches, the small kind I grew up with. The kind I hated. The roaches had shown up and eaten the ants.

Later, the roaches started to disappear, and I noticed water bugs. The giant, prehistoric flying type that don't die. They were eating the roaches. And me. Water bugs bite, and they'll crawl on you at night and nibble. Thankfully, their time didn't last long. Seemingly overnight they disappeared, and for a while, I thought I might be done with the plague of insects. In a sense I was, because next came the reign of the mice. They came in for the winter and feasted on the water bugs, which is why those bugs seemed to disappear overnight. I lived in relative harmony with the mice for most of the winter, but come spring, they cleared out only to be replaced by heavy scratching and digging sounds under the floor in my bedroom. It kept me up at night. I mentioned it to Pretty Tony one day.

"Yo! Have y'all noticed squirrels around here? I think I got one living under my bedroom floor."

Pretty Tony laughed and called Johnny over. Johnny had worked in the parking lot the longest, on and off for over twenty years when he wasn't in jail. He'd briefly lived in the apartment himself.

Johnny laughed. "Squirrels?! Ha ha! You used to have mice, right? Now they're all gone, right? Where do you think they went? Well, let me tell you. It ain't no squirrels that made them disappear, my friend. You got *rats*!"

I never saw the rats. I only heard their scratching. Thankfully, their time didn't last long. The feral cats that had made the parking lot home for generations got them. Thus, it went season after season: ants to roaches to water bugs to mice to rats to cats and repeat.

I lived in that spot for over ten years. It became holy, sacred, and sanctified ground. At night, when the parking lot emptied and all the stores closed, it became a peaceful refuge. Downtown Brooklyn was a ghost town and my playground. My home was tucked away from the street and totally secluded. No one would ever have suspected anyone lived there. Friends started calling it the Honeycomb Hideout after the popular cereal commercial from the '70s. When I painted the front door red and put an *Om* sticker dead center, they began to call it Temple Red Door.

I grew into sobriety there. I grew into manhood there. I got a bank account. I got credit cards. I got a driver's license. And during my time there, I finished getting my teeth fixed. I had beautiful relationships and broken hearts there. I had deep conversations and made meaningful connections there. I sent up many, many prayers, burned much incense, laughed many, many laughs, and cried many tears in the place.

I made love, art, and music there.

God made a home for me in that little hidden illegal Brooklyn apartment.

Time went by, and my life bloomed and blossomed. I began to get better jobs, more prominent and prosperous positions. When I became the program director of a major nonprofit arts organization, I began to meet, work with, and get friendly with some of the city's most powerful politicians. I hobnobbed with the rich and famous, all while still living in the hideaway.

There was something alluring about the idea of attending a fundraiser held by the Rockefeller Foundation, sitting at a fancy banquet table with a Rothschild, discussing half-million-dollar grants, then returning home having to avoid puddles of piss and crack stems to get to my front door. I enjoyed the irony of having a one-on-one frank conversation with Mayor Bloomberg at Gracie Mansion about the injustices of his policing policies only to come home to an illegal apartment in the hood.

One time I was invited to a posh black-tie event hosted by a friend and was seated between David Bowie and Alicia Keys. I left the event in a brand-new limousine. The look on the limo driver's face when he dropped me off in front of my dilapidated, graffiti-covered apartment in the middle of a ghetto desert was priceless. It must've been an interesting visual, me in a tuxedo, stepping out of a limo and into a place that looked like a crack den.

Mi vida loca.

One of the downsides of living in a nonresidential neighborhood was there weren't any nearby food markets or restaurants. Finding food, particularly after 6 p.m., was a hassle. I would have gone hungry many a night if it hadn't been for Julio's, a little old-school Brooklyn Puerto Rican bodega about six blocks from my crib. The bodega came complete with a cat sleeping on the bread shelf, salsa music, and guys sitting on milk crates out front wearing guayabera shirts and playing dominoes, smoking cigars, drinking cerveza, and arguing in broken English. There were even congas, bongos, and cowbell jams out front in the summer.

Salted codfish and overripe bananas made Julio's smell like a real bodega, but there was always another smell underneath that, and it smelled delicious. Julio, who spoke only a little English, had been cooking in the back of the store for well over a decade. I would sometimes see guys out front with plates of food, and after a couple of years, I got up the courage to ask if I could buy a plate.

"No, papi, is no for esale. Is just for these guys, thas it," Julio said, pointing to the regulars.

"C'mon, papi! I'm hungry, and there's nothing else around here. Hook me up, Julio!"

He smiled and shook his head, then went in the back and returned a minute later with a to-go container loaded with food. "Okay, dame five dollars. You make too much problem for me!" he said, but I could tell it made him happy to feed me.

I went to Julio's two or three times a week for a plate. Five dollars would get me enough food to last two days. Rice and beans, plantains, cassava/yucca, avocado, and baked chicken or roast pork. I hadn't eaten swine since I was a kid, but there was something about Julio's roast pork (that he had to shoo the flies from before he cut into it) that was irresistible. It was delicious. Spicy, salty, greasy, and made with love. Sometimes he wouldn't even take my money.

This went on for years until there was a fire in the kitchen in the back of the store, after which there was no food for a while, but then Julio moved the whole operation to the front of the store. He still wasn't officially selling plates, but he was out in the open now. People could see that he was making food. Alas, as Bob Dylan sang, "The times they are a-changin'."

When I first moved to the parking lot, the strip along

Fulton Street was known as Black Brooklyn's main shopping district. It had been so for decades. The five blocks between Flatbush Avenue and Jay Street generated more money between Thanksgiving and New Year's than the whole country of Haiti did in a year. When I was growing up, Albee Square was our mecca. Dangerous and exciting. It was where we went when we wanted to get the freshest and flyest. It was lined with Black Muslim street vendors selling oils and incense. We could get cheap hot dogs, hear boom boxes blasting the latest jams, and watch pretty fly girls and stickup kids stroll the strip. It was music and movement and culture and style, and it was *Black*.

But that was changing. White folks were moving in. Hipsters who were too cool and edgy for Williamsburg moved into my neighborhood.

They "discovered" Julio.

He succumbed to their pressure and started selling them food, too. It was the beginning of the end.

The newcomers complained the food was too salty and spicy. It started to get bland.

They complained the food was too greasy. It started to get dry.

Julio was no fool. He realized these hipsters had money and he could be charging more. The price doubled and the portions got smaller.

When I went to get a plate one day and saw he was now making tacos, not even a traditional Puerto Rican dish, because some newcomer suggested it would make his business "hipper," I knew it was the end.

By this time, the neighborhood was almost unrecognizable, and Mr. Kim had tripled my rent. Hotels were going up, and upscale retail shops were moving in. Jimmy Jazz, the one-stop shop for all that was fresh and fly, was replaced with a Banana Republic. The famous funky hot dog spot now offered vegan options and fruit smoothies. White folks strolled the Fulton strip in flip-flops and sundresses, and there were police on every corner.

I mailed him my rent check every month, so I rarely had occasion to see Mr. Kim in person. He'd converted the Korean nail salon below me into a high-end deli that sold gourmet potato chips and kombucha. One day I ran into him in the deli.

I knew he liked me. For ten years of living in his little illegal apartment, I'd never once paid the rent late, and I'd never asked for anything to be repaired or replaced. I was a model tenant. When I walked into the deli, he greeted me happily. "Oh! Mr. Dougher! It's so good to see you!" We shook hands. "Wow! You been here a long time!"

"Yes, I have. Thank you!"

Mr. Kim nodded and rubbed his chin. "Neighborhood change! Much better now, yes?"

I agreed it did seem to be getting cleaner and safer.

He said, "Good! Now you move."

He evicted me.

Crawling Back

I HAVE NOT done the "sober thing" perfectly. In fact, the only thing I have done perfectly is not drink. I've gotten better in many ways, but my sobriety is a daily reprieve contingent on my spiritual condition. I have a dormant terminal disease that waits ever so patiently to awaken and devour me. It is a ravenous, murderous sleeping giant, and if I'm not diligent in my practice of sobriety, it will most certainly awaken.

Sobriety is balance. Its fruits are the happiness, serenity, and joy that come from being granted freedom from a deadly disease. When I am balanced and on the sober beam, I experience all those things. When I am off the beam, all my character defects come to the surface and I'm in a very precarious and dangerous place. I stay on the sober beam by continuing to improve my conscious contact with my higher power through prayer and meditation, by trying to the best of my ability to practice the principles of AA in all of my affairs, and by living in the virtues of service, humility, and fearless honesty. The easiest way for me to stay on the spiritual sober beam is to continue to go to and grow in AA.

I had to learn this lesson the hard way.

After eighteen years of continuous sobriety, I came very close to picking up a drink.

I had celebrated my fifteenth year of continuous sobriety, and my life was looking great. I'd just gotten a prestigious position as a program director of a large nonprofit arts organization, and I was making more money than I could have imagined just five years prior. I was in great health, my relationships with family and friends were solid, I was dating lovely women, and I had just moved into a spanking new apartment. I was happy, joyous, and free. I got the "promises" people in AA spoke about. I literally got the cash and prizes, but most importantly, the compulsion and obsession to drink had completely left me. I didn't "think drink." I was good.

So I asked myself, *Why do you need to keep going to AA meetings?* My life was full, the new job was time-consuming. I realized I'd much rather go out on a date or work out in the gym and hit the sauna than sit in a boring old AA meeting and hear the same old tired stories. I didn't think I had anything more to contribute to the meetings. I'd already done a ton of service in AA and had taken more than a dozen guys through the twelve steps, and the men's meeting I'd started was being attended by fifty guys a week and growing. I had nothing to share in meetings and nothing to complain about. I didn't need any support. My *alcohol-ISm* was starting to feel like *alcohol-WASim*. Past tense. I was good.

I started going to fewer and fewer meetings and eventually got to the point where months would go by without my attending a meeting or checking in with my sponsor. I began to ignore my sponsee's calls. I was too busy.

In my fifteenth year clean, I don't think I went to more than three meetings, and in my sixteenth year, I went to none. And nothing bad happened. I didn't feel like drinking. I wasn't hurting anyone. I was happy, healthy, and productive. I was good.

I'd heard of the "dry drunk" syndrome since the day I started counting days in AA. It refers to an alcoholic who doesn't drink but isn't working a program of recovery. Usually, a dry drunk is described as someone who is angry, irritable, and discontented. I was an alcoholic who had stopped working a program of recovery, but I wasn't any of those things. In fact, I was better than ever. So I stopped going to meetings altogether. I didn't need them anymore.

Alcoholism is an insidious sneaky bitch that manifests itself in the character defects of the alcoholic. A custom-tailored fit. My alcoholism is like a mushroom that grows in darkness and manure. My secrets are my darkness and my character defects the manure. The longer I stayed away from meetings, the more secretive I became and the more I acted out in dishonesty, ego, and self-centeredness.

Gradually, I became more manipulative and dishonest, greedy and lustful. But I didn't drink. I began to isolate myself from the world, and I was no longer interested in being of service to those who may have benefited from my experience, strength, and hope.

I still didn't drink, but after a nicotine-free decade, I began to smoke again and lie about it. I didn't drink, but after years of honest, loving relationships, I began to cheat and lie and manipulate. I joined online dating apps. They became my drug of choice. I was fucking everybody and they mama with impunity. One night I lay in my tub, taking a bubble bath while sexting three women at the same time. Sending dick pics and getting pussy shots. I got the texts mixed up and they busted me. I didn't care. I was high as a kite from all the sexual attention and distraction, and I knew I could talk my way out of it. I invited a woman over, and while she gave me head, I was swiping left or right on my phone. Like an addict, always thinking about the next one. I didn't even hide it from her. I was high.

I missed days at work and lied. My grandmother died a few times. I had to take my invisible dog to the vet on an emergency. I missed appointments, avoided family, and basically stopped showing up for friends. All with a growing ego that I masked with spiritual talk. But I didn't drink.

As bad as all of this was, what was probably the most soul-crippling part was the longer I stayed away from meetings and a spiritual program of recovery, the less happy, joyous, and free I became. I stopped laughing. I would never admit it because I tried hard to present a facade of a sober man with his shit together, but I was miserable. I didn't slip and pick up a drink, but I had a spiritual slip. I had become a dry drunk.

Toward the end of my sixteenth year without a drink, I met a young lady. She was intelligent, tough, quirky, and kind. She was stunningly beautiful, and she dripped with sex appeal. Nicole was half my age. She was also a dry addict. We fell deeply in love as quickly and passionately as only addicts can do. There was a deep, undeniable connection between us.

She became my everything. My higher power. I treated her like shit.

She fed my ego and became my drug of choice. I loved her with my whole being. I treated her like shit.

I was grumpy, controlling, miserly, and moody with her. I

wanted her attention when I wanted it and on my terms. She was loyal and devoted to me. She was my showpiece. We would walk into a room and every head, male and female, would turn to look at her. She was my pride. Having her on my arm confirmed my coolness and manhood. She was how I justified my misery. The fact that such a gorgeous, sexy woman was with me proved I had my shit together. After a night out, we'd go home and I'd berate and belittle her, tell her she wasn't smart and that her beauty was all superficial and fading, lest she begin to feel too special. I treated her like shit.

But I didn't drink!

Nicole had been struggling with a cocaine addiction when we met, and I became her de facto "sponsor." I charged myself with the task of keeping her clean and sober. I took her to her first Narcotics Anonymous meeting. I told her which meetings to go to. She started to get better and build a community in NA. She invited me to go to meetings with her, but I declined because *I* didn't need meetings. After all, I was now eighteen years clean and sober.

She met a guy at one of those meetings who promised to treat her like the queen she was. I saw all the signs. She asked me to show up for her, to give a little more of myself. To be kinder to her and pamper her occasionally. My alcoholic ego said, *Fuck that noise! She won't leave you. She knows you're Superman. Just cut her off, and she'll come crawling back to you.* I listened to my fragile facade of an ego. I cut her off.

She never came back to me.

It was the overwhelming pain of losing a beautiful woman who loved and adored me and whom I loved that initially drove me to AA and sobriety, and eighteen years later, it was the loss of a beautiful woman who loved and adored me and whom I loved that drove me back again. Both times, my life was saved.

I think, for whatever reason, my higher power knows that only the pain of devastating heartbreak can truly motivate me to change. I have a high tolerance for pain. I can be comfortable with being uncomfortable for a long time. I truly believe if Nicole hadn't broken up with me when she did, I would have picked up a drink again. For me, that is akin to a death sentence.

Instead of Nicole crawling back to me, I crawled back to AA.

In pain, desperation, and humility, I went to a meeting. I was shaking. I sat in the back of the room, hoping to be embraced and supported, and equally feeling that if anyone said anything to me, I'd leave and never come back. It was like starting all over again. I experienced the same apprehension and fear that I had at my first meeting all those years before.

As the meeting came to an end, the chairperson said, "We have time for one more share. Does anyone have a burning desire?" No hands went up except mine. I said, "My name is Patrick. I am an alcoholic, and I'm just grateful to be here."

I tried to get out of that room without speaking to anyone, but as I got to the door, an old-timer cornered me. He stuck out his hand for me to shake. He said, "I'm proud of you, kid."

He sounded just like my dad.

Godbody IV

IT WAS THE hottest day of summer and the hottest time of the day when I decided to go out and walk to the store. The heat literally made it dangerous to be outdoors. The sun burned like fire, and the air was dense and stifling. With every breath, I could feel the air roasting my lungs.

I'd lived on this block in Bed-Stuy for nearly ten years. I thought I knew all the neighborhood characters, the mentally ill and drug addicts, but I'd never seen this guy who turned the corner that afternoon. If I had, I would've remembered. He couldn't have been older than thirty, but it was hard to tell because of the state he was in. He was a big man, maybe six foot three or so. He was shirtless and muscular. His dark skin was made darker by a layer of filth. His hair was matted, and he had one dead white eye. One of his arms was twisted at an impossible angle. His pants were rags, his feet bare. Sweat streamed down his face as he approached me, throwing mighty punches at the air with his good arm, cursing at invisible demons. I could feel the anger radiating from him half a block away.

I began to pray for him. Scary-looking as he was, it probably would have made sense for me to cross the street, but I felt no fear. My heart melted like the asphalt. I felt a deep sense of compassion as we drew closer. I petitioned the Creator, the *One* with countless names, "Please help my suffering brother. He's in pain. Please ease his load and relieve him of his bondage. Please provide for your sick and suffering son. Bless him." I said this over and over as he got closer.

When we were within an arm's reach of each other, he stopped and mumbled some unintelligible words in my direction. I made out the word *dollar*. I pulled out my wallet and saw I had only a twenty-dollar bill. My last twenty dollars. I wasn't going to give this messed-up man my last twenty dollars. I said, "Brother, I need to get change. I'm going to the corner store. Stay here and I'll be right back. Wait right here."

He started to shuffle off, cursing and swinging at the blazing sun. It was clear he didn't understand me. I began to walk away but got only a few steps when it hit me. How could I let this suffering man walk away? How could I ask God to help him while I had the means to help in even some small way right in my pocket? It occurred to me I'd been asking God to bless him and that perhaps *I am* the living blessing I'd been praying for. Maybe I am God blessing him. I called him back. I gave him my last twenty dollars.

* * *

I remain without a religion. I've never put any box around my ever-flowing and growing understanding of the Divine, which I believe to be infinite, eternal, and unfathomable. I've never called myself Muslim, Five Percenter, Buddhist, Hindu, or Rastafarian, although I recognize all to be righteous paths to the Divine. I am so grateful for the teachers, gurus, and sages who have presented themselves to me in so many unlikely forms and from diverse faiths to teach me the basic spiritual truth that we are all one with God. Parts of the whole. God bodies.

I've never claimed Christianity, even as the child who was made to go to church and Kingdom Hall. In fact, those childhood experiences made me shun the idea of Christ for most of my life.

Just as the pandemic regulations were finally easing up, the Reverend Dr. Mark Bozzuti-Jones, an Episcopalian priest, discovered my art through social media and reached out to buy a painting. When I went to drop off the work to him, I was immediately struck with a sense of connection. He so reminded me of the unconventional spiritual teachers I've been blessed to encounter throughout my life. He embodied the honest, straight-talking wisdom and toughness of someone who has survived poverty, and the loving heart of someone who knows God.

Brother Marcus, as I affectionately call him, was born and raised in Jamaica. He is tall, mahogany-skinned, bald-headed, and white-bearded, and even in his elaborate priestly garb, he somehow conveys the humble and loving yet firm demeanor of a Rasta man. When he found out I was deep into writing this memoir of sorts, he invited me to the Trinity Church Retreat Center in Connecticut to allow me the space, support, and peace to concentrate and produce these pages. I was clear with him that I'm not a Christian, to which he replied, "Neither was Christ."

Over the course of my visits to the retreat center, Brother Marcus and I have had many openhearted, vulnerable, and deeply spiritual discussions about Jesus Christ. Brother Marcus explained Christ to me like this: "Jesus was a powerful example for us, for what we can be. He was *a* son of God, not *the* son of God." He continued, "Yeah, mon! Jesus said, 'The Father and I are one.' That's what the Rastas mean when they say I and I," he continued, "and for that, Jesus was labeled a heretic and blasphemer, but he was only using himself as an example of what we all are. We are *all one* with the Father." Then Brother Marcus pulled out a Bible and read from John 10:34: "And Jesus answered them, 'Has it not been written in your law, "I SAID, YOU ARE ALL GODS."'"

Through these discussions and Brother Marcus's wisdom, I've been given a new *over*standing, appreciation, and love for Jesus Christ. Truly, Christ was the embodiment of God. Jesus was God body.

Coming home after a week at the spiritually uplifting and breathtakingly beautiful Trinity Church Retreat Center, which is situated by a flowing river and surrounded by virgin woods, to find myself in the gritty, grimy, greasy belly of the city was a shock to my system. Paradise to Babylon in one short train ride. I went from the Eden of the Trinity grounds, where I wrote quietly and peacefully for days at a time, hearing only the songs of birds and the symphony of nighttime insects, to the deafening, unnatural cacophony of New York City's Grand Central Terminal in an abrupt, unceremonious transition.

I got on a crowded A train, still basking in the spiritual glow of my interactions with Brother Marcus, and was immediately crushed and surrounded by aggressive, sour, suspicious faces. A little old woman got on the train and started working her way toward me. She was toothless, dirty, and disheveled. She looked like she might have mental problems, but she seemed harmless enough and certainly in need of some help. She asked for change as she worked through the crowd. No one paid her any attention. She finally got to me, and before she could ask, I pulled out my wallet and gave her all I had, which was less than five dollars. She lit up, beaming a big toothless smile. Then she looked deeply into my eyes, like she was contemplating something. Reading me like a doting mother would lovingly look at her baby. After a moment she said, "You are good! I'm so proud of you!"

I said, "Thank you, love."

She tilted her head slightly, still beaming with a mischievous glint in her eyes. Then she whispered, "You know I'm God, right?" And before I could respond, she said, "And so are *you!*"

God winked at me and exited the train.

Acknowledgments

I give thanks to the Supreme Source—the Infinite and Eternal ALL that is ONE.

My family, friends, and loved ones, who have been my rock and foundation. Thank you for giving me strength, encouragement, and advice, and for sharing this journey with me. There is no me without you all. Thank you.

My beloved sister Ms. Jacqueline Woodson, for being a source of inspiration, a guide, and an advocate, and for so graciously providing me with the time and space at Baldwin for the Arts to create this work. Your love and care have meant everything to me. My deepest thanks.

My dear brother the Reverend Dr. Mark Bozzuti-Jones, for his unwavering support and spiritual guidance, and for providing me refuge at the Trinity Church Retreat Center, where I was able to meditate, pray, and write. Your brotherhood

ACKNOWLEDGMENTS

was essential to the process of writing this book. Give thanks and praises.

My amazing agent, Ms. Regina Brooks at Serendipity Literary Agency, for her excellence and expertise, and for her guidance and resourcefulness. Thank you for working so hard to make this all possible and for helping to make my vision a reality. I literally couldn't have done this without you.

Ms. Tracy Sherrod at Little, Brown / Hachette Book Group for the acquisition of my book, for believing in my story, for your input, and for the initial editing. Thank you so much for getting this journey started.

Ms. Jodi Fodor. Thank you for your hard work, dedication, and editing expertise. Your meticulous attention to detail, your prompts, and your suggestions truly elevated my writing in ways I could have never imagined. You are a gift.

A special thanks to all at Little, Brown / Hachette Book Group. You have all been blessings.

About the Author

PATRICK DOUGHER is a self-taught fine artist, musician, poet, and actor. He has performed and recorded with Sade, the Grammy Award–winning Dan Zanes, Black Uhuru's Michael Rose, Steel Pulse's David Hinds, and hip-hop star Chuck D of Public Enemy. His art has been featured in numerous exhibitions, as well as on television shows, including *First Wives Club* and *Riches*. He created the cover art for the reissues of Zora Neale Hurston's *Their Eyes Were Watching God* and *The Mis-education of the Negro* by Carter G. Woodson and illustrated the children's book *Hold Them Close: A Love Letter to Black Children* by Jamilah Thompkins-Bigelow. His visual art can be seen on his website, www.godbodyart.com.